ANGLICAN CHURCH PRINCIPLES

ANGLICAN CHURCH PRINCIPLES

BY

F. J. FOAKES JACKSON

WIPF & STOCK · Eugene, Oregon

Wipf and Stock Publishers
199 W 8th Ave, Suite 3
Eugene, OR 97401

Anglican Church Principles
By Foakes Jackson, F. J.
ISBN 13: 978-1-62032-385-4
Publication date 6/22/2012
Previously published by Macmillan, 1924

PREFACE

The object of this work is to present certain features characteristic of the Church in England at different periods of its long and eventful history. No church has had a more continuous or more varied life; for its story begins before that of the English nation, which it called to a sense of unity when that people consisted of scattered tribes isolated from one another. It has passed through many changes without abandoning its continuity any more than has the civil government; for the medieval and Tudor Parliaments no more resemble those of the present day than does the Church of those periods, and yet the continuity is unbroken.

The great crisis of the Reformation was passed through by the English Church in a manner very different from any other. It declared its independence of Rome without abandoning its claim to be a branch of the Universal Church. At the same time it accepted the Protestant view that the Scriptures are the supreme tests of the lawfulness both of doctrine and practice. As a result the Church of England has always acknowledged that the Church of Rome has conserved much that is important, and that the Protestants have rendered an immense service to religion by taking a firm stand on the authority of the Bible. In consequence Anglicanism is in sympathy with both aspects of Western Christianity. Towards the venerable Church of the East it has repeatedly shown a friendly interest.

There is no church which has been more sharply criticised by its own sons than that of England. This spirit of disparagement of one of their national institutions is characteristic of Englishmen and not unwholesome. But it must be remembered that the Church has more than once saved the country in a great crisis. An archbishop of Canterbury incurred the wrath of the worst of Kings and the most powerful of Popes by carrying through the Magna Charta. The Church settlement helped materially to save England from civil war, and thus to make the Elizabethan age possible. The resistance of the Seven Bishops to James II was a main factor in restoring civil liberty. And in days like the present the principles of the Church may draw together in closer bonds the Anglo-Saxon race, and thereby secure the peace of this distracted world. No one can despair of the future who knows the past history of the *Ecclesia Anglicana*.

The rough sketch maps are intended to bring into prominence two important facts. One is the immense influence which St. Columba and the Scots of Ireland had on the spread of Christianity. The other is to show how marvellous has been the growth of English Christianity and the expansion of the British people within a very short period. When the extraordinary growth of the episcopate is considered, and it is remembered that our Church has not been more, but possibly less, active in missionary work than some other English-speaking Protestant bodies, no one can continue to be altogether discouraged by the slow progress of missionary labour.

Ten chapters of this work have been published in the *American Church Monthly* and appear here by the kind permission of the editor, and one has been printed in the *Churchman* (New York).

The author desires particularly to offer his thanks for the assistance given him by Mr. W. H. Murray, the Religious Editor of The Macmillan Company. He must also express gratitude to his colleague, Professor Johnston Ross, for reading the whole in proof and making very useful suggestions.

CONTENTS

CHAPTER   PAGE

I   INTRODUCTORY   1

English character revealed in Church and State alike—Remarkable continuity of English life despite changes—The one English Pope Hadrian IV (1154–1159)—Respect for Rome in England—The parish priesthood—Persistence of the medieval tradition—What are the fundamentals of Christianity?—Phases in our inquiry: (a) Celtic and Roman Christianity, (b) Relations with Rome, (c) The Norman Conquest, (d) The Reformation, (e) The Age of Elizabeth, (f) Action and reaction in the seventeenth century, (g) The Wesleys, (h) The evangelicals, (i) Reversion to Catholic ideals: the Oxford Movement, (j) Ritualism, (k) Church expansion, (l) Modern criticism.

II   THE PRINCIPLES OF THE PRIMITIVE CHURCH . . .   10

The Reformers aimed at primitive doctrine and practice—Position of Anglican Church at the Reformation—What was the original belief of the English Church?—The Creeds (a) The Apostles Creed, (b) The Nicene Creed, (c) the Athanasian Creed—Heresy—Anglican orthodoxy in Pearson and Bull—Orthodoxy in (1) Faith (2) Practice—Faith unchanged—Tendency to superstition in practice—Practices not primitive in vogue when the English accepted Christianity (a) Adoration paid to the Blessed Virgin, (b) Images, (c) Roman obedience.

III   EARLY CHRISTIANITY IN BRITAIN AND IRELAND . .   18

The early Christian Church in Britain—The Celtic monasteries—Monasteries in Ireland—Importance of Scotic Christianity—Misapprehensions to be avoided—Alleged isolation of Ireland—The Eastern question—Clan system adopted in monasteries—St. Columba—Columba leaves Ireland—Hii or Iona—Adamnan's Life of Columba—Character of Columba—Jurisdiction and influence of Iona.

IV   THE ROMAN MISSIONARIES.   26

Rome still the capital of the world—Gregory I compared with Columba—Early life of Gregory—Gregory and Gaul—Gregory I's claim to jurisdiction—Augustine more papal than the Pope—Augustine and the British bishops—What Gregory's mission accomplished—The new church monastic—Sees founded.

viii   *Contents*

CHAPTER   PAGE
V THE RELATION OF THE SAXON CHURCH TO ROME   34

Merits of the Roman Church—Trials of the Popes—Papal interest in England (1) Choice of Theodore to be Archbishop of Canterbury (2) The keeping of Easter—St. Wilfrid—(3) The Archbishopric of Lichfield (4) Pilgrimages to Rome (5) Coming of the Benedictines (6) Norman Conquest.

VI THE NORMANS   43

Ability shown everywhere by the Normans—The conquerors of England had become Frenchmen—Friendly relations toward the Papacy—Roman intercourse salutary—The Abbey of Bec—William aimed at an efficient but subject church—Papal claim of homage—Church courts—Royal officials protected—The Conqueror's rule severe but just—Papacy on the whole popular—William II unscrupulous—Henry I and investitures—Papal legates—Papal encroachments due to royal blunders—Expense of papal rule a grievance—Progress after the Conquest.

VII MEDIEVAL CHRISTIANITY   51

Little known of the people of the 11th and 12th centuries—People in England devoted to the Church—The bishops—Election—Importance of the bishops—Cardinals—The Higher Clergy—The Archdeacon—Monasteries—Benedictines—Cluniacs—Cistercians—Carthusians—Canons—Friars—Universities—Parish Clergy—Vicars.

VIII RELIGION AT THE EVE OF THE REFORMATION . .   60

Magnificence of the parish churches—Educational value of churches—The Mass—Sermons—Purgatory—Confirmation—Penance—Extreme Unction—Feeling toward the Clergy.

IX HENRY VIII.   68

Popularity of Henry VIII—Character of the breach with Rome—Henry VIII always "orthodox"—Precedents for Henry's action—Henry VIII supported by Parliament—The Medieval Church expensive—The Church and the nobility—Henry VIII's vigorous action—How far Henry VIII was a reformer—No new church set up—An imaginary concordat between Henry VIII and the Pope—Significance of Henrician reformation.

Contents ix

CHAPTER   PAGE

X THE PROTESTANT AND CATHOLIC REACTIONS . . . 77

Disastrous reigns of Edward VI and Mary 1547–1558—Henry VIII's policy reversed—Edward VI's reign called "the Protestant misrule"—The first step was a gradual change of the mass into a communion—The first Prayer Book—The Articles—Extreme Protestant reform—Reunion with Rome—Persecution of Reformers—Three Experiments (1) The Six Articles (2) Uncompromising Protestantism (3) Return to Rome—Reason for failure: A *via media* necessary—Elizabeth's balancing policy.

XI THE ROMAN SECESSION 86

Apparent indifference to religion in England—Why the Romanists broke off from the English Church—Elizabeth contrasted with Mary—Elizabeth identifies her interests with her people's—Position at her accession—The rebellion of the northern Earls—Pius V excommunicates Elizabeth—The counter-reformation.

XII SEPARATISTS 95

Three classes of Protestants—Sectarianism illegal but inevitable—The Anabaptists—Puritans and Separatists—Reformation without tarrying—Northampton—The Wandsworth presbytery—Sufferings of the Independents—Prophesyings suppressed—Separation could not be open—Presbyterianism—Independency—Anabaptism.

XIII PURITANISM 104

Spirit of Puritanism—The influence of Geneva—The Vestment Controversy—Parker's *Advertisements*—The Puritans Approach Parliament—Need of more discipline—The Church of England a middle path—Puritan pamphlets—Reaction against Puritanism—The Government harsh but in the end beneficial—The nation always supported the Tudors.

XIV ANGLICANISM 114

The Church of England professes primitive doctrine of Christendom—The royal supremacy—Consecration of bishops—The other orders—Position of the clergy—Religious foundations—The Church's year—Religious life of an Anglican—The Calendar—The Eucharist—Occasional offices—Things prohibited—Elevation of the Host—Prayers for the Dead—Anglicanism a compromise.

x · Contents

CHAPTER		PAGE
XV	THE HIGH CHURCH PARTY	124

How had church continuity been maintained?—Church settlement England at first distrusted, grew in favor—Early High Churchmen anti-Roman—Andrewes—Laud—Principles of Caroline divines—Predestination a popular doctrine—Reaction against it—High Churchmen after the Restoration—High Church sympathizers at the Revolution of 1688—High Church ascendancy under Anne—Intolerance, the cause of a reaction against the Church.

XVI	LOW CHURCHMANSHIP	133

Typical High Church leaders—Low Church hard to define—George Abbott—Abbott's promotion—Williams—Burnet—Tillotson—Downfall of the Whig spirit—The Church and the leisured class—Hoadley—Opposition to Deism—Tolerant spirit encouraged.

XVII	LATITUDINARIANISM	142

Meaning of Latitudinarianism—Jeremy Taylor—The Cambridge Platonists—The new natural philosophy—The importance of "Reason"—Profligacy of the Restoration—Tillotson—Trinitarian controversies—Bangorian Controversy—Subscription to the Articles—Good work of English divines—Weakness of Deism.

XVIII	THE NON-JURORS	151

Importance of the Non-jurors—The strength of their Anglicanism—Origin of the Schism—Oath of allegiance—Non-jurors ejected—Perpetuation of the Schism—Ability of the Non-jurors—No Rome-ward leanings—Ken and Nelson—Sancroft, Hickes, and Brett—Hickes and Dodwell—Jeremy Collier—Ideal of the Non-jurors—The Non-jurors' overtures to Scotland and the Eastern Church.

XIX	THE WESLEYS	161

The Wesley family—Samuel Wesley, the younger—John and Charles at Oxford—John—The two Wesleys go to Georgia—Whitfield as a preacher—Dislike of "enthusiasm"—Condition of England—The Methodists—Wesley and the Bishops—Macaulay's criticism—Activity of the Wesleys—Methodism considered Popish—Wide spread of Methodism—Churchmanship of John Wesley.

Contents

CHAPTER	PAGE

XX EVANGELICALISM 171

Scepticism of the age—Abuses tolerated—Strength of Calvinism—Evangelicalism not favoured by authority—Evangelical clergy scorned—The Clapham sect—Life at Clapham—The Cambridge Evangelicals—Isaac Milner—Charles Simeon—Evangelicals sentimental but practical—Humanitarian reforms—Slave trade—Prison reform—Misery of the poor—National education—Criminal law reform—Bible Society—Missions.

XXI OXFORD MOVEMENT 180

Apathy of Oxford and Cambridge—The High and Drys—Older High Churchmen—Gothic revival—Liberalism materialistic—The "noetics" of Oriel—John Keble—Hurrell Froude—Froude and Newman abroad—The Assize Sermon—Tracts for the times—Dr. Pusey—Tract 90—Tractarians condemned—The High Churchmen do not secede.

XXII RITUALISM 189

Tractarianism academic—An eighteenth century church—Object of ritualism—Symptoms of ritualism—First ritualistic churches—The vestments—Action taken in the courts—Meaning of the Royal Supremacy—Court of Delegates abolished in 1833—The Lincoln Judgment—Widespread effects of ritualism—Activities of ritualists—Dangers: Intolerance; Submission to Rome.

XXIII THE NEW THEOLOGY 198

Little essential difference of belief before the new science and criticism—Evolution—Inerrancy of Scripture—Legal questions involved—*The Origin of Species*—*Essays and Reviews*—Colenso and the Pentateuch—The new liberalism—Its opponents—Religious belief materially affected—The Old Testament—Danger of the Higher Criticism of the Old Testament—The New Testament believed to be secure—Present indifference to theology—Substitutes: Mysticism; Sentiment; Attractive worship; Social Service.

XXIV EXPANSION 208

Little desire for expansion both at home and abroad—Romanism in England—Natural tendency of the British to keep themselves separate—The expansion of the British of recent date—English speaking Protestantism reproduced—Extension of the Anglican Episcopate (1) Irish (2) Scottish (3) In United States of America (4) Colonial (5) India (6) Missionaries—G. A. Selwyn—Mission to Central Africa—China and Japan (7) Native episcopate.

xii   *Contents*

CHAPTER   PAGE
XXV THE PRESENT SITUATION 218
  National sentiment always strong—Individuality—Unity
  with diversity—Religion not now a serious cause of disunion
  among Anglo-Saxon peoples—Union with Rome—The Future
  —The task of civilization—Adaptability of Anglican Church—
  Comprehensiveness—Recuperative power—Periods of reaction
  —Subservience to party in power—Political complications—
  Dangers of disruption—Non-jurors: a warning—Dogmatic
  differences—Need of a message to the world.

ANGLICAN CHURCH PRINCIPLES

I

INTRODUCTORY

ENGLISH CHARACTER REVEALED IN CHURCH AND STATE ALIKE—REMARKABLE CONTINUITY OF ENGLISH LIFE DESPITE CHANGES—THE ONE ENGLISH POPE, HADRIAN IV (1154–1159)—RESPECT FOR ROME IN ENGLAND—THE PARISH PRIESTHOOD—PERSISTENCE OF THE MEDIEVAL TRADITION—WHAT ARE THE FUNDAMENTALS OF CHRISTIANITY? —PHASES IN OUR INQUIRY: (A) CELTIC AND ROMAN CHRISTIANITY, (B) RELATIONS WITH ROME, (C) THE NORMAN CONQUEST, (D) THE REFORMATION, (E) THE AGE OF ELIZABETH, (F) ACTION AND REACTION IN THE SEVENTEENTH CENTURY, (G) THE WESLEYS, (H) THE EVANGELICALS, (I) REVERSION TO CATHOLIC IDEALS: THE OXFORD MOVEMENT, (J) RITUALISM, (K) CHURCH EXPANSION, (L) MODERN CRITICISM.

The Church of England is one of the most remarkable examples of the characteristic qualities of the English people. Founded in a small kingdom, which occupied the southeastern corner of the island, it witnessed the growth and consolidation of the nation. Submerged by the piratical invasion of the Danes, it rose from its ashes to promote the glory of the Anglo-Saxon monarchy in its palmy days. Denationalised by the Normans, it became the champion of national liberty under the Plantagenets. Bound by the closest ties of gratitude to the Roman Church, to which it owed its foundation, it always was intensely English in spirit. For centuries it produced no heretic, few grave scandals, only rarely a saint, and

scholars out of proportion to its size. Common sense
characterised the best English Churchmen. John of
Salisbury, the humanist and the wise friend and adviser
of St. Thomas Becket; Robert Grosseteste, the most eru-
dite man of his age and the reforming bishop of Lincoln;
Stephen Langton, the saintly statesman, Archbishop of
Canterbury; Roger Bacon, the pioneer of modern science;
William Occam, one of the earliest political philosophers;
Duns Scotus, the Franciscan master of the schools, are
typical products of the *Ecclesia Anglicana*. Good men
and devout Christians, none of them ever became the
centre of a cultus. No one worshipped at their shrines
or found protection in their relics. Yet posterity has not
allowed their memory to perish; and they are as much the
fathers of the Christianity of England as the Conqueror
and Simon de Montfort are of its civil polity, or Bracton
and Fortescue of its law. Whilst no nation has changed
more with circumstances, the remarkable thing about the
history of the English people is that none has altered less
in disposition, or stamped its characteristics more indelibly upon its institutions. From the earliest time no
Englishman of sense has ever wished to change or abolish
any custom or institution unless his comfort, convenience,
or independence demanded it.

Thus the history of the Church, like that of the Constitution or the Law of England, is a revelation of the
national character, and a clue to the story of the development of the race. It may appear a strange paradox, but
the religious genius of the Anglo-Catholic before, and of
the Puritan after, the Reformation was practically identical. Both were serious in their religion, moral in their
intentions, narrow in their views, but unwilling to go to
extremities. It is a mistake to imagine that religion in
England was light-hearted before, and gloomy and sad
after, the Reformation. It was always a grave matter to
those who really desired to pursue it earnestly; and many
a parish priest under the Roman obedience deplored the
laxity of his flock, and their neglect of the Sabbath, in

a fashion not wholly unlike that of his puritanical successor. The Catholic Englishman of an earlier time was very little different from the Protestant Englishman of later days.

Only once did an Englishman become Pope of Rome. He was not a man of birth or position: he owed everything to his ability and character. His career in the twelfth century was unique and essentially English. In a pontificate of four short years he excommunicated the city of Rome for refusing to obey him; forced an arrogant German Emperor to walk beside his horse and hold his stirrup; executed Arnold of Brescia, a trouble-making politician, and died confessing to an English friend that the unscrupulous rapacity of the Romans had made his life intolerable. He did his duty with dogged determination, a stranger in a strange land, ruling his subjects justly, but apparently without sympathy. His reign was unique in the annals of the Papacy. Hadrian IV was an embodiment, nearly eight hundred years ago, of the best tradition of the just but not amiable type of Englishman.

The unforgettable epigram that, according to the Anglican party, the Church of England was Protestant before the Reformation and Catholic ever since, reveals the absurdity of many modern reconstructions of history. Till within a few generations of the great catastrophe the English were distinguished by their orthodoxy and respect for the Pope, for whose office they had a profound reverence. Their attitude was that of William the Conqueror to Gregory VII, when the King readily agreed to pay the arrears of Peter's pence, and absolutely refused to do homage because his predecessors had never done so. Except on rare occasions during the Middle Ages the Church of England enjoyed considerable independence and self-government. It is true that in theory and papal law the English were not members of a national Church, but Christians inhabiting two of the provinces under Roman obedience, and that the lightest command issued from Rome set aside the gravest decision of Convocation. But the Popes, as a rule, allowed the nation to manage its own ecclesiastical affairs. Any grievances the English had were not connected so much with religion as finance. They objected to the intrusion of foreigners into lucrative benefices, to the greed of the collectors of papal dues, and to the expense and delay of the legal proceedings of the curia. In a word, they revered the Pope and disliked his officials, which was precisely their attitude to their own sovereign.

There is a series of pictures of medieval rectors of Hertfordshire taking their contributions to the Abbey of St. Albans which are unmistakably portraits, and the faces are those of the country clergy of to-day. Great as were the changes effected by the Reformation—and the attempt to minimise them is unhistorical—there was very little break in continuity so far as the average parish priest is concerned. Whether the supreme authority over the Church was vested in Pope, King, or Parliament, mattered little to him, as an Englishman with duties to be performed unnoticed by the great world; and, upon the whole, the record of the obscure priesthood of England for many centuries has been highly creditable, and has had more far-reaching effects than is commonly imagined.

It is this continuity of religious life in the country that is of so much historical importance. The English Church is remarkable for the tenacious way in which it has refused to break with its past. Despite the fact that its medieval traditions have, from time to time, been submerged by Protestantism, they have always risen to the surface later, asserted their vitality, and found a ready response among the clergy, who have never acquiesced in the contention that they had neither part nor lot in that unreformed Church which had endured with little change for so many centuries. This persistent adherence to its belief in the national character of the Church is due to a nobler spirit than a narrow patriotism manifested in a selfish desire for an English religion for

Englishmen: it is, rather, the result of a feeling that, for the race and nation, their religion forms an unbroken link with the past. Even those who have severed themselves from its communion find it difficult to forget that, after all, they still belong to the same stock, and have a share in the common heritage. Throughout the country, the ancient churches, from the stateliest of cathedrals to the smallest parish church, defaced it may be, but never destroyed by fanatic violence, attest the permanence of the religion of the English.

In order to understand the English Church, one primary thing to be borne in mind is that in all its vicissitudes it never officially committed its members to any doctrine that was not considered indispensable by the primitive Church. Hardly any Protestant Church escaped this snare. The Lutherans stand for Luther's doctrine of justification, the Calvinists for their eponymous hero's view of predestination, both supported by an appeal to Scripture, neither insisted upon by the first teachers of Christianity. A careful perusal of the Thirty-nine Articles will show how cautiously doctrines, of cardinal importance in other Churches, are explained and never insisted upon as vital. For this reason it is necessary to discover what were the fundamental principles of primitive Christianity.

The next thing is to investigate the two main channels by which Christianity came to the English race, and to trace the influence of the Christian inhabitants of Britain, whom they supplanted, and that of the missionaries who came to them from Rome. The relations of the early English Church with the great patriarchal see of the West are as interesting as they are important, and these became closer after the Norman Conquest—the most important fact in the whole history of England, and a remarkable example of how a really great people can rise superior to what might appear an overwhelming calamity. The Normans broke the resistance without destroying the spirit of the conquered nation, and, by stern and salutary discipline, brought out its finest qualities. The English had the wisdom to appreciate the good government which the victory of the Normans secured to them, and the two races completely amalgamated to their mutual advantage. The next stage in our progress must deal with the Church when it was frankly medieval and in the course of transition. After that comes the first period of the Reformation, the iron reign of Henry VIII, and the attempt of the King to enforce simultaneously an orthodoxy of belief which Torquemada would have approved, with an anti-Roman policy which would have satisfied an Anabaptist. His two descendants gave the country a taste, first, of continental Protestantism, and then of continental Catholicism; and the result was that both were rejected with disgust. Thus we reach the Elizabethan age and the beginnings of the great differences of religious opinion in England. In the choice between allegiance to the Pope or the Queen, some chose the Pope and suffered under the imputation of disloyalty to England. Others preferred Geneva to Canterbury, and suffered as Separatists; others tried to reform Catholicism out of the Church, whilst others became more and more convinced of the excellency of its position. Thus we have the English Romanists, Dissenters, Low and High Churchmen. The next century witnessed the two great attempts to destroy the Church, and both aroused the opposition of the people by going to extremes. The success of the Puritans in the Civil War was followed by a general reaction against the very virtues of the party, and the utter folly of James II in trying to dragoon his people into the Church of Rome led to his own discomfiture and to much undeserved suffering on the part of his coreligionists. With the fall of the Stuart monarchy, and the advent of the toleration of Protestants, a new party made its appearance in the Latitudinarians, who sought to remove all barriers which divided Protestants. Churchmen, however, turned rather towards those who, like themselves, had rejected Rome and yet retained the Orders, Sacraments, and orthodoxy of the ancient Church. Approaches were made to the Gallicans of France, and to the ancient Churches of the East.

At this time occurred one of the most remarkable episodes in the long history of the Church. Two brothers, clergymen, and sons of a distinguished rector of a country parish, after careers of unusual brilliancy at Oxford, undertook the work of evangelising the entire country. The preaching of the Wesleys resulted in a revival which is still felt in the English-speaking world. Methodism is one of the most remarkable developments of religion in England; and though it separated from the National Church, it was, at least, nurtured in its bosom. Methodism is to Protestantism what Franciscanism was to the medieval Church. Akin to Methodism, though often opposed to it, was the Evangelical movement within the Church, characterised by the same fervour of appeal to personal emotion, and an enthusiasm for humanity, and the cause of missions. Probably no movement has contributed more to the general alleviation of the miserable and oppressed. At first, though opposed by the official rulers of the Church, Evangelicanism throve, but it gradually lost its vigour when hostility was replaced by approval, and this opened the way for a new force to manifest itself.

Even amid the strong Protestant prejudices of the eighteenth century, it was realised that the Church of England stood for the ancient principles of Catholicism. The rapid progress of liberalism in the agitation for reform (1830–1832), therefore, aroused the apprehensions of the more thoughtful clergy. They perceived the danger of losing their secular status and their endowments, or even if these were preserved, that their standing would be regarded as little better than subjects to a godless Parliamentary majority. From Oxford there then issued a series of tracts to remind them that their true dignity was due to the commission they had received from Christ, and not to the fact that they were ministers of a Church as by law established. This appeal was received with enthusiasm, and the Oxford Movement, as it was called, came into being.

The Oxford Movement, till after the secession of Newman, was mainly academic, with an appeal that was mainly to scholars. The *Tracts for the Times* were learned articles, some almost volumes in themselves, often reprints of half-forgotten writings of Anglican divines. These necessarily affected only the scholarly clergy and laity, for the public could not be appealed to successfully by such means. The worship of the most advanced of the Puseyites, as they were called, was as dull and decorous as that of their brethren, nor were their doctrines obvious to the ordinary man. Not till the churches were made attractive, the Communion Table arranged as an altar, and the vestments of the Roman priests assumed by some clergy, were the public drawn into the movement. Ritualism was furthered by the furious opposition which it provoked, which endeared it to its followers and advertised it to the world. By it many of the churches of England have been made to resemble, at least in appearance, the churches of Roman Catholic countries, and many practices that used to be abhorred have become parts of its ordinary devotion.

Another change came over the Church almost at the same period, a change of attitude toward those of other nations. Since the Reformation the Church had become increasingly insular. Its clergy were bred up in hatred of Rome, and in dislike of foreign Protestants, who were regarded as little better than the Dissenters at home. Gradually the barriers broke down. The missionaries were the pioneers in this respect and through them the growth of the Empire was followed by that of Church expansion.

From a Bishopric in South Africa a critical movement in theological inquiry arose in Anglicanism; and the old

Introduction

Latitudinarians became the new Modernists. These various subjects will be treated under twenty-four chapters, at the end of which it will be necessary to arrive at some conclusion as to the result of our completed extensive, if not intensive, study.

II

THE PRINCIPLES OF THE PRIMITIVE CHURCH

THE REFORMERS AIMED AT PRIMITIVE DOCTRINE AND PRACTICE—POSITION OF ANGLICAN CHURCH AT THE REFORMATION—WHAT WAS THE ORIGINAL BELIEF OF THE ENGLISH CHURCH?—THE CREEDS: (A) THE APOSTLES' CREED, (B) THE NICENE CREED, (C) THE ATHANASIAN CREED—HERESY—ANGLICAN ORTHODOXY IN PEARSON AND BULL—ORTHODOXY IN (1) FAITH, (2) PRACTICE—FAITH UNCHANGED—TENDENCY TO SUPERSTITION IN PRACTICE—PRACTICES NOT PRIMITIVE IN VOGUE WHEN THE ENGLISH ACCEPTED CHRISTIANITY: (A) ADORATION PAID TO THE BLESSED VIRGIN, (B) IMAGES, (C) ROMAN OBEDIENCE.

Here it is not necessary to consider the results of criticism because we must put ourselves in the place of the early reformers and try to discover what the primitive Church meant to them. They regarded the religion of the Middle Ages as a perversion of primitive Christianity, and their great object was to find out what the life and practice of antiquity was. It is characteristic of the Reformation that the chief humanist pioneer, Erasmus, chose Jerome as his favourite author, and Luther chose Augustine. This difference means that, given their way, learning and scholarship would have led to reform of abuses, whilst piety led to one of doctrine. But both the fathers mentioned flourished in the fifth century at the time the Church was pronouncing a final verdict on the Creed and the Canon of Scripture. Shortly before Augustine's death, the General Council of Ephesus decreed that no one should ever produce a creed to supersede that of the Council of Nicæa. After Jerome no further discussion arose as to the acceptance of all the books of our New Testament as canonical. That is to say, henceforward no disputes might be allowed as to the meaning of the New Testament and the Nicene Creed.

Now, this was exactly the position assumed by the Anglican Church at the Reformation, from which it has never officially receded, and it is virtually that of all orthodox Protestant bodies, Lutheran, Calvinist, Anglican, Baptist, Congregationalist, and Presbyterian. In so far as they accept the scriptural and the credal doctrine of the Church they are free from the imputation of heresy, for the declaration in the Sixth of the Thirty-nine Articles of the Church of England, that "the canonical books of the Old and New Testament as they are commonly received" are those "of whose authority there was never any doubt in the Church," takes us virtually back to the days of Jerome and Augustine, since our present canon of the Old Testament is that of Jerome.

To understand the story, from the earliest days to the present time, of the Anglican Church, it is necessary to begin by stating what beliefs it professes to have held from the first, and never to have relaxed. In the present day we realise neither the importance of orthodoxy nor even its meaning. Orthodoxy has to do entirely with faith: its ultimate basis is Scripture, and its explanation is found in the Creed. There are points of doctrine on which a difference of opinion is permissible, and there are others on which none is allowed by the Church. The Reformed Church of England has exercised a wise discrimination. The questions which most tormented the minds of Christians during the Reformation have been left open—notice the extreme caution of the Articles on the topic of Grace and Free Will—because these had never been finally decided. On the subjects on which the first four Councils have pronounced definitely, such as the

Divinity of Christ, the Church permitted no controversy.[1]

Luther and the Reformers acknowledged the three Creeds enumerated in the Articles of the Church of England as "the Nicene Creed, Athanasius's Creed, and that which is commonly called the Apostles' Creed." The first of these is the Creed of the First General Council, not verbatim, but appearing in its present form about A. D. 381, with the exception of the unfortunate *"filioque"* clause. This is, in truth, the Creed of the Universal Church, the one public declaration of the Christian faith. The Athanasian Creed was, at the time of the Reformation, accepted as the genuine production of the Bishop of Alexandria, and used in the Hour services of the Breviary, as that of Nicæa is in the Mass. The other Creed, termed with commendable caution, "that which is commonly called the Apostles' Creed," is based on the Baptismal Creed of the Roman Church, and was the one in popular use, taught to the laity, and made the basis of Christian instruction. It takes its name from the legend that each of the Twelve Apostles contributed an article before starting on their missionary labours; and it is not found in exactly its present form till the middle of the eighth century.

In sentences, admirable for their majesty, terseness, and arrangement, the Nicene Creed sets forth the Catholic faith in metaphysical terms dear to the Greek mind. It is a Creed essentially suited to a service of stately dignity and to music which can do justice to its profound and triumphant profession and faith. But as a document it is unsuitable to put in the hands of the uneducated: its philosophical phraseology is designed to answer objections which can have little or no meaning to the plain man. To many Protestant Christians it is now almost unknown; and even some theologians seem scarcely to realise that it is essentially "the Creed."

The Athanasian Creed is really a hymn designed for

---

[1] Whatever the opinions of individual members of the Church may be, this fact cannot be disputed.

the instruction of the clergy, as an exposition of the doctrine of the Trinity and of the relation of the Godhead to the Humanity of the Second Person. It has been forgotten by most Protestants; and it is little used even in the Roman and Anglican Churches. Its damnatory clauses render it so unpopular that it is now rarely alluded to, and St. Athanasius is certainly not its author. Although it is an admirable statement of obscure points of doctrine, its use never penetrated to the Eastern Church.

The Apostles' Creed, like the Athanasian Creed, is unknown to the Eastern Church; but its brevity and apparent simplicity have made it suitable for the laity.

The Creeds are the test of orthodoxy which the Church of England accepts, not because of their conciliar authority or antiquity, but because "they may be proved by most certain warrants of Holy Scripture." The orthodoxy it professes is that of the Scriptures, interpreted by the Creeds, as is shown by the punishments which our ancestors, to our shame, inflicted upon those who refused to accept the doctrine and discipline of the Church. Since the days of Mary I, no one has suffered the death penalty for heresy on account of alleged errors in respect of the Sacraments. Roman Catholics have been put to death and cruelly oppressed, but never as heretics, though their doctrine of Transubstantiation was violently reprobated alike by Puritan and Anglican. When they have endured imprisonment, torture, and death, it has always been as traitors or violators of the law, and not as heretics. The Protestant opponents of the English Church endured much the same sufferings as the Roman, and the penalty of death for their religion has never been inflicted on them, but has been reserved for those who denied the doctrines of the Creed; the last fires were lit in 1611, for two men who denied the Divinity of our Lord. For more than a century after this, Unitarians were liable to be treated as heretics; and in the eighteenth century it was declared as a legal opinion that those who denied the Trinity could be indicted for felony.

Two seventeenth century divines may be cited to show how orthodoxy was supported by the great teachers of the Church of England, Bishops Pearson and Bull. The first named delivered a series of sermons to his congregation in the city of London on the Apostles' Creed. Later, George Bull wrote his defence of the Creed of Nicæa in Latin. Each of these books is a monument of erudition. Pearson takes up every article of the Apostles' Creed and proves it from Scriptures. He discusses the Jewish commentators in his references to the Old Testament, and collects the opinions of the Christian fathers, afterwards explaining the sense in which he himself accepts the dogma. Bull writes to refute the view that the doctrine of Nicæa in regard to the Second Person of the Trinity was not that of the earliest fathers of the Church. His way of vindicating the Council is to show that the teaching of the New Testament and the fathers (implied, if not expressed) was that the Lord is of one substance with the Father. He received the thanks of the French Church, for his defence of the Faith was as valuable to the Roman as to the Anglican Communion.

Modern criticism might question the correctness of the view that the doctrine of the primitive Church was the same as that of the fourth and fifth centuries, just as it might the methods by which the Scriptures were received and interpreted from that period to the close of the eighteenth century and later. But this is immaterial for the present purpose, which is to show what was interpreted to be primitive orthodoxy. In our attempt to define it we may divide the subject into (1) faith, and (2) practice.

(1) How far would a well-instructed member of the Anglican Church admit that the Faith preached by Augustine to the Anglo-Saxons, under the superintendence of Pope Gregory the Great, was primitive? The answer would be unhesitatingly in the affirmative in every point, with the possible exception that he might not agree with

Gregory's view of the state of the dead, though it was only an outline of what later became the more fully developed doctrine of Purgatory. As regards belief in God, in the Trinity, the Person of Christ, etc., there was no departure.

(2) As regards practice, just before the mission of Augustine there had been a remarkable growth of superstition; and Christianity, as a working religion, was not such as would have commended itself to the leaders of the Church in early times. With the vanishing of civilization in Western Europe the world had indeed fallen on evil days, and ignorance had necessarily produced superstition. Great as was Pope Gregory, and few men in all history have played a better or more useful part, the famous St. Augustine of Hippo, in Africa, would have been astonished by his credulity; nor can such ready belief in the constant intervention of the miraculous in life fail to affect practice. The trust placed in relics, the constant recurrence of dreams, portents, omens, miraculous cures or equally miraculous deaths, influenced almost every act of life; and the men who came to convert the English had lived in this atmosphere of marvel. Thus while the belief of a man like Hooker, who was alive in Kent a thousand years after Augustine preached there, may have been identical externally, it was in certain respects, also, fundamentally different. The two might have subscribed to a common creed; but their practice, as manifested in ways of life, could not be the same. As far as the English people were concerned, it was not possible for them not still to continue to be partially heathen long after their nominal acceptance of Christianity. When thousands were baptized in a single day along with their king or chieftain, most would naturally retain at least privately their ancestral belief. Many customs, heathen in the beginning, remained for centuries and were never, perhaps, really Christianised. Though some of these became perfectly innocuous, the Puritans of Hooker's day were waging unceasing war against them.

The question how far an Anglican could have assented to the practice of the Church at the time of the Reformation in matters which were deemed to be contrary to the principles of the primitive Church, must now be considered.

First is the adoration paid to the Blessed Virgin. The Church of England has never denied that high honour was due to the Mother of the Lord, as the festivals observed or noticed in the Calendar attest. It does deny that prayers should be addressed to her. By its acceptance of the Council of Ephesus, the Third General, the Church has implicitly recognised her as "She who gave Birth to God" (*Theotokos*), and allows to her all the honour she received in the primitive Church. By the time of Gregory the Great, while the reverence for Mary was increasing, it did not begin to approach that of later centuries. Although it was agreed that she was the greatest of the Saints, who were already believed to exercise supernatural powers on earth; as yet, there was scarcely a cultus which one who was attached to the Catholic traditions of England, as opposed to Puritanism, could reprobate.

The Roman missionaries approached King Ethelbert in procession, with a cross borne in front, and a standard of wood on which was painted the figure of the Crucified "depicted beautifully and with gold (*auriose*)," says one life of Augustine. At a later date the use and adoration of pictures, strenuously upheld by Rome, became the cause of one of the most furious and embittered controversies in ecclesiastical history. By the final decision, they might be retained and adored, but not with the worship due to God alone, and withheld from all Saints. A post-Reformation Churchman could not assent to this decision and Pope Gregory's attitude was not dissimilar. Representations of sacred subjects, he taught, were useful, especially to the ignorant, and were not to be destroyed by fanatic zeal against idolatry, but they were to be used to instruct the people.

Augustine and his companions received their commission from Rome, and were in the closest communion with the church over which Gregory presided. To them to be independent of the Pope was an idea too terrible to contemplate. Augustine, indeed, seems to have been "more papal than the Pope," and Gregory's good sense checked his ardent insistence upon Roman uniformity. Provided the unity of the Church was preserved, and the Faith unimpaired, Gregory was too great a man to care about the minutiæ of ritual or practice. Nor must it be forgotten that a close connection with the centre of Western Christianity was of extreme necessity to the infant Church of Teutonic Britain, for it meant discipline, organisation, reverent worship, the arts of life—in a word, civilisation. In the nine centuries which elapsed before the Reformation much happened which rendered connection with Rome an undoubted benefit to the English Church. Whatever, therefore, the attitude of an Anglican in the seventeenth century might have been to the Roman Church, he would probably have approved of Augustine's obedience to Gregory the Great, who is still acknowledged in the English Calendar to be a Doctor of the Church.

Allowing, therefore, for the difference of time and circumstance, the lack of civilisation, the deplorable ignorance spreading over Europe, the semi-paganism of the Christian world, there seems to be little to which the Church of England in modern times could take exception in the Christianity which Gregory sent Augustine to preach to its remote ancestors. Most of the doctrines of so-called medieval Christianity were not in evidence, and, if believed by some, had never been formulated. We have to wait six centuries for Transubstantiation to become a dogma of the Church of the West.

III

EARLY CHRISTIANITY IN BRITAIN

THE EARLY CHRISTIAN CHURCH IN BRITAIN—THE CELTIC MONASTERIES—MONASTERIES IN IRELAND—IMPORTANCE OF SCOTIC CHRISTIANITY—MISAPPREHENSIONS TO BE AVOIDED—ALLEGED ISOLATION OF IRELAND—THE EASTERN QUESTION—CLAN SYSTEM ADOPTED IN MONASTERIES—ST. COLUMBA—COLUMBA LEAVES IRELAND—HII OR IONA—ADAMNAN'S "LIFE OF COLUMBA"—CHARACTER OF COLUMBA—JURISDICTION AND INFLUENCE OF IONA.

There is so much obscurity in regard to the origin of Christianity in Britain that the legends concerning it may here be disregarded. We shall assume the Church was in existence there by the opening years of the fourth century. Tales of Apostolic missions to the island, of correspondence between a British King Lucius and Pope Eleutherus, the martyrdom of St. Alban, the presence of British Bishops at early Councils, whether fabulous or well attested, the story of Pelagius and Coelestius, and their famous controversy with St. Augustine of Hippo, are to be found in any history. The important point for us is that before the Romans abandoned Britain there was a Christian Church planted in the island which had taken such firm root that it survived disastrous invasions by heathen pirates, who drove the inhabitants into the infertile mountains of the West and established themselves in the country. Although the invaders obliterated every trace of Christianity as they advanced, and isolated the British Christians from the rest of the world, they could not destroy either the Christian community or the Latin

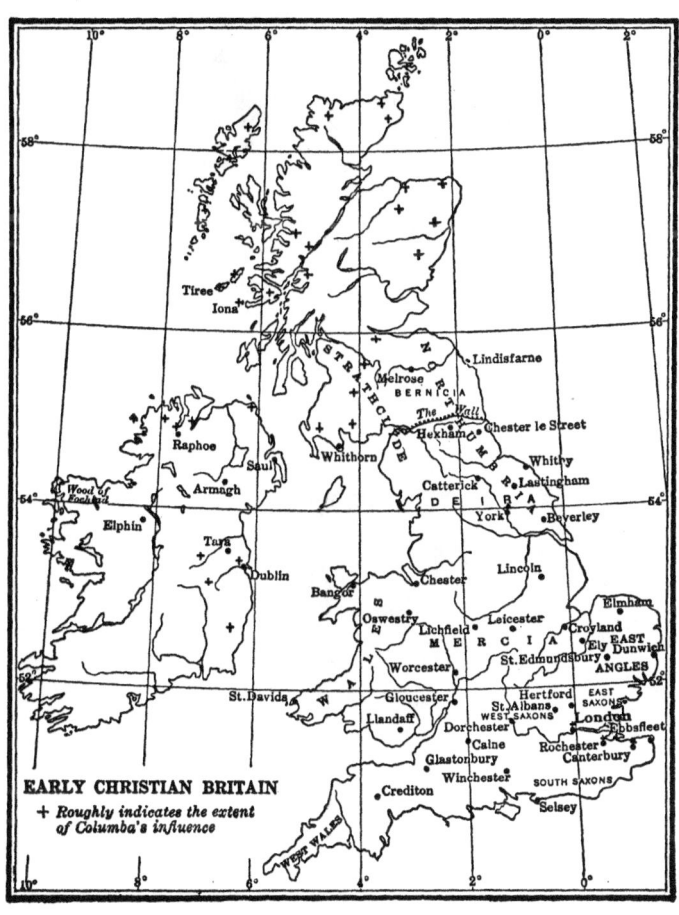

Early Christianity in Britain

language in which its services were conducted. To discover the cause of this marvellous vitality, the historian has to grope in the darkness of the fifth and sixth centuries.

In Celtic Christianity, the monasteries were of more importance than the bishoprics. The monastic movement came very early to Britain and spread rapidly. Shortly after St. Jerome was commending the austerities of Syrian and Egyptian ascetics to his admiring disciples in Rome, a monk of British birth was preaching there against what he considered to be the immoral tendencies of the predestinarian doctrine of the great St. Augustine of Hippo. Pelagius and his friend Coelestius had long been prominent as monks in Italy before their heresy provoked St. Augustine's indignation.

We find it hard to realise that in Ireland, between the days of St. Patrick, that is, in the fifth, and the close of the eighth, century, more monasteries were founded than in any other country in the world. Many of them can only have been cells, occupied by a very few monks; but even so, their number is staggering. A list of monasteries established before A. D. 800 throughout Christendom is given in Smith's *Dictionary of Christian Antiquities*. It enumerates upwards of fourteen hundred, scattered throughout the ancient Roman Empire and in Georgia, Armenia, Arabia, Persia. They were numerous in Egypt, Syria, Greece, Italy, Gaul, as also in Wales, and later in England and Scotland. Naturally, many were established in Rome and Constantinople. But in other countries or great cities nevertheless, they were numbered by tens, whereas in Ireland they were reckoned by hundreds. And the leaders of this extraordinarily fertile movement, not content with progress in their own country, or with the practice of private devotion and asceticism, traversed Europe, founded monasteries in Italy and Switzerland, taught and encouraged the arts, studied Greek and perhaps Hebrew, when these languages were hardly known in Western lands. They braved the storms of the northern ocean and traversed Scotland in boats of oxhide, which they carried from loch to loch, by its great central waterway to Inverness. Their great settlement at Iona was selected with all the strategical skill of sailor pioneers of Christianity. Elsewhere the important personages were the bishops, but in Ireland the great abbots were the leaders. It should not be forgotten that early Christianity in England was mainly the fruit of the labours of the Scots or Irish, and was almost entirely monastic.

The activity of these Irish monks and their disciples abroad was so remarkable that more attention than is usually given in accounts of the rise of the English Church ought to be paid to their labours. One reason for this omission is the belief that they were opposed to the pretensions of Rome, and therefore the decision of the native Teutonic Church to adhere to the Roman Easter developed the crisis which caused English and Scotic Christianity to part company. The genius of the Teutonic race assuredly moulded its Christianity on lines different from that of the Celts. Nevertheless, in the seventh century the Scotic or Irish Church was naturally more influential than was the Roman in missionary work among the English, and it is only right that full justice should be done to the extraordinary piety, devotion, and vigour with which the monks of Ireland toiled to extend the empire of the Gospel. The student, therefore, of the growth of the English Church should pay particular attention to the constitution of Irish Christianity.

Against two misapprehensions it is particularly necessary to guard. (I) The first is that Irish Christianity was a purely local development of the Faith due to the isolation of the island from the rest of the civilised world. (II) The second, that the Scots, as they were called, deliberately severed themselves from Rome, because of a difference as to the time of observing Easter, a question so extremely difficult that only a long treatise could do justice to it, which cannot here be attempted. The more the facts are known the harder it is to reach a decision.

All that we shall try to do is to clear the ground, by explaining the attitude of Scotic Christianity toward that professed by the Church in the West.

(I) The isolation of Ireland was far less complete than is generally assumed. Although the Romans had not attempted its conquest, there were traders settled along the coast, and Christian Churches were in existence, for whose benefit Pope Celestine I consecrated Palladius, the predecessor of St. Patrick. It would seem as though the Easter observance, peculiar to the Celts, which followed an earlier calendar than that used in Rome, was adopted before the preaching of Patrick, and that he found it in use when he began his missionary work in Ireland. Among the Saints of the First Order, who are regarded as the fathers of the island Church, many are said to have belonged to different nations, including Egyptians. It is, therefore, possible that the peculiarities of the Irish religion were due to foreign influence, perhaps from as far distant as the desert homes of the first Christian solitaries. Patrick himself was trained on the island monastery of Lerinum in the south of Gaul.

(II) Certainly the Christians in the far West evinced no desire to sever themselves from communion with Rome. After all, the Easter dispute, though, like other ecclesiastical controversies it led to much bitterness, was about a custom on which Christians had long been at variance. The Celtic bishops never questioned the supremacy of Peter's chair, nor denied that it was the ultimate court of appeal in matters of Faith. But in this matter they were convinced that they possessed the true interpretation of the ecclesiastical tradition. They appealed, as was often done in later times, from the Pope ill-informed to the Pope well-informed, if his authority was quoted against them.

The Church in Ireland was monastic in organisation, more so than in any other part of the world, and the authority of the great abbots was a marked feature. Ireland was divided among a number of tribal Chieftains, called "Kings," culminating in the High King (or *Ard-ri*) at Tara, to whom all the subordinate Kings paid service, at least when he was able to enforce it; that is, the basis of society was tribal, and the clan was the unit. The same thing appears in the monasteries, in which the clan spirit was as strong as elsewhere. The founders of a religious establishment gave its lands for the benefit of their own relatives, one of whom generally presided over the society, which tended in this way to become a sacred clan, bound together by blood as well as by spiritual affinity. As there were practically no cities, the bishops counted for less than the abbots, who were themselves, in a sense, chieftains. The episcopal office, however, was recognised and considered indispensable, and its dignity highly esteemed; but the real power was in the hands of presbyter-abbots, who for some reason refused the higher dignity. Eligibility to this office was often confined to a single family; at any rate, every one of the successive abbots of some monasteries could trace descent from a common ancestor. A general knowledge of the system, however, can best be presented by relating the story of a single great abbot who is typical of an Irish Church ruler of the sixth century, although his most glorious labours were in Scotland. St. Columba is not only a worthy example of Celtic monasticism, but the subject of much literature still accessible. The facts of his life will be briefly set forth, and more special attention given to his monastery in Iona and to the description of the Saint in his *Life* by Adamnan.

He was born at Gartan, in a remote part of Donegal, the son of a chieftain of the northern branch of the O'Neills connected with the reigning families of Dalriada in Scotland. His mother, Eithne, was related to the kings of Leinster. In a word, he belonged to the most distinguished families in the land. He received the name of Crimthawn (the wolf), but was afterwards known as Columcille (Column of the Church), or Columba (the dove). Educated by the most celebrated men of the time, by St. Finnian, Bishop of Moville, by the bard Geruman (Columba was himself a bard), afterward he betook himself to Clonard to study under another St. Finnian. He entered the monastery of Glasnevin, near Dublin, but owing to a pestilence left it and went back to the north. There he founded many monasteries, notably his central house at Durrow. In his forty-second year (A. D. 563) he left Ireland to go to Scotland, where a branch of his family had its kingdom, in order to preach the Gospel to the heathen. The reason for his doing so is said to have been a quarrel over a copy which he had made of a Psalter belonging to Finnian of Moville. Finnian claimed the work of Columba, and Diarmaid, the King, decided that, as the calf belongs to the owner of the cow, the copy should go to Finnian. In Ireland this decision was quite sufficient as pretext for war; and the two saints received each the support of his clan. Diarmaid was defeated, and Columba, though his prayers had secured the triumph of his tribe, was ordered as a penance for the bloodshed he had caused, to leave his country and never to return. He accordingly settled at Hii, an island off Mull, and, with his twelve companions, founded the famous monastery generally known as that of Iona.

The spot was well chosen; for it was accessible from Ireland, and near the estuary of the Great Glen of Albyn, now the Caledonian Canal, the artery which leads to the heart of Northern Scotland. Columba and his monks were sailors, and their mission was full of maritime adventures. Many of the Saint's miracles had to do with stilling storms and securing favourable winds.

Fortunately, one of his successors as Abbot of Iona, St. Adamnan, has left a Life of Columba, from which we are able to gather what manner of man this typical saint of Scotic Ireland was. Adamnan's work is not a biography in the modern sense, but a recital in three books of Examples of Prophetic Revelations, Miracles, and Visions.

Columba was no conventional saint. He united with a commanding presence an heroic voice, capable of terrorising his opponents. He was a fighter, haughty and, like other Irish saints, not free from Celtic vindictiveness. Yet, through the cloud of miracle which envelops him, we can discern a character with many truly Christian qualities. The first book relates prophecies, most of them being manifestations of second sight. The Saint sees guests at a distance coming to visit the monastery, he foretells when and how men will die, he sees battles being fought afar off and tells their results. He rebukes those who come to him and are not truly penitent. But Adamnan gives one example of the kindness of the Saint, trifling, he admits, but too beautiful not to relate. Once, it is said, Columba entrusted a tired crane to the care of a monk, because it came from Ireland, and told him to nurse the weary bird till it should be able to fly home to their beloved country. Adamnan's preface contains a beautiful description of the great missionary—"And still in all these he was beloved by all, for a holy joy ever beaming on his face revealed the joy and gladness with which the Holy Spirit filled his inmost soul." How the old horse who used to carry the milk to the monastery bewailed his death, is related with unforgettable pathos. The miracles in the second book, and the visions in the third, are neither improbable nor extravagant upon the whole, and though Adamnan was ninth abbot in succession to Columba, and was born nearly thirty years after his death, he does not seem to have been unduly credulous or uncritical in relating the traditions of the monastery of Iona about its founder.

A presentation of the extent of the jurisdiction of Columba's abbey, and of the veneration in which the Saint was held, will give the best idea of the influence of Celtic monasticism.

The monastery, where Columba settled in Scotland, is situated on the small island of Hii or Iona about three miles and a half in length, about 600 acres out of its 2,000 being fit for cultivation. In 1842 the population reached five hundred. The abbey was enclosed by a rampart or *vallum*. It had its church, abbot's house, refectory, library, guest chambers, rooms for the monks, barn, kiln, and smithy. The life was prayerful, but at the same time industrious. The monks tilled the soil, took care of the cattle, copied manuscripts, and built boats. The abbot was almost invariably a scion of an Irish royal house, but never assumed episcopal rank. Bishops, however, were received with deep respect, and Columba gently blamed one of these visitors for his humility in concealing his office. The authority of Columba, both in his old Ireland home and in the extent of his missionary labours, may be judged by the number of the churches and monasteries which boasted of him as their founder, or bore his name. When the monks of Iona went forth to convert the English, there was a perfect ring of Columban foundations extending from the south of Ireland along the west shores of Scotland, round the Orkneys and down the eastern coast, and then across to the Solway. But a glance at the map will do more than any enumeration of names to show what Columba meant in the work of converting the British Isles. Nor must it be forgotten that, great as he was, he is only one of the great monastic saints of Ireland, and is not even included in the Saints of the First Order. Because the Irish Church fell on evil days in the Danish invasions from which it never recovered in the Middle Ages, its importance from the fifth to the eighth century cannot be ignored.

IV

THE ROMAN MISSIONARIES

ROME STILL THE CAPITAL OF THE WORLD—GREGORY I COMPARED WITH COLUMBA—EARLY LIFE OF GREGORY—GREGORY AND GAUL—GREGORY I'S CLAIM TO JURISDICTION—AUGUSTINE MORE PAPAL THAN THE POPE—AUGUSTINE AND THE BRITISH BISHOPS—WHAT GREGORY'S MISSION ACCOMPLISHED—THE NEW CHURCH MONASTIC—SEES FOUNDED.

The sending of missionaries in answer to the request of "King" Lucius of Britain by Pope Eleutherus, 177-190, is the earliest hint that the early Roman Church regarded Britain as a field for missionary enterprise. This story, however, belongs to the domain of legend rather than history, while our subject is the work actually done by those who were sent from Rome to convert Teutonic Britain.

The Roman see had already become accustomed to the extension and consolidation of its spiritual dominions. Despite the extraordinary misfortunes which had befallen the city since its capture by Alaric in 410—the sack by the Vandals under Gaiseric in 455, the removal of the last puppet Emperor in 476, the foreign domination, first of Odovacer and then of Theodoric, the war between Justinian and the Ostrogoths, the taking and retaking of the place by Belisarius and the barbarians, the depopulation of the city, the oppression of the Byzantines and the invasion of the Lombards—the Romans never forgot that their city was the capital of the world and the head of Christendom. When Gregory the Great ascended the papal throne, Rome was ruled, if not by the most power-

The Roman Missionaries

ful, certainly by the greatest man in character and spirituality in the known world.

The points at issue here that seem to be of especial significance to the historian are: What knowledge could Gregory the Great have had of Britain? What jurisdiction did he claim over the bishops of remote countries? How did he plan and foster the conversion of the Anglo-Saxons? The story of the actual mission, as told in the unrivalled account of Bede, must be studied apart from these less interesting but important questions.

Gregory the Great and Columba were contemporaries, and so alike, though living under totally different conditions, that if a Christian Plutarch arose he could easily make parallel lives of the Pope and the Irish Saint. Both were men of the world, in the sense that they were conversant with the politics of their respective countries, and each, in his own field, accustomed from youth to associate on equal terms with kings and princes, shaped the course of secular as well as religious history in the double capacity of statesman and ecclesiastic. Both enjoyed every possible advantage of birth and position. Both sacrificed all worldly prospects to religion. Both were enthusiastic in missionary enterprise. Both shared in the credulity of their age, without for a moment failing to take a wise and practical view of the situation. Both found time for the labour of the scholar and scribe in the midst of an extraordinarily strenuous life. And, taking everything into account, it would be difficult to decide which of the two was the better or the abler man. It seems quite possible that had Gregory been born in Donegal he would have been a Columba, and had Columba been a Roman he would have become a Gregory.

Gregory the Great, like Columba, was highly connected, and belonged to one of the ruling patrician families of Rome. He was a wealthy man and was singled out by the Emperor for the great position of Prefect of Rome. He resigned in order to enter religion and devoted his large property to the founding of monasteries, especially the one to St. Andrew on the Coelian Hill. But he was too able a man to be overlooked and freed from executive office in the Church. He became one of the great deacons of the Roman see who assisted the Pope in the work of administration, and was sent as his representative (*apocrisarius,* the regular Greek word for ambassador) to Constantinople, where he remained for six years. When he was elected Pope in 590, he was no obscure cleric, but already one of the best known men in the Roman world.

Since the mission which he sent to Britain was in truth no more than an episode in a crowded pontificate of fourteen years, the care with which it was planned and carried out is amazing when we recollect the extraordinary difficulties with which Gregory was surrounded. In protecting Rome against the Lombards, he was hindered, rather than aided, by the Byzantines, who were jealous of the influence of the Pope, although powerless to protect the city. He had also to defend his dignity against the pretensions of John the Faster, Patriarch of Constantinople. He was virtually forced to feed Rome from the produce of the vast estates which made the Pope one of the richest men in the world. He administered these estates with a businesslike capacity and prudence, which made him a model ecclesiastical ruler. Among other things, the Pope had a difficult schism to deal with in Istria over the condemnation of what are known as the Three Chapters, in which the Roman see had been forced to acquiesce at the Fifth General Council in 553. It would not be necessary so much as to allude to this dismal controversy but for the fact that it brought Gregory into connection with the Irish Church, which was opposed to the action of the Council. The Irish had written to Rome to ask for help, apparently to meet some persecution, and Gregory in his reply complained of their departure from Catholic orthodoxy. This was in 592, five years before the arrival of Augustine in Kent. It would, moreover, have been impossible for Gregory to have been ignorant of Irish Church matters, owing to the presence in Northern Italy of another Columba, known as Columbanus, who had left Ireland in 583, not a youth, but already a man of fifty, as a missionary to Gaul. He had brought from his native land a power of writing good Latin, a knowledge of Greek and Hebrew, and a considerable acquaintance with the classics. The severity of his morals astonished the degenerate clergy of the Continent, and his sterner monastic rule might well have supplanted the more tolerant laws of St. Benedict.

Gregory, therefore, had some knowledge at least of the widespread and energetic Church of Ireland before he sent Augustine to Britain, and he was also in active correspondence with the rulers of Gaul, who were of the same Teutonic stock as the Anglo-Saxon conquerors of the island. Bertha, the Queen of Ethelbert, King of Kent, was the daughter of Caribert, King of the greater part of Western Gaul, the son of Lothaire and grandson of Clovis; but, as he died in 567, nearly thirty years before Augustine arrived in Britain, Bertha can have had little intercourse with her continental relations who were engaged in deadly feuds with one another. She seems to have lived contentedly to a mature age with a pagan husband in the unostentatious practice of the Christian religion. Her aunt by marriage, Brunichildis, the most vigorous, able, ruthless, and religious of the Merovingian rulers, was a friend of Pope Gregory, who admired her talents for government and friendship for the Church, and maintained a constant correspondence with her. He, therefore, already knew something of the people whose conversion he so earnestly desired when he saw the Angle children in the slave market at Rome, who were subjects, by the way, not of Ethelbert, but of Aella, King of Deira, with York as its capital. The fact is that Eastern Britain was separated from Christendom temporarily by the Saxon invasions, and its reconquest by the Faith was a task somewhat analogous to the reconquest of the dominions of Clovis a century earlier. There is a story in Procopius, the historian who lived a generation before Gregory, which implies that there was an island in the North Sea to which the Spirits of the Dead were ferried. Gibbon applies this reference to Britain, but such ignorance in regard to that country can never have existed even in Constantinople.

It is not possible fairly to discuss Gregory's claim of jurisdiction over other Churches in the light of more modern controversies. But there is no question, as far as England was concerned, that the Church was founded on his initiative and by his orders. For this reason it was markedly Roman, and the words of an English council, "Gregory, our father, who sent us Baptism," are peculiarly applicable. The Pope, moreover, had no doubt that he presided over the first Church in the Christian world and spoke with an authority derived from the Prince of the Apostles. But everything we know of this great man shows that he was a combination in a rare degree of opposite traits. He could attend to detail and he could take a comprehensive view of the situation. He had a high sense of his office, and he had a very real personal humility which appears in his rebuke of John the Faster, Patriarch of Constantinople, for assuming the title of Universal Bishop. Gregory knows of no see which is not subject to the Roman Bishop; but neither he nor his predecessors dared to claim the name "Universal" (i.e. œcumenical). Rather than be so styled the great Pope prefers to be the "Servant of the Servants of God," a title continued to this day. As he writes to Eulogius, Patriarch of Alexandria, when he addressed Gregory as "Universal Pope," "if you give more to me than is due to me, you rob yourself of what is due to you. Nothing can redound to my honour that redounds to the dishonour of my brethren. If you call me Universal Pope, you thereby own yourself to be no Pope; let no such titles be mentioned or even heard among us." Possessed of such a spirit, Gregory was ready enough, as his advice to Augustine shows, to allow a newly founded church to develop on native lines, and gave his emissary an even freer hand than he probably desired. But for us it is important to inquire as to Gregory's attitude to the Christianity already in Britain.

Augustine was evidently under the impression that, when Gregory founded the English Church by his agency, part of the Pope's design was to establish a sort of Roman colony, to which all the surrounding Churches in Britain and Gaul were to look for direction as from Rome. As himself a Roman and a member of the *clerus Romanus,* sent specially by the Pope, invested with the *pallium,* a token of authority over other bishops, Augustine must have regarded the bishops of Gaul as barbarians. Sooner than invite them to consecrate him, he had left the scene of his labours and gone to Arles, in Southern Gaul, to obtain Orders from the representative of the Pope. It is not, therefore, so unnatural, or even so presumptuous, as is sometimes asserted, for Augustine to ask Gregory whether he had authority over the bishops of Gaul. The Pope told him to confine himself to Britain, and sketched out, as his idea of the constitution of a Church in the island, a plan by which it was to consist of two Provinces, one at London, the other at York, each with twelve suffragans. Augustine was to have precedence over York for life; afterwards the senior archbishop was to take the first place. Like most paper schemes, this one came to nothing, and the mission only established two permanent sees. It would have an important bearing on the questions resolved for us if we could learn whether Gregory was aware of the organisation of the British Church in Cornwall and Wales, or intended Augustine to include their sees in the twenty-four in which he proposed to divide the island. Probably the Pope had only a vague notion of the actual condition of affairs.

Augustine's interview with the British bishops, as described by Bede, is of great interest. He found their practice differed in three important respects from the Roman, and that they were unwilling to abandon their ancestral customs in deference to his authority. The three distinguishing characteristics of British Christianity did not touch doctrine at all. Their manner of administering the Sacrament of Baptism differed from that of the Roman Church; their monks and clergy shaved the head not on the top, but from ear to ear; above all, they dated Easter by a different reckoning. This last proved the fatal bar to union, and continued to be so for more than a century. The intense British hatred against the Saxon invaders made the bishops the less ready to receive Augustine's suggestions that, if they would co-operate in evangelising the heathen Saxons, conform to the rest of the Church on the date of Easter, and adopt the Roman ceremony in Baptism (he said nothing of the tonsure), the British might retain their customs. Thereupon the British refused to accept Augustine as their archbishop, and the conference broke up. The Roman mission had to carry on the work of conversion unaided by the Welsh, who contributed little, if anything, to the subsequent spread of the Faith among the English.

Gregory's object to plant a Church among a thoroughly heathen people is of special interest as being the one great missionary enterprise which went forth directly from Rome. The coincidence is worth noticing that Gregory I sent missionaries to the English, Gregory II ordained Boniface, the great English missionary to Germany, and Gregory VII, while not yet Pope, supported the policy of sending the Normans to restore England to the unity of Christendom. The chaotic state of the world, together with the extreme difficulty of communication, combined to make the elaborate organisation of the Church of the Middle Ages impossible in the sixth and seventh century. At the same time the necessity of Christian unity was strongly felt, and the primacy of Rome, the only Apostolic Church in the West, was recognised as the chief means of securing this ideal. But the Roman Church did not possess the required means of exercising its legitimate authority in the evil days after

Gregory the Great. It remains to be seen what the mission sent by Gregory actually accomplished.

The Celtic system of evangelisation, which was entirely monastic, was common to the Church throughout the world. From the Western shores of Ireland to the Nestorian Settlements advancing toward China in the far East the monastery was at the centre. Gregory's ideal was an episcopal abbot. Augustine and his successors were expected to share the life of their fellow monks, and to receive from them the unquestioning obedience due to the ruler of a monastery. The ordered life of a religious house was to be kept before the people, and by it they were to judge of the charm and advantage of the Christian religion. The monks were to elect their abbot, who became a bishop by consecration, and an archbishop on receipt of the *pallium* from the Pope. A certain unity and continuity was thus given to the evangelisation of the country, and the ideal of the bishop living in community with his priests long continued. As the monastery would be naturally recruited from the neighbourhood, the ministry must tend ultimately to become almost entirely native. At first it was almost entirely Roman.

The success of the original band of missionaries was at first partial and temporary. All it really accomplished was the permanent establishment of two sees, Canterbury and Rochester. A third at London had but a short life. In the second generation Paulinus was for a few years Archbishop of York. By its means the knowledge of the Gospel crept into the Kingdom of the East Angles. Further overtures were made to the Christians of Wales; but the fatal question of the date of Easter made them of no avail. Within thirty years of the death of Augustine (635), the scene of Christian endeavour had shifted to the north, and Irish monks from the islands of Scotland were the chief actors. In another generation, however, Roman missionaries were again in possession of the field.

V

THE EARLY ANGLO-SAXON CHURCH AND ROME

MERITS OF THE ROMAN CHURCH—TRIALS OF THE POPES—PAPAL INTEREST IN ENGLAND (1) CHOICE OF THEODORE TO BE ARCHBISHOP OF CANTERBURY (2) THE KEEPING OF EASTER—ST. WILFRID—(3) THE ARCHBISHOPRIC OF LICHFIELD (4) PILGRIMAGES TO ROME (5) COMING OF THE BENEDICTINES (6) NORMAN CONQUEST.

There are historians who deem it was almost the first duty of every branch of the Western Church to show independence toward the centralising policy of the Roman patriarchate. Their attitude reveals a lack of historical perspective. The Church, in the sense of the local organization presided over by the Pope, could not have secured its immense authority in the Church at large, either on the basis of the Lord's promise to Peter or of those legendary imperial donations to the Romans see, except it were constantly doing something to merit its preëminence and win the respect of other Churches. To account for the undisputed fact that the supremacy of the Church at Rome was acknowledged far and wide in those days, it is necessary to bear in mind certain facts which happened centuries later.

In the first place, the Church of Rome, from the days of Gregory the Great to Charlemagne, owed little to its worldly advantages, or even to any personal greatness in the Popes. In the whole seventh century hardly one left behind a name to be remembered. Very few of them occupied the Chair of St. Peter for more than a few

The Early Anglo-Saxon Church and Rome

years, and they were all nominees of a far distant Emperor at Constantinople. As a rule they were less conspicuous for their exploits than for their sufferings. Further, the Roman Church found that the Emperors proved more effective as tyrants than as protectors: for the Lombard invaders of Italy were pressing constantly toward the City and threatening to become masters of the Papacy. Again, Rome was so poor a city that its clergy were unable to take the lead in directing the thought, even of a dark age; and the Pope, Agatho, had to apologise for sending simple and ignorant priests to represent him at Constantinople. The strength of Rome as a Church seems to have been due to her retention, even in the distressing days of the seventh and succeeding centuries, of much of the tradition of order and government, and her ability to take a broad view of the needs of humanity.

The Celtic Church, then so energetic and enthusiastic for learning, piety, and real devotion, was provincial, partly by necessity but also by temperament. The newly converted English were more drawn to the distant Church, from which the first effort to win them had come, than to the one nearer home, so closely allied by blood and speech to the British whom they had subdued. Therefore, no sooner had Christianity been accepted in most Anglo-Saxon kingdoms, mainly by the energy of Celtic missionaries, than the Roman influence began to overcome the Celtic policy of isolation and to advance by rapid strides. The landmarks, which can here only briefly be indicated, are: (1) The mission of Theodore, whom the Pope sent as Archbishop; (2) The settlement of the Easter controversy; (3) The Archbishopric at Lichfield; (4) Pilgrimages to Rome; (5) The coming of the Benedictines; (6) The irregularity of Archbishop Stigand's appointment.

From Bede, two consecutive chapters (II, 18–19), it is evident that the affairs of Britain occupied the attention of the Roman Church. In the first there is a letter from

Honorius, then Pope (638), to his namesake, the Archbishop of Canterbury, occasioned by the sending of a *pall* to be used by Paulinus as Archbishop of York at his consecration, which directs the senior Archbishop in England to take precedence of the junior. The second contains another letter to the Scotic prelates on the subject of the observation of Easter, and the spread of Pelagianism, which was written during an interim in the succession to the papal throne by the Archdeacon and *Primicerius* of the Roman Church. Moreover, Pope Honorius had only recently acted on the petition of Birinus that he be allowed to go to Britain to preach where no one had preached before. He was ordained by the Bishop of Milan as a "regionary bishop," and went to Wessex in 634.

Up to this point, however, the missionary work accomplished by the Romans in Britain had been inconsiderable; for, in 633, a general apostasy occurred, owing to the victories of the pagan King, Penda of Mercia. The work of conversion passed into the hands of the Scotic monks, and the Romans confined their labours to the two sees of Canterbury and Rochester in the Kingdom of Kent, together with the East Anglian bishopric, founded by the Burgundian, St. Felix. As an indication of the vitality of the new Church, it is worth noting that by 654 all the sees in the east of England were filled by natives who had been trained in the monasteries of Canterbury.

(1) Though Oswy, the Bretwalda or head of the confederacy of the Teutonic kings in Britain, had been educated in the Faith by the Scottish monks, his sympathies leaned toward Rome. In 664 he rejected the Celtic Easter under the influence of Wilfrid; and when Deusdedit, Archbishop of Canterbury, died, Oswy in 667 held a conference with Egbert, King of Kent, at which the two agreed to send a presbyter of the clergy of Deusdedit, named Wighart, to Rome for consecration. This was a very important step, as it deliberately brought the English

Christians into close connection with the parent see of the West. The Pope to whom Wighart was sent was Vitalian (657–672), and his letter to Oswy, as given by Bede, is curiously instructive. He refers to Wighart, who died at Rome, not as Archbishop-elect, which is the way that Bede introduces him, but as the bearer of Oswy's gifts, with instructions to petition the Pope to send out a suitable archbishop. But whatever the position of Wighart was, it was not to assert the claims of his see that Vitalian acted. To appoint an archbishop did not mean to him to put a friend into a desirable post, but to find a man with sufficient zeal to go into exile into a barbarous and unknown country. After much trouble Theodore of Tarsus was discovered and sent with Hadrian, a learned African, and it would be hard to imagine a wiser or happier choice.

(2) It is very difficult for some of us to understand the extreme importance of the Paschal question at the time when the Anglo-Saxons were being converted to the Faith. On this question, till the Council of Nicæa, the primitive Church had agreed to differ; and, did not the experience of our own day prove how the bitterest ecclesiastical disputes do arise from the most trifling causes, we should find it impossible to credit that so much trouble could have arisen on so slight a pretext. However, without entering into the complexities involved, it is sufficient to say that in Britain whether Celtic or Roman Christianity should be supreme depended on what cycle was to be used to determine the date of Easter, for it was considered heretical to celebrate the Christian Passover on the 14th day of the moon, if that day happened to be a Sunday. The protagonist of the Roman party, Wilfrid, was a native Northumbrian, and one of the most attractive figures in early British Christianity, a truly astonishing man, if we recollect how recently the stock to which he belonged had all been heathen barbarians.

Wilfrid is an extraordinary example of the power of attraction that Rome had for his people. Although educated at Lindisfarne, the home of Celtic missionary labour, whence Aidan had gone forth to convert Northumbria, Wilfrid's one desire was to see Rome. At the age of nineteen, or in 654, he went there with Benedict Biscop and after many strange adventures returned full of enthusiasm for all things Roman, and of contempt for the usages peculiar to Celtic Christianity. At the synod of Whitby he was the leader of the Roman party, and it was due to his persuasion that King Oswy decided in favour of their method of reckoning the date of Easter. Colman, the Bishop of Lindisfarne, who had supported the customs of Columba, then retired to the Scots, who upheld their own rule as to Easter for more than fifty years, or till 716. The South Irish had yielded to Rome thirty years before, the North conformed in 704. But Wales adhered to the old Celtic custom for fully a century, and did not come into line with other churches till 777.

It is not easy to pass by such a personality as that of St. Wilfrid, or to omit the story of his long dispute with Theodore, and incidentally to recount the great services rendered by this Archbishop of Canterbury, who may justly be called the second founder of the Church of the English. But we must not be turned aside from our main purpose, which is to show the relationship of the Saxon Church to that of Rome. It is now evident that the bond was a close one, and that succeeding Pontiffs took an intelligent interest in the Church which Gregory I had founded. Wilfrid's appeal against Theodore's somewhat arbitrary action in dividing the north of England into dioceses was decided by a Council at Rome in the pontificate of Agatho (678–681). To Wilfrid was given the right of setting the limits of the dioceses to be formed in Northern England. Of the surviving eight letters or decrees of Agatho no less than four relate to Saxon England, as they are grants of privileges to the abbeys of Peterborough, Hexham and Ripon, Wearmouth, and St. Paul's, London. This indicates the interest shown in England by the Popes, whose solicitude for its Church was repaid in the next century by the devotion of the greatest of early medieval missionaries and reformers, Winfred of Crediton, better known as Boniface, who did more to convert the Germans and reform the Churches of Gaul than any one of his age. He also helped prepare the way for the raising of Pepin to the Frankish throne, and thus for the subsequent reëstablishment of the Roman Empire in the West by Pepin's son, Charles the Great.

(3) By the close of the eighth century the connection between England and Rome appears to have become very intermittent; but Offa, King of Mercia, was all powerful in England; he obtained authority from Rome to set up a third archbishopric in England at Lichfield, naturally to the detriment of Canterbury. After Offa's death, Ethelhart, Archbishop of Canterbury, laid an appeal before Pope Leo III, who decreed that Lichfield should cease to enjoy metropolitan rights.

(4) The immense influence of Rome on the imagination of the Anglo-Saxon Christians is seen in the general desire among them to pay a visit to the Eternal City. Not only did enthusiastic monks, like Wilfrid and Benedict Biscop, make pilgrimages to Rome, but, to quote Bede, "In those days many of the race of the English, high and low, laymen and clergy, men and women, were accustomed to resort thither eagerly." The relics which it was the custom of the Popes to send freely to favoured Princes did much to stimulate the desire to see the City, which contained so many tokens of the triumphs of the Faith, valued not only as evidences to the facts, but for inherent powers of their own. Above all, to die under the protection of these inestimable treasures was to secure salvation, and fortunate indeed was the visitor who not only saw the tomb of the Apostle, but also received baptism at the hands of his representative, the Pope. This was the happy fate of the first royal pilgrim to Rome from England, Cadwalla, King of Wessex. He was a somewhat ferocious monarch, and though he had enjoyed the friendship of St. Wilfrid, he resolved to defer his

baptism till he could obtain it from the Pope. It appears, therefore, that, even as late as 688, the year of his visit to Rome, a King of Wessex could remain a pagan for the greater part of his life. The story of his baptism is thus briefly told by Bede: "For on his arrival in the pontificate of Sergius he was baptized on the holy Sabbath (Saturday in Holy Week) of the Passover, in the year of the Incarnation of the Lord 689. And whilst he was still wearing the white robe (*in albis adhuc positus,* or, as the Chronicle says, 'under Christ's clothes'), he was delivered from the flesh, and joined the Kingdom of the Blessed in Heaven. And when he was baptized, the Pope gave him the name of Peter, to commemorate the fact that he had come from the ends of the earth in pious love of his most holy body, in order that he might be united to the Apostle by sharing his name. And he was buried in St. Peter's Church and by the order of the Pontiff an epitaph was placed on his tomb, in order that the memory of his devotion might abide for all time, and that the example of what he had done might kindle in those who read or heard it zeal for religion." Ini, the successor of Cadwalla, abdicated in 725 in order to make his exit from the world in the holy place and obtain a more friendly reception (*familiarius recepi*) in heaven.

These cases will suffice, especially as the *Ordo Romanus* for the administration of baptism in the Lateran by the Pope is available for study. Nothing was omitted which could help to make the scene impressive. Day after day was spent in elaborate preparation and mystic ceremonies; anointing, exorcising, committal of the Creed, and the like. The day, or rather the night, of the baptism, was impressive in the extreme. The priests and deacons prepared and instructed the numerous candidates for the ceremony in the great baptistery, where the Pope presided in person. Clothed in white robes, and bearing tapers, the newly baptized followed the clergy in procession into the Church which bears the proud inscription— "Chief and Head of the Churches in the World"—and received the Sacrament of the Body and Blood. No wonder kings left their kingdoms to enter the Church under such auspices, and that pilgrims flocked to witness all this splendour of the Roman religion.

(5) The seventh and eighth centuries may rightly be called the golden age of early English Christianity. Nothing can be much more remarkable than that a nation described as utterly barbarous should produce, in scarcely more than a generation, missionaries, men of letters, poets, scholars, and saints who were the glory of the entire Church. The women, notably the great abbesses— Hilda and Etheldreda are but examples—were as distinguished as the men. And the moral record of the Church is as creditable as its display of intellect and achievement. One has only to compare Bede with Gregory of Tours to see what a different story the two historians have to tell. The earlier historian of Gaul has a record of crime and bloodshed to relate, in marked contrast with the gentler records of the monk of Jarrow. In Gaul, bishops and ecclesiastics were almost a match in ferocity for the Merovingian kings.

But the wonderful Christian civilisation of Irish and Scotic and English Christianity was destined to undergo a sudden eclipse. Successive waves of invasion from northern pirates swept away the monasteries and churches and with them the learning which had made these islands famous throughout Europe. There would be, it is true, gleams of the old glory in the reigns of Alfred and his great successors, and here and there a notable saint would appear; but the Christianity of the Church of England needed to be reinforced from the Continent before it could again display its pristine vigour. This began with a revival of monastic life through the efforts of St. Dunstan and his friends, who reintroduced the severer discipline of restored Benedictinism that enabled Europe to emerge from the barbarism of the dark ages.

(6) The coming of the Normans was the second step. They maintained that the English were in schism, owing

to the usurpation by Stigand of the see of Canterbury. The Conquest was actually a crusade undertaken by command of Pope Alexander II against a rebellious Church; and it marks the beginning of constant and direct intercourse between England and Rome. The effects it entailed can only be rightly judged in the light of a full statement of the facts. It is enough to say that never was a nation more benefited by a great and humiliating catastrophe than the English.

VI

THE NORMANS AND THE PAPACY

ABILITY SHOWN EVERYWHERE BY THE NORMANS—THE CONQUERORS OF ENGLAND HAD BECOME FRENCHMEN—FRIENDLY RELATIONS TOWARD THE PAPACY—ROMAN INTERCOURSE SALUTARY—THE ABBEY OF BEC—WILLIAM AIMED AT AN EFFICIENT BUT SUBJECT CHURCH—PAPAL CLAIM OF HOMAGE—CHURCH COURTS—ROYAL OFFICIALS PROTECTED—THE CONQUEROR'S RULE SEVERE BUT JUST—PAPACY ON THE WHOLE POPULAR—WILLIAM II UNSCRUPULOUS—HENRY I AND INVESTITURES—PAPAL LEGATES—PAPAL ENCROACHMENTS DUE TO ROYAL BLUNDERS—EXPENSE OF PAPAL RULE A GRIEVANCE—PROGRESS AFTER THE CONQUEST.

The Normans brought England into touch with the larger world of the Continent. This extraordinary people were for about a century mainly responsible for the revival of civilisation in Western Europe, and the inspirers of medieval culture. Wherever they went they naturally took the lead and made the best of the institutions of the nations among which they took up their abode. The Northmen who settled in France became thoroughly French by the time their descendants had conquered England. In Celtic countries they developed into hereditary chieftains, notably in the Scottish Highlands. In the Lowlands they were the leaders of the native patriots against England. In Sicily they saved the island from Islam and revived the glories of the ancient Magna Grecia in the fields of art and science. But the scene of their greatest triumph was England. After showing that they were not men to be trifled with, they won their way by giving the Anglo-Saxons an excellent government which the conquered appreciated the more because it respected their ancient customs; and in a few generations victors and vanquished became indistinguishably mingled in one nation. Yet the Norman spirit outlived the Norman race, and to this day is in active strife with the less adventurous temper of the older inhabitants. The Englishman in India and elsewhere engaged in administering the Empire is a Norman; at home he is apt to be under the heavier influence of the Anglo-Saxon spirit, just as his religion in so far as it is Catholic is Norman, whilst on the Protestant side it is eminently Teutonic.

From the days of Ethelred, the Unready, England had been continually overrun by the Danes, and even under the dominion of Danish Kings; but, though the Danes were foreigners, their language was akin to that of the English, and they could easily adapt themselves to the customs of the people among whom they settled. Not so the Normans. It is true they were of the same stock as the English and the Danes, but they had long abandoned their Norse language. They were known as Frenchmen in England and gloried in it, for they despised its older inhabitants as barbarians, ignorant of the very language of civilised men. But this extraordinary people had remarkable powers of assimilation: as they had become Frenchmen in Gaul, Italians in Sicily, Scottish in Scotland, and Irish in Ireland, they became English in England. Everywhere they took the lead and formed an aristocracy, but never an entirely exclusive one.

With their usual sagacity, the Normans early recognised that the Pope, in his capacity of a political power, was a most useful ally. A little before their invasion of England they had been at war with Pope St. Leo IX, in southern Italy, and had taken him prisoner after the battle of Cividale. But, being not only a most politic but also a sincerely religious people, they treated their captive with deep respect, and obtained from his successors recognition of their right to occupy their conquests in South Italy and Sicily. Consequently their Duke, William, was delighted to conquer his new kingdom in the name of the Holy See, and to unite the English Church to that of Rome by the closest ties consistent with his royal rights. It was his policy to retain every institution which he considered useful, whilst depriving it of all its objectionable features; and, even when he introduced real changes, to make them appear consistent with precedents taken from the past.

The aspect of the Norman Conquest which concerns us here is the closer relations which it brought about between England and the Roman see; and at this point a reminder is desirable that we cannot judge what happened more than eight centuries ago by using what happened many generations later as a standard. Because the breach with the Papacy in the sixteenth century was advantageous to religion in England, it by no means follows that it was an evil to be united intimately with the Roman Church in the eleventh. The nation had suffered by reason of its isolation from the larger life of Europe and when forced back into the general current by the rough discipline of conquest, gained incalculably in art, scholarship, energy, and, it may be added, in religious fervour.

The home of the best religious culture in Normandy was the Abbey of Bec. The "pirates"—for this is what the native French persisted in calling the Normans—possessed the art of combining ferocity in war with a real zeal for education, which disdained no foreign aid that would foster the advancement of learning. A knight, named Herluin, full of religious zeal, embraced the monastic life and founded a monastery remarkable for the austerity of its discipline. He was not a scholar, but a simple-hearted, pious soldier, yet he could attract men to him of world-wide reputation for their learning. Conspicuous among these were two Italians, Lanfranc of Pavia, and Anselm of Aosta, both of whom became successively Archbishops of Canterbury. The Normans encouraged these two great men—William made Lanfranc his chief adviser and the Primate of his new kingdom, and the Norman nobles insisted on Anselm for Archbishop in the days of Rufus—which is proof sufficient that the conquerors were determined to employ the best talent at their command.

The policy of William I was to do everything that would render the Church efficient; but he was determined to make the clergy, as well as the nobles, obedient to him. He would tolerate no feudatories to be practically independent of the Crown, nor any bishops who presumed to flout his authority. His principle was to establish a feudalism in England in which every landowner would be directly responsible to the King, and the clergy would be recognised as a separate Order, with their own courts and privileges; but always ultimately under his control. On three points, the Chronicle says, he always insisted: that no new Pope should be recognised by his subjects, that no new law should be enacted by his bishops, and that none of the royal barons or ministers should be excommunicated without the consent of the King.

The first point covers the attitude of England to the Papacy. The Pope was to receive all the money dues customary in antiquity; but was practically to be inaccessible save through the King, and by his consent. William absolutely refused to recognise the Pope as his feudal superior (*fidelitatem facere*), as no precedent could be cited that an English King had ever done so.

As to the second, the King's policy was to permit the bishops liberty in the executive, but not in the legislative, domain. Their courts were to be distinct from those of the King, but by no separate enactment could they extend their authority. Like the barons, their property was to be held direct from the Crown, through the symbolical ceremony of investiture by ring and staff, a method that enabled the King virtually to prevent the election of any person distasteful to himself.

Finally, the King's secular officials were not to be coerced by the Church under threat of ecclesiastical censure for crimes which popular opinion might attribute to them, unless the King gave his assent.

This strong assertion of royal supremacy no one disputed as long as the Conqueror lived. Apart from his personal force of character, he justified his arbitrary claims by the justice of his rule, by his sincere anxiety to do the best for religion, shown in his careful choice of bishops, and by his scrupulous care not to abuse his power for his personal advantage or profit. The evils of such a system only became apparent in the days of his successors.

The interference of Rome in the affairs of England as the Norman regime continued seems to have been generally beneficial, though the royal power suffered by the increasing demands of the Pontiffs; and it is necessary to note how and why the Pope's authority waxed stronger under the later Normans and early Plantagenets. For the first part of the period it was not, for various reasons, unpopular with the people, whose reverence for the Roman Church, which had sent the first missionaries to their ancestors, was unabated. Further, there was nothing particularly national about the English monarchy to counteract it. To the Saxons, the Norman Kings were victorious oppressors, and the Plantagenets were neither Norman nor Saxon, but Frenchmen, whose ambitions were continental rather than insular. As long, therefore, as the Church, supported by Rome, was in controversy with the Crown, Rome was decidedly popular: not till the wickedness of John and the weakness of Henry II made the Crown rely on the support of the Papacy did any anti-Roman feeling become manifest.

The policy of William Rufus was so unscrupulous that almost any appeal by the Church to the Pope or other external authority could plead justification. This King possessed much of his father's ability, and none of his integrity. His conception of royal supremacy allowed

him to use every pretext to enrich himself by keeping
church benefices vacant to his own profit. The story of
Anselm's appointment as archbishop and his subsequent
expulsion from the realm is the disgraceful record of an
attempt on the part of a tyrant to oppress a defenceless
Church. Here the Pope could do little: all he was able
to effect was to show his respect for the persecuted archbishop, and to recognise in him the most famous Christian
teacher of his age. The result, however, was to create a
general distrust of the secular power where the Church
was concerned.

The continual sufferings of Anselm in his dispute
about investitures under Henry I helped to advance the
papal claims to control over English ecclesiastical affairs.
Henry I, like his namesake, the Emperor Henry V, gave
up the right of investiture by ring and staff, though he
retained the old substantial influence in the appointment
of his bishops. There is nothing, however, to show that
the abuses of royal power which had prevailed under Rufus
were discontinued, for Henry I kept bishoprics vacant,
much as his brother had done, in order that he might enjoy
their revenues. Consequently, papal interference on this
point would have been a benefit to the Church.

Rome now began to resume regular correspondence
with foreign churches, including England, by sending
ambassadors or legates, who, as the personal representatives of the Pontiff, were recognised as the superiors of
the native clergy. It was, however, necessary for them
to obtain permission from the Crown to visit England,
and the Kings were very sensitive on this point. In 1176,
not long after the death of St. Thomas Becket, though at a
time when Henry II was extremely desirous of concili-
ating the Pope, a legate on his way to Scotland entered
England without leave, and was sternly rebuked for his
presumption. In process of time the Archbishop of Canterbury was made a legate of the Pope, *ex officio,* and the
same dignity was often conferred on York. Even Mary,
the last Sovereign under whom relations with Rome were

The Normans and the Papacy

legal, for all her devotion to Rome, asserted her right to exclude a legate sent in 1557 by the Pope. The Conqueror forbade any letter from the Pope, which had not passed through his hands, to be received by an English prelate. The higher clergy were also prohibited from leaving the kingdom without a royal license.

Nevertheless, the weakness or follies of the Kings gave the Popes constant opportunities for encroachment. The murder of Becket undoubtedly weakened the authority of Henry II, but did not increase the papal power as much as might have been expected; for the Constitutions of Clarendon, the cause of Becket's exile and, indirectly, of his death, were never repealed. The real debacle of the royal power came when John, to save himself from his subjects and from foreign invasion, surrendered his kingdom to the Pope, and did homage for it to Pandulf, the representative of Innocent III, in 1216. Then a steady reaction set in: exactions of the Pontiffs and the appointment of Italians to English sinecures provoked resentment, till, under Edward I (1272–1308), the law of the land was invoked to restrict the power of the Roman see.

Thus far we have dealt with the importance of the Conquest for the Church in bringing England into close contact with the Holy See. The fact that in Saxon times the English looked to Rome with deep feelings of veneration is undoubted; but the circumstances, both of the country and of the Papacy, made intercourse very difficult in that age, though the archbishops still went to Rome for the *pallium*. After the Conquest the connection was better regulated, but the Church now had less cause to complain of the Papacy than of the encroachments on its liberty by the Crown. Possibly the only time in the Middle Ages that the influence of the Roman see was really oppressive in England was in the middle of the thirteenth century, when their necessities made the Popes, in their quarrel with Frederic II and his descendants, reckless as to whom they despoiled. Complaints at other times usually deal with the expense of appeals to

Rome, the exactions of the Popes' proctors, and the veniality and corruption of the Roman chancery.

A short space may here be given to pointing out some of the advantages of the Conquest to the Church. The Norman cathedrals are a standing testimony to the progress made in architecture. The foreign bishops whom William appointed were almost all mighty builders, and chose the most advantageous sites for the cathedrals they erected. The worship gained in dignity and beauty. An immense impulse was given to education through the contact of the English clergy with the rising continental schools. At first the natives were oppressed in Church as well as in the State, but they rapidly asserted themselves and became men of mark again throughout Europe, as they had been in the palmiest days of Anglo-Saxon Christianity. The fact that Lanfranc, one of the most influential ecclesiastics in Europe, renowned far and wide for his legal and theological learning, was Archbishop of Canterbury, and that he was followed by St. Anselm, to whose genius the rise of scholasticism may be attributed, is a proof that the Normans had the interests of religion at heart, or they would not have chosen Italy's best to preside over the English Church. The contrast between these great men and their obscure predecessors is very marked. But the most valuable work of the Norman Kings, both in ecclesiastical and civil matters, was their success in consolidating their English kingdom by their stern and judicious rule. The awe which the Conqueror inspired is shown by the hostile character given him by the Saxon Chronicles. Not only the oppressed Saxon, but the conquering Norman felt his heavy hand. "The rich men moaned and the poor murmured; but he was so hard that he recked not the hatred of them all." Yet the old writer ends with a prayer that God will have mercy on his soul. And he was right: for he laid effectually the foundation of the greatness of the nation which victors and vanquished at last combined to make.

VII

MEDIEVAL CHRISTIANITY

LITTLE KNOWN OF THE PEOPLE OF THE ELEVENTH AND TWELFTH CENTURIES—PEOPLE IN ENGLAND DEVOTED TO THE CHURCH: THE BISHOPS—ELECTION—IMPORTANCE OF THE BISHOPS—CARDINALS—THE HIGHER CLERGY—THE ARCHDEACON—MONASTERIES—BENEDICTINES — CLUNIACS —CISTERCIANS— CARTHUSIANS — CANONS—FRIARS—UNIVERSITIES—PARISH CLERGY—VICARS.

What was the actual religion of Medieval England? Not, assuredly, that which the Catholic party have eulogised, not that which Protestants have decried. For the early Middle Ages our information is comparatively scanty, as the laity were too ignorant to give expression to their hopes and fears and the clergy were the only people with even a pretence of education. In the eleventh and twelfth centuries there was practically no middle class of importance, and till the thirteenth century, when the rolls of the courts and manors furnish a fund of information, little can be said of the life of those working on the land. Even the mass of the clergy is practically an unknown factor, and our knowledge is confined to the educated and highly placed priesthood and the aristocracy.

At the time of the Conquest, the Church had a varied history behind it in England, extending over almost five centuries, or since the coming of Augustine. The limits of the dioceses were becoming practically what they were at the Reformation, the parishes had been organised, and the monasteries were arising again after their ruin at the hands of the Dane. The clergy were ignorant, but the people were well disposed, there was no heresy and little complaint. In this respect, England was certainly exceptionally favoured, as heresy was making rapid strides in Italy, France, and in the busy cities of the Netherlands; and it often took the form of violent anti-clericalism. After the Conquest the chief grievance against the superior clergy was the fact that they were not Englishmen, but complaints on this score soon died down.

In the survey that we shall now make, we may take things in the following order: (1) The bishops, (2) the higher clergy, (3) the monasteries, (4) the parishes.

(1) The interest in a diocesan map, even of modern England and Wales, lies in the fact that for many centuries some dioceses represented, not shires or early political divisions, but nations—Chichester, for example, was the diocese of the kingdom of the South Saxons; Winchester, of Wessex; Norwich, of East Anglia; London, of the Middle and East Saxons; Canterbury, and its dependent Rochester, of Kent. A diocesan map of England before the dissolution of the monasteries recalls the days of the old Anglo-Saxon kingdoms, when shires and counties were unknown. The only difference is the tendency, just before and after the Conquest, to move the see of the bishop from obscure villages either to cities or to places of strategic importance. Thus, Canterbury, Winchester, and London were always the seat of bishops, as well as the capitals of nations or towns of commercial importance, and so was York, one of the greatest of the ancient Roman cities. But Exeter, Norwich, Lincoln, Durham, were all sees transferred to the strong cities that could be well fortified, and the importance of their bishops was due, not only to their sacred office, but to their possession of military strongholds. After the Conquest, the bishops were great feudal nobles, and their friendliness or neutrality of the utmost importance to the King, who, naturally, demanded a share in their appoint-

ment. This explains the keenness of the dispute about investitures under the Norman Kings.

In theory, every bishop was elected by his flock, or rather by his clergy, in whom the right of choice, even at Rome, was ultimately vested. He was the head of the church of his see, either as its abbot, if they were a body of clergy, or of those who, as canons or prebends, served the Church. But, though these were the electors, it could hardly be expected that bodies, like the monks of Canterbury and the canons of York, would be allowed to impose on the Church whoever they chose as primates, or the monks of Ely to select anyone they preferred to hold some of the strongest castles in the kingdom. As a matter of fact, the King usually assembled a committee of electors at his palace and directed them whom to elect; and, at a later period, the Pope "provided" the bishop himself, and the chapters had no share in his election. These "provided" bishops were, as a rule, recommended by the King to the Pope, and disputes between Rome and the English Crown on this point seem rare. The bishopric of Rochester was appointed by the Archbishop of Canterbury.

A medieval bishop was a truly great man. He was the head of a vast administrative organisation, a judge, often a military commander. His estates were scattered far and wide, and he moved from manor to manor with his vast retinue, as no one property belonging to him could long support his following. He was often absent from his diocese in order to hold some important office of State, or to act as ambassador, and, large as his revenues often were, he had need of them all because of the heavy expenses of his office. The clergy under him were numerous, and we often find that he ordained men, even priests, literally by the hundred. The bishop was assisted, not by suffragans, but by what were termed bishops *"in partibus,"* that is to say, by men with titular sees of places in the far East. Some bishops possessed extraordinary privileges and jurisdiction. Canterbury had the precedence of all archbishops, and sat at the right foot of the Pope. The archbishop had also a primacy over all bishops in the dominions of the King of England, which included, according to the claims of Henry II, a territory extending from Scotland to Spain. His also was the duty of crowning the King. His great rival at York, because of his remoteness from the King's Court, was relatively a petty monarch. Till very recent times, whenever he condescended to visit his cathedral city, he was received with partially royal honours. He disputed the right of Canterbury to precedence over him, and claimed jurisdiction over Scotland, with but little success, however. His suffragan of Durham was a prince-palatine, whose mitre bears a ducal coronet; as a lieutenant of the King, he commanded his own army. Ely, as occupant of the royal lands of the sainted Queen Etheldreda, exercised sovereign rights down to 1835. He had his own judge and prison, appointed his magistrates, and ruled over what was known as the Isle of Ely. Unlike the German prince-bishops, these English princely prelates were never chosen solely from noble families, and some of the greatest bishops were humbly born.

An English bishop sometimes became a cardinal but, till the fifteenth century, this promotion entailed the resignation of his see and residence in Rome. Stephen Langton, in the thirteenth century, seems to have retained his cardinalate after he was made Archbishop of Canterbury. It was not till after the Council of Constance (1417) that it became customary, when great foreign prelates were raised to the dignity of cardinal-priests at Rome, to allow them to retain their positions at home.

(2) The bishop presided over a great church bureaucracy, at the head of which was a dean, if his cathedral was served by canons, or a prior, if it was a monastic church. The cathedral clergy were supposed to act as advisers and helpers to the bishop, and the dean was really the arch-presbyter of the diocese. This ideal of loving coöperation was seldom realised, and for many centuries

Medieval Christianity

the dean and his chapter were, in practice, almost the natural enemies of the bishop. The most memorable dispute between a bishop and his chapter occurred in the thirteenth century, when Robert Grosseteste, Bishop of Lincoln, tried to exercise his authority as visitor. A chapter was made up of the clergy of the cathedral and formed a corporation to administer its estates.

The most important functionary in the diocese, next to the bishop, was the archdeacon. He was the eye (*oculus*) of the bishop, and it was his duty to make visits of inspection to the parishes and to correct abuses. He had, and still has, his own courts. His visitations were dreaded because of the expense they entailed on the parishes, and the office was unpopular. The question, Can an Archdeacon be saved? was generally answered in the negative. A vast amount of business fell to the ecclesiastical courts, as shown by traces which survive in English, and even in American law. Marriage, wills, contracts (because they involved the guilt of perjury), shipping (because lighthouses were under a church corporation), as well as heresy, church property, and questions of morality, all came within the scope of the "Courts Christian," and as a consequence there was an immense army of clerical officials whose duty it was to report violations of the law and to summon the accused to answer to the charges against them. The clergy, further, claimed and maintained the right to be tried by their own courts, as not amenable to lay jurisdiction, and "benefit of clergy," so called, long existed in England, even till the beginning of the nineteenth century. It is not too much to assert that, whilst many of the higher clergy were not theologians, hardly any of them were without a knowledge of law, either civil or ecclesiastical.

(3) England was filled with monasteries of every description, including establishments of canons, regular and secular, and of friars of different Orders. Hermitages were numerous and a very large proportion of the population, male and female, were devoted to what was techni-

cally called "religion." There were religious houses of every kind, from the great Benedictine Abbeys to the cell of the anchoret. The most important abbots and, in earlier times, even abbesses, were summoned to Parliament to serve as representatives, not so much of religion as of property. The heads of the larger monasteries were often fully the equals of the bishops in rank, though it is remarkable how often bishops, and how rarely abbots, played a leading part in secular affairs. The importance of the monasteries was on the wane in the late Middle Ages, and by the time of the Tudors the heads of only twenty-six were summoned to Parliament.

(a) The most ancient and important monasteries, including those of the cathedrals, were subject to the Benedictine rule. The Benedictine was the most ancient and sensible of all monastic Orders. It restrained all excesses, even of devotion; it encouraged industry, whether in the management of the estates, or in the field of learning. A monk of one of the chief houses belonged to the higher class of society and was a person of importance. If the popular tale be true, Nicholas Breakspeare, who became Pope Hadrian IV, was not socially eligible to be admitted to the Abbey of St. Albans. Chaucer's Monk is evidently a Benedictine. He is a scholarly gentleman, an excellent judge of a horse, pompous and so prosy that he never could have pushed his way into the position he graced. He was next in social rank among the Canterbury Pilgrims to the Knight. The poet's Prioress, with her priests and nuns as attendants, is evidently a highborn lady worthy of every consideration. Almost all of the abbots in the House of Lords were Benedictines.

(b) The first Reformation of the Benedictine Order at Cluny, a monastery in Gaul, was founded early in the tenth century. The Cluniacs, unlike the Benedictines, were not independent communities; all their abbeys were subject to the parent house.

(c) The Cistercians, whose great saint, Bernard, virtually ruled the Western world from the Abbey of Clair-

Medieval Christianity

vaux, which was dependent on that of Citeaux, were a severer Order than the Benedictines, or even the Cluniacs. One of the first of its founders was an Englishman, St. Stephen Harding. Though St. Bernard had denounced the luxury of Cluny, whose church was one of the finest in Europe, the Cistercians have left in Fountains Abbey the most beautiful monastic remains in England.

(d) The Carthusians, or monks of the Charterhouse, tried to combine a society of monks living together with the solitude of the hermit. The courage displayed by the London Carthusians in the days of Henry VIII was remarkable.

After the monks came the canons. A canon is a person subject to a rule (*canon*). The title is applied to members of a collegiate church the services of which are conducted by them in common. Though canons were originally priests who lived with the bishop and assisted him in his church, there were afterward many canons' churches without any bishop in residence. Canons were secular and regular. A secular canon lived in his own house like an ordinary priest, and assisted his colleagues in the services of the church, whilst a regular canon lived a semi-monastic life. The most important order of canons belonged to the rule of St. Augustine, and were called Austin Canons. There was also one, a purely English Order, founded by St. Gilbert of Sempringham.

At the beginning of the thirteenth century friars (*fratres*) make their first appearance. The most important were those of St. Dominic (preachers) and of St. Francis, whose glory was their imitation of the poverty of Christ. The friaries were mostly to be found in the towns.

The ecclesiastical names of London landmarks which still survive are an evidence of the influence of the religious Orders. Gray Friars, Black Friars, Austin Friars, the Minories, Crutched Friars, the Temple, the Charterhouse, and others, testify to their presence, whilst Abbot, Prior, Friar, Frere, Canon, so common as English surnames, prove how strong was the influence of the Orders on the minds of the people.

The English Universities of Oxford and Cambridge are always popularly regarded preëminently as monastic institutions; but, as a matter of fact, the colleges at these seats of learning were founded, not in order to uphold, but often as a protest against, monasticism. The architecture, except where an old monastery has been changed into a college, is domestic rather than conventual. Walter de Merton, the founder of the earliest regular Oxford College, specially ordered that none of the society should be monks. In the later Middle Ages the monks were accustomed to send their novices to the Universities, just as some religious bodies, both Catholic and Protestant, have done in later times.

There remain the parish clergy of England, or, as Chaucer would call them, the "parsons of the towne." The origin of parishes in Western Europe is obscure, as is that of patronage.

To speak generally, the landowner who built the church claimed the right to appoint the priest, and the bishop, on his petition, instituted him. Although it was not always necessary that the man presented should be in Orders, he could be deposed if he did not qualify after a certain time. The parish priest was the head of the parish, which was recognised to be, not merely an ecclesiastical but a civil unit for Government. The parson and his churchwardens were responsible for the good order of the parishioners, and often for the performance of their military duties. Naturally the conduct of worship was the duty of the parson.

The word "parson" is now used almost contemptuously; but really it connoted originally a clergyman's importance. He was the *persona* or person of the parish, the great man held legally responsible for its welfare. The more modern equivalent is the rector. But rectors were less common then than vicars. Vicar (*vicarius*), of course, means a deputy. It became the practice to give the benefices to religious houses and colleges which appropriated their revenues and appointed deputies to do the work. So these "vicars" were assigned, as a stipend, what were called the "lesser tithes." At the Reformation the greater tithes, the property of the rectors, were given to the holders of monastic lands, and the real ministers were paid the lesser tithes for their compensation. There were some very wealthy medieval rectors, but at all times the average parish clergy were poor. The abuses of pluralities; that is, of the same man holding many ecclesiastical sinecures, was by no means unknown in the Middle Ages.

On the whole, the English clergy seems to have been respectable in character throughout the Middle Ages. There were undoubtedly exceptions, but we hear of less serious abuses considering their number, than those prevalent on the Continent. The bishops' registers convey a high idea of the general efficiency of church administration.

VIII

RELIGION AT THE EVE OF THE REFORMATION

MAGNIFICENCE OF THE PARISH CHURCHES—EDUCATIONAL VALUE OF CHURCHES—THE MASS—SERMONS—PURGATORY —CONFIRMATION—PENANCE—EXTREME UNCTION—FEELING TOWARDS THE CLERGY.

The remarkable fact about the Reformation is that, violent as it was, complete as was the religious revolution in many countries, it was not accompanied by any actually anti-Christian movement. So far as the Creed was concerned, the Protestants were as orthodox as the Catholics. When it is remembered that the entire fabric of the Western Church was shaken everywhere to its foundation; that institutions men had been for centuries taught to revere were ruthlessly destroyed; that the rulers of the Church were held up to contempt; that the buildings hallowed by the reverence of ages were defaced and sometimes ruined—it is hard to believe that Christianity, as a religion, was never so much as questioned! Even at its chaotic worst there was nothing as heretical in the sixteenth century as the Catharism of the twelfth and thirteenth; for the Anabaptists and Socinians differed essentially from the heretics of Southern France, Northern Italy, Albigenses, Patarines, and Bogomili. Our conclusion must be that, when the Reformation came, most of these people were well grounded in the fundamental truths of the Christian revelation.

We know something of the attention given to religious instruction in England in the last days of the ascendancy

Religion at the Eve of the Reformation 61

of the Old Church, from the way in which it practically silenced the once popular heresy of the Lollards. Many a church in England still remains as evidence to the desire that the people should be instructed in doctrine and even in Scripture. There still exists a considerable amount of medieval devotional literature and instruction in Christian duty. It is evident that the services of the Church were intended to be followed with attention, for these were often explained in language familiar to the humblest.

The centre of all Christian worship in the Middle Ages was not the sermon, but the Sacraments, and the priest's first duty was not so much to instruct his people as to administer to them the means of Grace. People went to church when the Mass was offered, more for prayer than for edification. Religion seems to have been generally normal in England on the whole, so far as priest and people were concerned. There was little or no heresy till the social discontent which followed the Black Death. The disputes which occurred were among the clergy, and any startling opinion, being concealed in the decent obscurity of a learned language, did not disturb the even tenor of the lives of the people. Except London, there was not one considerable city; for Bristol, Norwich, and York can hardly have had large populations, nor could they compare with the great manufacturing centres on the Continent. Life in England, in the main, ran its normal course; and the parishes may be considered as a rule to have been rustic ones.

When we recollect all this, we are amazed at the magnificence of many of the parochial churches, which almost rivalled those of the cathedrals and monasteries. In the least frequented parts of the country, small villages possess churches of surpassing beauty, and, despite the defacing hand of centuries, the remains of once sumptuous decorations—altar scenes, font-covers, wood-carving, stone tracery, bronzes, altar tombs. The visitor to-day can see that the walls were once covered with paintings; and the windows filled with glass which is to us as valuable as jewels, for no maker can reproduce it. We can only marvel, with the roads mere tracks, how the stone was carried from great distances with which to construct these churches, and the vast amount of labour procured when the smallness of the population is taken into account. The parish churches of England are really more wonderful than the cathedrals themselves.

The main object sought in making these magnificent churches was educational; and one sometimes wonders whether less money was not wasted then on the most expensive parish church, than is expended now on many a cheap and hideous parish school. In those days, when reading was a rare accomplishment and the price of a book prohibitive, the churches were popular manuals of instruction. Religious education had practically to be conveyed through the eye: the story of redemption in the Old and New Testaments, heaven and judgment, the legends of the saints, the main duties of religion, all were depicted in the church and explained to the people. Much that was superstition, no doubt, got mixed in with instruction otherwise salutary; but even the pilgrimage to the wonder-working shrine had its educative effect. Grant that the Bible was rarely read; its contents were familiar, as we can see from Chaucer's Wife of Bath, who is too natural to be untrue to life. A vulgar, worldly, coarse-minded, but extremely clever woman, for all that she has her biblical arguments at her fingers' end.

The service to which the people were accustomed was the Mass. The primitive Communion, of which all the faithful partook, had given place to a sacrificial act, pronounced inaudibly by the celebrant, in which the ministers at the altar alone had a share. The people attended, but took no part: they said their private prayers and trusted to the efficacy of the priest's acts. Only the very devout communicated, save at rare intervals. But by the fourteenth century, efforts were made to render the acts of the priests intelligible. Books, naturally, were only avail-

Religion at the Eve of the Reformation

able for the rich and readers were few; so the service was explained in simple rhymes, easy to commit to memory, gathered together in what is known as the "Lay Folks Mass Book."

Although the clergy rarely preached, sermons were decidedly popular; and those with the gift of eloquence were subject to the same temptation they are to-day. The friars were especially popular in the pulpit, and cultivated preaching as an art. It was customary to enliven the sermons by stories, and collections of anecdotes for the use of preachers were circulated. Some moralists complained that often the story was more considered than the moral, if the latter was insisted upon at all. Some popular preachers were censured as Sabbath breakers, because they travelled from church to church on Sundays, in order to display their gift. The last of the Canterbury Tales is a sermon by the "Persone of the towne," an excellent specimen of medieval teaching. It deals with Penance, and the seven deadly sins, and is clear, practical, and full of sensible advice given by a man of piety and learning.

Medieval religion played a great part in man's life, and kept him close company from the cradle to the grave. His very amusements were devised for his edification by the priest. Scarce a week could pass without some day marked for special devotion by the Church. Every trade or profession had its patron saint. It is not true that the people were encouraged to believe that religion was an easy thing, provided the commands of the Church were fulfilled and its dues paid. On the contrary, the doctrine of many priests was almost Calvinistic in its severity, and gave stern warning that few indeed would be saved. This is certainly the tone that runs through the collects which reflect strongly the influence of the teachings of St. Augustine. With the appearance of Wyclif and the Lollards, insistence upon the doctrine of predestination began to be suspected as heretical in tendency. There was also a feeling growing that the Sabbath ought to be observed with the same strictness as the Puritans of a later date required.

But though there was this decidedly Puritan strain in English medieval religion, and a troubled feeling that many would be lost forever, it was hard for anyone to imagine that so terrible a fate could after all overtake a Christian man and his relatives and friends. But, if hell was problematical, there was no doubt that purgatory, its alternative, was sufficiently terrifying. For no one entertained a doubt that the sufferings of those who were expiating their sins after death were neither light nor of short duration. In A. D. 1300, Dante saw Statius in purgatory which meant that the poet had already endured nearly twelve centuries of pain, and was by no means ready yet for heaven. The mercy of the Church, however, provided a means of escape from purgatory. By the prayers of the faithful, and especially by the merit of the offering of the Mass a speedier deliverance might be secured. To hasten their release people were ready to pay heavily for Masses to be offered for the beloved dead, and the rich were anxious to secure the aid of a priest to pray for their own personal deliverance. For this purpose they endowed what came to be called chauntries, chapels with an altar, where Mass would be said, for the benefit of their souls, by a priest who received his stipend from the income of the fund they had provided. Thus the number of clergy attached to churches with no particular duty save that of offering the Mass for their benefactor, grew to be large. Nothing stirred the reformers more than this situation, and to the spread of this practice is due the violent prejudice felt by Protestants toward the very natural desire to pray for the dead.

The idea that there are seven Sacraments is common to both the Eastern and Western Churches, and is but another instance of the tendency to group things in Threes, Sevens, Tens, and Twelves. Of those not accepted by Protestants, Matrimony and Holy Orders were for special

Religion at the Eve of the Reformation

states of life, and the three others, Confirmation, Penance, and Extreme Unction, alone demand our present attention.

Of Confirmation, it is enough to say that most Protestants, who accept infant Baptism, make use of something analogous to it, as do also the Jews. It is inevitable that a child who has been admitted to the fellowship of a religion in infancy should have, at an age when he is capable of understanding its privileges and responsibilities, an opportunity of acknowledging them; and, when the idea of a Sacrament is introduced, of receiving special Grace. In the West, children were, and are, brought to the bishop for that purpose when they are old enough to understand what it means. It is an instance of the practical Western mind changing an ancient custom for the sake of edification.

Penance was originally a merciful concession by which a baptized person, who had fallen into sin, might be restored once, and once only, to Communion with the Church. In process of time sincerity compelled the admission that all, without exception, needed to realise constantly that they were sinners, and stood in need of pardon and restoration to Christian fellowship. In the Middle Ages Penance was two-fold in character, public and private. Public Penance was prescribed for grievous and open sins, and was practically the alternative of excommunication, whereby the sinner was cut off from all communion with Christians. It often took a degrading form, as wearing some badge to show that the man was under ecclesiastical censure. It was especially imposed as the penalty of heresy. Sin was expiated by scourging, or heavy payments to charity, or pilgrimages, and the like. Private Penance was imposed for sins confessed to the priest, in accordance with the canon of the Fourth Lateran Council (1215), by which everybody was compelled to resort to auricular confession at least once a year, under severe penalties. In the days of the Reformation no objection was made to the severity of church discipline, but to the manner of its administration. The

Puritans, indeed, complained that it was not severe enough.

The scriptural authority quoted for Extreme Unction is the Apostolic injunction to a sick person to call the elders of the Church in order that they may anoint him with oil, calling on the name of the Lord. "And the prayer of Faith shall heal the sick man, and if he hath committed any sin it shall be forgiven him" (James V, 13–15). The meaning of the rite appears to be that sickness is due to sin, and the presumption is that the prayers of the elders ensure the pardon of the invalid while the oil is used in part remedially. Restoration to health is declared to be the result of the visit of the elders to the sick bed. The warrant of Christ is claimed for this Sacrament because it is said that His Apostles, after He had commissioned them, anointed with oil many that were sick, and healed them (Mark VI, 13). In the Eastern Church the practice of the primitive Church is continued in its literal form. The priests come to the sick bed and anoint the man, in the hope that he may recover. The Latin Church regarded the ceremony, not as curative, but as a preparation for death, the *viaticum,* something that the traveller to the next world takes with him, as a protection on his journey into the unknown. This Sacrament, it may surprise some to learn, was not eagerly sought, because of the popular superstitions connected with it. Some supposed that, like Baptism and Holy Orders, it could never be repeated, and that those who did not happen to die after receiving it could not be similarly prepared for death again. Consequently, they would be expected to live a life of severe mortification for the rest of their days, which might not prove convenient. The clergy had to urge those in peril of death to seek the Sacrament, and as additional persuasion to insist that it was capable of repetition.

The points emphasised in the religious life of the Middle Ages can only be understood in the light of the heresies and revolts then current which were symptoms of the coming Reformation in England and elsewhere. As a popular movement, the Reformation was not so much a movement against the Pope as against the clergy. The only ones in England who could have any possible grievance against the Roman court were ecclesiastics in high places. The exactions which the laymen felt were not those of a distant prelate, but of clergy with whom he was in immediate contact. The wealth and power of his own church were the object of his resentment rather than abuses of authority in distant Italy. The last days of the fourteenth century had been marked by outbursts, not only of religious discontent but of social dissatisfaction. They witnessed an attack on property which it required the iron hand of the first Lancastrian sovereigns to suppress, and the Church, as the richest institution of the day, shared in this hostility. Since the centre of the power of the priesthood was the Mass, as long as the priest alone was recognised as able to offer the sacrifice, and to call into being the mysterious Presence of the Saviour, on which the salvation of the world depended, so long would the Church possess powers coercive in the strongest degree. But if once belief in the Mass as a saving sacrifice were to become relaxed, the priest would be reduced from the only possible mediator with Heaven to the position of a minister to his congregation. The popular attack on the priesthood, therefore, concentrated its efforts on the attempt to change the Mass into a Communion, and to combat the doctrine that the priest changed the elements by the words of the Canon of the Mass. Thus began, with the Lollard movement in England, a determination to destroy priestly authority that grew and spread. The Reformation at first directed itself not against Rome, whose authority troubled only kings and prelates, but against the Mass, and this determined its whole course rather than any patriotic zeal for the national liberty of the English Church.

IX

HENRY VIII

POPULARITY OF HENRY VIII—CHARACTER OF THE BREACH
WITH ROME—HENRY VIII ALWAYS "ORTHODOX"—PREC-
EDENTS FOR HENRY'S ACTION—HENRY VIII SUPPORTED BY
PARLIAMENT—THE MEDIEVAL CHURCH EXPENSIVE—THE
CHURCH AND THE NOBILITY—HENRY VIII'S VIGOROUS
ACTION—HOW FAR HENRY VIII WAS A REFORMER—NO NEW
CHURCH SET UP—AN IMAGINARY CONCORDAT BETWEEN
HENRY VIII AND THE POPE—SIGNIFICANCE OF HENRICIAN
REFORMATION.

No King ever ascended his throne with brighter prospects than Henry VIII. He owed much both to the wisdom and to the unpopularity of his father. Henry VII was one of the most prudent princes of his time. His right to reign was dubious, to say the least, but he kept his position to the last, and left the monarchy stronger than ever. If his government was oppressive to individuals, it was always economical; unlike most kings, he left behind him a full treasury. There was little to fear from any of his subjects: the Church was docile and submissive, the nobility exhausted and almost obliterated by the Wars of the Roses, the middle class rising in influence, but as yet without much political power. With the country at peace, the King was more indisputably supreme than he had ever been before in English history. But Henry VII was not an attractive ruler. His greed for money was notorious, and his two infamous ministers were objects of detestation and dread. The new spirit which was spreading throughout Europe had received little encouragement under the efficient tyranny of this able monarch. At his death hope revived, and in his son the nation found a young king after its own heart. Henry VIII had everything to commend him to an enthusiastic nation. He was young, good-looking, believed to be good-natured, an excellent scholar, since he had been bred, as a younger son, for the Church, a first-rate athlete, and gracious of manner to men of every degree. It seemed as though the land was to be blessed by one of the ablest, most popular, most amiable, and most religious rulers who had ever occupied the throne of Edward I, Henry V, or Edward the Confessor. Men might have wondered at the beginning of his reign whether the young Henry VIII would end as the arbiter of Europe, or as a canonised Saint. That a king who had come forward as the champion of the church against Luther, thirteen years after his accession in 1522, and been honoured with the title of Defender of the Faith by the Pope should be the one to sever England from the Papacy would have seemed incredible.

Our object here is not to relate the course of events; but to indicate the significance of the breach between Henry VIII and the Papacy, and the position in which it left the Church in England. The King sundered the connection which, for centuries, had been maintained between England and the Roman Pontiff, subjugated completely the clerical estate of the realm, and accomplished the partial spoliation of the Church. In all this work he made no attempt to alter the doctrine of the Catholic Church, nor were the theories on which he acted novelties, in the sense that they had never been broached before in Western Christendom. Further, even what appear to us now to be the more arbitrary of the acts of Tudor despotism were done in legal fashion, and with the consent of both houses of Parliament.

Henry VIII had been trained as a younger son for the Church. He belonged to a political party and represented a family renowned for its orthodoxy. Of the Lancastrian sovereigns, Henry IV and the victorious and beloved Henry V were full of zeal against Lollardy, and the piety of Henry VI was signal enough to make his canonisation a possibility. Henry VII was most scrupulous in the discharge of his duty as a Catholic, and, though parsimonious elsewhere, his religious benefactions were lavish. The teaching of Luther and the continental reformers had nothing attractive to offer to his successor, who loved magnificence in all things, and the fact that the Princes of the Empire used religion as a pretext for rebellion against their lawful sovereign made Lutheranism absolutely repulsive to one who held the Imperial dignity of his own Crown in the highest esteem. To the day of his death Henry VIII believed that he had never been unworthy of his title of Defender of the Faith.

There was precedent enough on the side of great monarchs who defied the claims of the Pope to control them. Emperors had repeatedly set up anti-Popes. Philip the Fair, of France, had not scrupled in the person of his agents to treat Boniface VIII with insulting brutality, nor to coerce Clement V to do his will. The proposal had actually been made in Parliament to seize the entire revenues of the Church in England in order to devote them to secular purposes, so that the suppression of the monasteries finally was only part of a project suggested in 1400. Even earlier, proposals had been made to reduce the Pope to a state of apostolic poverty so as to use the wealth of the Church for the furtherance of the Crusade against the advance of the Turks.

In his church policy Henry had to secure the support of his Parliament for every step taken by him. The power of the Upper House, however, had been reduced to a shadow of what it was before the Wars of the Roses, and the Commons could be coerced and bullied to an almost incredible extent; for one reason because many of them had been nominated by the King. At the same time, Parliament could, and did, show itself independent on occasions where the interests of property were concerned, and formidable risings during his reign warned Henry that he could not safely act in opposition to the will of his subjects. The title of the House of Tudor to the throne was not a good one, and had Henry VIII really provoked general indignation, the nation would undoubtedly have united as one man to set up some pretender in his place. But he possessed, in a rare degree, the gift of anticipating the popular will and of posing as its representative. Arbitrary as his acts seem to us, he was never universally execrated personally, and his worst actions always displayed a show of legality. Each one of the many important persons who were executed in his reign had some sort of a trial before he was condemned, and the King's claims, even to act in defiance of precedent, were expressly sanctioned by his Parliament. A King of France might have proclaimed himself "Head of the Church"; the title was conferred by Parliament on Henry VIII.

What is the explanation of this acquiescence on the part of the realm? Certainly not indifference to religion. The clergy and the monks may have been unpopular, but not the doctrines of the Church. There are no indications of any great hostility to Rome. The Pope was unable to exact money from England as he had done in the thirteenth century; and as far as the laity were concerned, it was just as objectionable to them to pay mortuary and other fees to the clergy at home as to anybody else. What the average man wanted was a less expensive church, in which he could worship as his ancestors had done. Certainly, he had very little sympathy for heretics and religious innovators. If the King wished to curb the power and reduce the wealth of the clergy, he was welcome to do so. As regards the breach of relations with the Pope, probably Henry's most unpopular act was the putting away of Catherine of Aragon, and his marriage with Anne Boleyn.

The Church and the greater nobles had, till the close of the Wars of the Roses, been the two influences which limited the power of the Crown, which, both in England and France, was finding its best support in the commercial and middle classes. The Commons had not yet sufficient power to interfere much in the government of the country, and saw that the king was best able to give them the security and tranquillity which they desired. They realised clearly that the despotism of a single ruler was less of an evil than a war of succession, and for this reason the Tudors, who were at least an able family, could rely on their support. At the accession of Henry VII the nobility was almost powerless. There were not thirty lay members of the House of Lords against fifty-two bishops and abbots. The Church, to all appearances, was as powerful as ever; but it had lost the spirit of independence of the Middle Ages, as well as the confidence of the people. Far-sighted statesmen, like Wolsey, foresaw what was going to happen with a prince of Henry's ambition if he took control of affairs, and with the fall of Wolsey in 1529 the King was free to pursue his own policy.

Once embarked upon it, Henry carried it through with a consistency for which he is not usually credited. He broke relations with Rome; induced Parliament to give him the revenues which the Pope had enjoyed in the form of Annates, First Fruits, etc.; allowed Cromwell, as his Vicar-General, to take the place of a papal legate above the Archbishop, and then he struck the clergy down with a series of smashing blows. He ordered his judges to declare them all guilty under the Premunire Statute; laid on both Convocations an enormous fine; forced them all to acknowledge him as "Supreme Head of the Church of England," and struck terror on every side by executing as traitors the London Carthusians, the holiest monks in the land, including Bishop Fisher, whom he himself had declared to be the most learned and best in his dominions, and his old friend and Chancellor, Sir Thomas More, the most honoured lay scholar in the world. His next step was to arrange for a visitation of the monasteries, and after a case against them had been devised, to force some to surrender their charters, and to suppress others without pity. It was all done in a constitutional way, with the consent and approval of the representatives of the people. With the Church awed into subjection, he turned on the heretics. As Cromwell was of no further use, he was executed after persuading his master to ally himself with the Protestants. The Six Article Act was passed, making it a felony to deny Transubstantiation—notice that the bishops were not now the judges—and a crime to consent to Protestant innovations. To prove that all who resisted him were in equal danger, he dragged Protestants and Catholics as heretics and traitors respectively to their deaths on the same hurdle.

But Henry VIII was, in one sense, a reformer as well as a tyrant. He desired the Church to be humbled, but also to be purified and rendered more efficient by his reforms. With this in mind, he increased the number of bishoprics out of the monastic revenues, encouraged the translation of the Scriptures into English, and the issue of books which would make the doctrines of Faith and the duties of a Christian plain to all. He destroyed objects of superstitious veneration which were impostures; he even allowed the Litany to be published in English; and except that he removed the name of the Pope from the service books and declared the Church of Rome to be abominable, he did nothing which was contrary to Catholicism as understood in the West. In other words, had at any time Henry agreed to a concordat with Rome, he had done nothing which could not have been sanctioned, except his taking the title of "Supreme Head" and his vilification of the Pope. As a matter of fact, when Mary once more acknowledged the papal supremacy, the price demanded for reconciliation, and conceded, was the recognition of the dissolution of the monasteries, and the confiscation of their estates for lay purposes.

It must not be forgotten that Henry had the co-operation of his bishops, not one of whom, except Fisher, seem to have had any religious scruples over breaking with the Papacy. Some of those who upheld the doctrine of the Mass most staunchly, Gardner and Bonner for example, were entirely with the King in the matters of the marriage suit with Catherine, and of the royal supremacy, and do not seem to have been taken back as repentant schismatics in the days of Mary. The only bishops who were deposed by Henry were Latimer and Coverdale, who were in sympathy with the Protestants. His chief religious adviser was Cranmer, who played so important a part in the next reign. Cranmer is by no means an attractive character—few people were at this period; but he was undoubtedly a man of great ability and learning. His worst trait was his lack of courage. A man might well be humble before Henry VIII, whom Cranmer sincerely admired and even loved; but he was equally submissive to the two protectors, in the reign of Edward VI, in whose rapacity and injustice he usually acquiesced. Under Henry he did as much to encourage reformation as was consistent with his own safety.

The theory that Henry VIII set up a new Church in England is entirely untenable. He had no idea of doing anything of the kind. His quarrel with the Pope was a diplomatic one, and was healed in the reign of his daughter. Princes whose orthodox faith was never questioned had resisted the Pope by force of arms. Rome itself had been captured by the soldiers of Charles V only a few years before the rupture with England. Divines honoured as doctors, nay, even as saints, had denounced the Court of Rome and compared it to the harlot city of the Apocalypse. Violent and unscrupulous as was the King of England, he was a well-read theologian and had no desire to separate himself and his kingdom from the Church of antiquity by denying its fundamental doctrines.

It may be fanciful, yet not wholly unprofitable, to try to imagine a concordat between Henry VIII and the Roman see, had he lived to old age. It would probably have been like the one under Mary, only the king would have permitted no foreign interference. At such a conference he would probably have insisted on the nomination of all bishops by himself, and on a Praemunire Statute far more drastic than that already in existence. He might have set up a claim to act himself, or through his representative, as papal legate and he might even have insisted that English should be used in part of the liturgy. In return he would have consented to the collection of the customary dues, given up the title of Supreme Head, and acknowledged in general terms the papal authority. No more than his predecessors, would he have allowed a Roman inquisition, but his severity to heretics would have left no excuse for this outside interference. He would have humbly, but successfully it is probable, requested the canonisation of Henry VI, to the honour of the House of Lancaster, which he claimed to represent. Whether England, under such conditions, would have ever become Protestant is open to doubt. Certainly, Catholicism would have been safe as long as the strong hand of Henry protected it. But these are, after all, at best, ingenious surmises.

Let us now put the question, What was the position of the English Church at the death of Henry VIII? Though the King and his supporters claimed that supremacy of the Crown over the Church was no new thing, it had become infinitely more thorough in practice than anything previously known. In the language of the Middle Ages, the *Ecclesia Anglicana* meant the clergy, and these were absolutely under the authority of the Crown. The supremacy was personal, not constitutional, and a present king really exercised all the arbitrary power over their acts and persons which an absent Pope might, in theory, claim. Before Henry VIII, an ecclesiastic oppressed by the Pope might appeal to the King, and *vice versa;* under him there was no appeal to any authority but his own. In one matter an empty freedom was granted. The chapters were allowed to meet and choose their bishops, but woe to them if they failed to select the King's nominee. This apparently absurd, but not entirely useless, fiction is still kept up. The essentials of doctrine, as has been shown, were preserved in their integrity. Save that all the churches were to use the ritual of Salisbury, and that the Pope's name was omitted, all went on as before. The position of the secular, as contrasted with the monastic clergy, was virtually unaltered, save that the king's judges, and not the bishops, decided cases of heresy, now regarded as a criminal offence. Protestantism was as illegal in the dominions of Henry VIII as it was in Spain. The cults of some saints, notably of Thomas Becket at Canterbury, were suppressed, as encouraging superstition, or because the pilgrimages to them might result in disturbances, or the questioning of the royal power. All connection with Rome was, of course, a penal offense, and any special value to devotions performed there was expressly denied. But as yet there was no legal recognition of anything like continental Protestantism, and the Church of England continued its course unbroken, unless it is held that a breach with Rome annihilates a Church, a view apparently not entertained in the sixteenth century.

X

THE PROTESTANT AND CATHOLIC REACTIONS

DISASTROUS REIGNS OF EDWARD VI AND MARY, 1547–1558—HENRY VIII'S POLICY REVERSED—EDWARD VI'S REIGN CALLED THE PROTESTANT MISRULE—THE FIRST STEP WAS A GRADUAL CHANGE OF THE MASS INTO A COMMUNION—THE FIRST PRAYER BOOK—THE ARTICLES—EXTREME PROTESTANT REFORM—REUNION WITH ROME—PERSECUTION OF REFORMERS—THREE EXPERIMENTS (1) THE SIX ARTICLES (2) UNCOMPROMISING PROTESTANTISM (3) RETURN TO ROME—REASON FOR FAILURE: A *via media* NECESSARY—ELIZABETH'S BALANCING POLICY.

It matters little whether his sympathies are Catholic or Protestant, no Englishman can fail to pronounce the reigns of Edward VI and Mary I the most regrettable in the history of the nation. In the first place Protestantism appears at its worst. Its leaders in the State were cruel, arbitrary, and rapacious: those in the Church, subservient and, at the same time, intolerant. Under Mary the party of reaction, starting with everything in its favour, completely alienated the nation by severity toward its opponents, and by drawing England into the war which Spain was waging with France. The Queen's unfortunate marriage to her cousin Philip formed ties between the old religion and an un-English policy, between Protestantism and patriotism, which made the breach with Rome irreparable.

All that was done for ten years after the death of Henry VIII was done in opposition to the policy of his later years, which aimed at securing control of the Church for the Crown, without allowing it to depart from the ancient Faith. In appointing a Council of Regency, in which both sides were represented, the King's object was to see that England, after his death, should, so to speak, mark time, till it became plainer in which direction an advance should be made. Perhaps he hoped for a settlement with Rome, by which the King of England would be recognised in his own dominions as the representative of the Pope, and the power of the Curia, as a court of appeal, transferred to the ecclesiastical courts of England. The unscrupulous men, however, who seized the government at the King's death, allied themselves for their own ends with the continental Protestants.

When one realises, as anyone may by a little study, the sort that the men were who surrounded Henry VIII in his later days, some excuse is possible for the brutality which characterised the King. His death was the signal for an ignoble scramble to retain wealth and power on the part of men whom he had ennobled and left as guardians of his youthful heir. The Court was an intricate mass of intrigue. It set the country seething with rebellion and discontent, coerced Scotland into hostility, and made the whole reign of the boy king one of the most discreditable in English history. It has been called, justly, "the Protestant misrule." But whatever motives guided the leading men in those miserable years, the Church of England emerged from them with a permanent and ineradicable stamp of individuality. Had the misrule lasted much longer very little of the Church in the island would have been left by the so-called reforming nobility. The dissolution and spoliation of the monasteries would have been followed by the same treatment of the churches and cathedrals, and England would have become a land of ecclesiastical ruins. When it is remembered that the ultra-reforming Protector, the Duke of Northumberland, conformed to the old religion under Mary, the sincerity of the convictions of the lay spoliators

The Protestant and Catholic Reactions

may be suspected: the Edwardian bishops, at least, testified to their faith by their deaths.

The beginning of the Reformation under the new regime was marked by a wise discretion. Whatever may be the faults of the King's uncle, who assumed the titles of Duke of Somerset and Lord Protector, and there can be no doubt as to his rapacity, he had some high ideals. He aimed at a social, as well as a religious reformation, and interested himself in the condition of the poor, and in the abolition of the savage repressive legislation, which had disgraced the last days of Henry VIII. His first step in changes in worship could not be seriously reprobated by anybody. The Mass was to be said as heretofore, but an English service was added to enable the people to communicate, as the Missal makes no similar provision. The Communion of the laity was ordered henceforward to be in both kinds, but this was admittedly the primitive practice.

Next came the publication in English of all the services necessary for the conduct of worship for use throughout the realm. The First Prayer Book of Edward VI may lay itself open to objection on the part of the supporters of the old religion, especially the rubric forbidding the elevation of the Host. But even this was not a primitive practice. Provision for the exorcism of infants before Baptism was made, and the sick might receive Extreme Unction if desired. The Mass, for the name was retained as an alternative, was to be celebrated by the clergy in their ancient vestments. As the congregations had never heard the words of the "Canon" pronounced, they would scarcely notice the omission in two places of the names of the saints, and so might attend and find no offence in the new form of service. The men of Cornwall rebelled against the new book, and called the service a "Christmas game"; but as they did not speak English, one foreign language had only been substituted for another. Bishop Gardiner, one of the strongest opponents of the new religion, was not averse to the new book.

The Articles, forty-two in number, were drawn up by Cranmer and his friends, and though the clergy were called upon to agree to them, they do not seem to have had the authority of Convocation or Parliament. This document is much abused as an intensely Protestant confession, but, when carefully studied, it seems moderate and mediating, and no Christian could raise any objection to many of its cardinal clauses. These are the abiding results of the Edwardian Reformation.

But the extremists were not content with anything so moderate. The bishops of the old religion (all, by the way, had agreed to the Supremacy of Henry VIII, and were technically in schism) were thrown into prison, the churches were despoiled by mobs or greedy nobles. Orders were given that no clergyman might so much as own a Missal or a Breviary. Foreigners were invited from abroad in order to instruct the English, under the patronage of Cranmer, and churches were given them for their peculiar services. These men were to aid in the extension of Protestant principles, and the First Prayer Book made way for the Second, in which extreme Protestant doctrines were insisted upon. All observers are agreed that the moral condition of the country was at its lowest ebb; and that the sudden and unwise annihilation of the old authority of the Church, to which men had for generations been accustomed, produced most deplorable results. Protestants and Catholics concurred in this opinion.

That the changes thus brought about were not in accordance with the will of the nation is evident from what followed. The whole country declared for Mary against Lady Jane Grey, and as a matter of course, the old religion was restored. Had not the Queen married her cousin, Philip II, there would have been scarcely a voice raised in favour of the new religion. Reunion with the Roman see was agreed to with remarkable unanimity in Parliament. Once the Pope consented to regard the seizure of the monastic lands as an accomplished fact, there were no further serious difficulties in the way of restoration of his authority to the place it occupied in the twentieth year of Henry VIII. The annates and first fruits were not restored to him, and they were, by the advice of the Primate, Cardinal Pole, devoted to the augmentation of the smaller benefices of the native clergy when Mary's scruples made her give them up. In fact, under Mary, the Pope's power in England was as inconsiderable as it had been in the late Middle Ages, and with all her bigotry, the Queen was too much a daughter of Henry VIII to allow her prerogative to be unlawfully diminished. In addition, the Spanish clergy were not by any means Papalists, though their fanatical devotion to Catholicism is proverbial, and they were disposed to uphold the authority of their monarch and of the Spanish episcopate. Before Mary's death her husband Philip was actually at war with Paul IV, and Cardinal Pole's orthodoxy had been called in question by the Roman Curia. The real conflict between the two religions was, as has here been constantly asserted, not so much over the Pope as over the Mass.

The savage persecution of the Reformers in this reign, which was as impolitic as it was cruel, was condemned even by some of the Spaniards about the Court. Though the pathetic retractation by Cranmer of his recantation and the fortitude displayed by him at the last won popular sympathy, it was not so much the dramatic execution of the bishops and leaders of the Protestant movement, as the sufferings of hundreds of humble people, innocent of any political crime, which inspired such universal horror. Mary was not by nature cruel or vindictive. In purity of life, in the true dignity of high-born virtue, in generosity, and in most other amiable qualities, she was the superior of her sister Elizabeth. Yet she has left a name of abiding terror in England. The hatred of Rome, and all that Church connotes, became indelibly ingrained owing to persecutions which bear her name. They proved an effective barrier against all later attempts to restore the papal authority, especially as her reign was also connected with the humiliation which England endured in the war with France, undertaken by the Queen in the desperate hope of regaining, if she ever possessed, the affection of Philip II. People did not forget that for the aid which the English infantry had contributed to the great Spanish success at St. Quentin, the only fruit of the war England reaped was the loss of Calais, the last remnant of her great French possessions in former days.

It now remains to consider the effect of these two brief and disastrous reigns on the subsequent history of religion in England. Three experiments had been tried, if we include the one in the closing days of Henry VIII. All had proved failures. Whatever was now to be done to secure religious peace, none of these experiments could safely be tried again. Each will be discussed in turn, and why it proved a failure explained.

(1) The remedy proposed by Henry VIII was the famous Act of the Six Articles, in 1538. Henry felt that the Reformation had then gone far enough in England. The supremacy of the Crown was established, the Pope thrown over, the monasteries dissolved, the clergy reduced to complete docility and the Bible translated. Further than this the King was not prepared to go. Accordingly, he persuaded Parliament to make it a felony to deny the doctrine of the Mass, which practically made Catholicism, *minus* the Pope, the religion of England. The more severe provisions of the Act were seldom enforced in its actual operation and few suffered under it. It might have succeeded with a Henry VIII at the head of affairs. But England could not permanently remain a Catholic land which was at war with the Pope and rigidly excluded Protestantism in every form. It apparently considered it, however, a good arrangement and there were agitations for its restoration in later days.

(2) The Edwardian policy was to insinuate an uncompromising Protestantism into the Church. Like every other religious movement in this age, it was guilty of a

reckless disregard of private conviction and much brutality. Even Cranmer was ready to burn people for their opinions, and under him two heretics (one a woman) suffered at the stake. The whole attempt to change people's religion by the action of the Privy Council was bound to be a failure. That it was unpopular is proved by the enthusiastic welcome Mary received as Queen. This reign was to show that continental Protestantism, imported from Geneva, Poland, and elsewhere, was never likely to win the very conservative English, but that they preferred the old way of worshipping God, provided it was not, in their opinion, contrary to Scripture or truth.

(3) Less successful than either of the above was the Marian method. The Spaniards were greatly feared at this time for their power, enterprise, and cruelty, and their influence about the Court and among the clergy was hotly resented.

The manly fortitude shown by such men as Ridley, Latimer, Hooper, Rogers, and Rowland Taylor appealed to the best instincts of the nation, and the cruelty of the persecution aroused its undying detestation. These things gave the death-blow to Rome and the Mass in England.

Some sort of *via media* had then to be discovered, not only if the religious but the political unity of the nation was to be secured. The obvious way to us would have been to grant toleration to all, and exhort them to live together in amity as Englishmen. But this was so contrary to the spirit of the age as to be unpracticable. It was tried in France, and resulted in three religious factions at war with one another. A Church was necessary to the country, and a variety of churches, living side by side, was impossible in those days. The only workable solution was to make the Church very comprehensive and inclusive, in order that those who remained outside should have as little reasonable excuse as possible for dissatisfaction. To have established the old religion with Rome and the Mass would have alienated a powerful part of the nation, the rising middle class; to impose Edwardian

Protestantism would have alienated all the old families of the kingdom; to give either the supremacy would have been to set up an ecclesiastical tyranny, and the people were equally resolved to submit neither to Rome nor Geneva. The only feasible alternative was to retain the bishops, whose presence in the Lords was necessary to the Crown; to leave unchanged the Cathedral establishments and the remains of the ancient hierarchy; to keep the Church Courts—in a word, to alter as little as possible. On the other hand, the people must have the services given to them in their own language, they must not be forced to observe customs contrary to Scripture or leading Romewards, nor must they break away entirely from all friendship with the Protestants of the Continent. Such was the tangled problem which faced the advisers of Elizabeth at her accession. Whatever the solution they devised, they had to bear in mind that her only friend in foreign affairs was her brother-in-law, Philip II, who was the staunchest upholder of Catholicism in Europe. Before dealing with the results of their attempt to arrive at a settlement, it is desirable to review what was done to calm the Church.

In the first place, Elizabeth wisely refused to assume the title which had been borne by Henry VIII and Edward VI, and also by Mary till she resigned it; and instead of Supreme Head, she called herself Supreme Governor. In the second, she took great pains to see that her bishops were canonically ordained by the laying on of hands by men with episcopal ordination. She summoned Convocation to decide on the Articles of Religion, and to sanction her arrangements for the establishment of order. She would have preferred the First Prayer Book of Edward, but gave way to the Protestants by agreeing to a modification of the Second Book, with an implied permission to use the older vestments at the Communion. She allowed the names of many of the old non-scriptural Saints to remain in the Calendar, whilst providing no service for their festivals. According to the Puritan complaints, the Communion was in several churches celebrated much as the Mass had been. The Queen showed a disposition to favour the ancient ceremonials; indeed, her political necessities rather than her convictions made her concede anything to the Protestants. Her attitude to her bishops has been much misrepresented. This is largely due to an eighteenth century fiction that she threatened to unfrock the Bishop of Ely in a speech beginning "Proud prelate." On the contrary, she never sought to relegate her bishops to any such humiliating position as Edward VI's guardians had sought to reduce them. Her object was to make arrangements for all men to live at peace in the Church of England, and to give them as much liberty as was consistent with conformity. Her policy was not ideal, but it saved the country from civil war and left the door open for Christian reunion. The appearance of three great parties—the Romanists, the Independents, the Puritans—was the result, each of which, in the following century, had the opportunity of ruling in England, and all proved equally distasteful to the nation. This is a testimony to the far-sightedness of the Queen and her advisers, and to the government they designed for the Church of England.

XI

THE ROMAN SECESSION

APPARENT INDIFFERENCE TO RELIGION IN ENGLAND—WHY THE ROMANISTS BROKE OFF FROM THE ENGLISH CHURCH—ELIZABETH CONTRASTED WITH MARY—ELIZABETH IDENTIFIES HER INTERESTS WITH HER PEOPLE'S—POSITION AT HER ACCESSION—THE REBELLION OF THE NORTHERN EARLS—PIUS V EXCOMMUNICATES ELIZABETH—THE COUNTER-REFORMATION.

A remarkable characteristic of the Reformation in England was the general indifference of the people to the religious changes. Not that they were irreligious; but they cared little for the forms which religion assumed. Keenly tenacious of their civil liberty, the mass of the nation seemed ready to accept whatsoever religion the Government imposed, and it was less dangerous to propose to restrict "uses" or charges on estates for the benefit of the younger children, than to introduce a new Prayer Book. In the days of Edward VI, the ancient worship was abolished without any serious disturbances, and it was restored with scarcely any trouble under Mary. Even at the accession of Elizabeth, religion was less important than might be expected in shaping the course of events. The Queen herself hardly knew whether she was at heart Catholic or Protestant. For some years the Roman Catholics were not much molested, and they did not formally secede from the Church. Parish priests were to be found who had remained in the Church from the days of Henry VIII, conforming in turn to whatever service the Government in power required to be performed.

What lies before us next is to describe the course by which the Anglo-Romans separated completely from the Church, and became a small but in the main aristocratic sect in the realm. This was accomplished by gradual stages during the reign of Elizabeth. The agencies responsible were the vigilance of the Protestant party and the mistakes of the Roman Curia, whose policy aroused the suspicion of the nation, till it became not a little difficult to be at the same time a good Englishman and a good Catholic. The Catholics who remained in the country gave, as a rule, but little trouble, and, but for the interference from outside, would have probably been practically unmolested. The rebellions and the sufferings of the Roman party were mainly due to interference from the Continent and the activity of the religious Orders.

It is hardly too much to say that, had Elizabeth possessed the virtues of her sister Mary, her reign would have been a short one. It is true that the late Queen had been a ruthless persecutor; but at least bitter disappointment and a sincere fanaticism excuse somewhat her unpolitic and cruel treatment of the Reformers. Mary was naturally humane and, as the opening years of her reign showed, averse to shedding blood. To sacrifice human life to expediency would have been repugnant to her nature. She laboured, as far as possible, for the welfare of her subjects, was pure in life, and generous beyond her means in her benefactions. Elizabeth was the reverse. Her religious convictions often yielded to political expediency, and if her feet were not swift to shed blood, she did not refuse if it were necessary to her safety. Her personal extravagance was as great as her parsimony in other respects was detestable. She could be false, ungrateful, and deceitful beyond description, and her caprices were the terror of her ministers.

The virtues of monarchs and rulers of men have rarely been as beneficial to their kingdoms as certain defects which have justly deserved the reprobation of posterity. Perhaps no ruler governs to more advantage than one

whose selfishness is sufficiently enlightened to realise that
his interests are identical with those of his subjects.
Probably nothing contributed more to give the world a
brief respite of prosperity and peace than the wise egoism
of Augustus, or to make a nation great than the consummate duplicity of Elizabeth. On the tortuous windings
of a policy which always moved in the direction of national progress the fate of the Romanizing Catholics in
England hinged. As we follow their course, we are astonished at the consummate ability of the great Queen,
though our admiration is intellectual rather than moral.

On her accession Elizabeth found herself in a strange
position. Her only ally was her brother-in-law, Philip
II of Spain, who offered to become her husband. To
offend Philip would have meant ruin, and yet he was,
both by disposition and circumstances, irrevocably committed to the old religion. On the other hand, though
named heir to the throne by her father's will, in the eyes
of all good Catholics she was undoubtedly illegitimate,
and her only firm supporters were the extreme Protestants who had returned from exile when she came to the
throne. The Queen and her advisers had conformed during the Marian persecution, and were rather opportunists
than fanatics in religion. Elizabeth herself had no love
for the Protestants. There was nothing puritanical in
her morals, and she enjoyed the pageantry and splendour
of her position. Had she been free to choose, she would
have preferred to go back to the policy of her father, of
a Church, Catholic in doctrine and ritual, subordinate to
her authority, with the repealed Six Article Act again
on the statute book, for use only if absolutely needed.
The reforming divines were singularly unattractive to a
young, energetic, pleasure-loving woman, but they were
at the head of the most active and able party in her
dominions. Therefore, though she respected the Catholics and despised the Protestants, she had the wisdom to
bow to circumstances, and partially to satisfy the reformers without entirely alienating Philip. For a few years,

therefore, there was a species of truce between her Catholic subjects and herself, due partly to the fact that no one believed that the Church settlement she had sanctioned could have any permanence. It always appeared possible that policy might dictate the advisability of making terms with the Roman Church. A good deal of controversy was carried on in volumes of theological literature; but there was no overt act of rebellion; and if the Romanists were annoyed by fines for not attending the new services, they were not seriously oppressed.

Upon the whole, in England, as elsewhere, the Catholics were strongest in the country districts and among the great families, and the Protestants in the towns and among the middle classes. The northern shires were still, in the main, feudal; and the people followed the old religion and the ancient nobility. Consequently, when Mary, Queen of Scots, was driven out of her country, her misfortunes and her zeal for the faith of her fathers aroused the sympathy of the northern Earls; and a rebellion resembling the Pilgrimage of Grace broke out, which was sternly repressed by Elizabeth's generals. After the usual series of executions, the Queen issued a proclamation, saying, as the historian, Lingard, reports, that "she assured her people that she meant not to molest them for religious opinions, provided they did not gainsay the Scriptures, or the Creed Apostolic and Catholic, nor for matters of religious ceremony, as long as they should outwardly conform to the laws of the realm, which enforced the frequentation of Divine Service in the ordinary churches." This was in 1569, and would have left the Catholics, provided they conformed in externals, free to worship as they pleased.

Such a policy was well calculated to bring about a satisfactory solution of the religious trouble. As a class, hardly any subjects have been less inclined to make trouble than the landed gentlemen in England who held faithfully to the ancient religion for generations, though subject to laws which excluded them from the privileges of their rank and impoverished them by unjust exactions. They were men whom persecution could not shake, but not the sort to engage in intrigues and conspiracies. Provided they were unmolested, they were likely to remain at peace, and even when Popery was most unpopular, they were, as a rule, respected. Left to themselves, they shared the prejudices of their neighbours, had no gift for conspiracy, and were intensely English in their distrust of foreigners. A century later, in the days of the Popish plot, when the Roman Catholics were recklessly accused and condemned on the slenderest evidence, the descendants of these men were, as a rule, unmolested.

It appears probable that the Queen's proclamation, even more than persecution, incited the zealous Catholics in England and the authorities in Rome to action. Had her policy been possible to execute it would have called into being a class of lukewarm Catholics who, after a formal appearance in the national churches, would hear Mass and receive the consolation of their religion in private. But the object of the zealots was, not to save the English Catholics from oppression, but to reconquer the island for the Church. Better that these men and their priests, who showed signs of acquiescence, should be persecuted and tormented, than that so great a prize should be sacrificed. Pius V, the Pope at this time, was no statesman, but a Saint, the last Pontiff who has won the supreme honour of canonisation. To the horror of all responsible statesmen in Europe, including Philip II, the Pope had Elizabeth tried and accused for heresy at Rome, and issued the bull *Regnans in excelsis,* declaring her excommunicated, and absolving her subjects from their allegiance.

From this time, the Roman Catholics in England were forced to choose between their religious conscience and their loyalty to their sovereign, since it was impossible to obey both the Queen and the Pope. They felt that there was now only one course open to them: definitely to renounce all connection with the Church of England, and take the side of the enemies of Elizabeth.

By the time of its conclusion, in 1564, the Council of Trent had finally shaped and stereotyped the doctrine of the Roman Church, and the Catholic "Counter Reformation" was at its height. The tide which had been running against the ancient Church had turned, and the Protestants were beginning to lose countries where they had hitherto been dominant. Poland, Bohemia, Southern Germany, and France were coming back to the Catholic fold; and hopes were cherished that England would do the same. The next heir to the throne, Mary, Queen of Scots, was a Catholic; Elizabeth was less and less likely to marry, or might marry a Catholic prince, and the country itself was by no means unanimously in favour of Protestantism. It seemed, in or about 1580, that the time had come for a vigorous effort to regain England for the Church. Although Elizabeth and Philip had hitherto remained nominally at peace, the day was approaching for a life and death struggle for existence on the part of England with Spain, the greatest power in the world; and the quarrel inevitably turned on a religious issue. The Protestants of every shade of opinion rallied round the Queen: conscience made some Catholics prefer their Church to their country, and thus drove them to side with Spain. Overt acts of hostility began the war. The ports of England sent forth vessels to prey on the Spanish settlements in the New World, and the Government at home disowned their acts and profited by their successes. Spain stirred up trouble in Ireland. Elizabeth encouraged rebellion in the Netherlands. Plots were hatched to assassinate the Queen, and to set the captive Mary, Queen of Scots, on her throne. The massacre of St. Bartholomew in France had previously raised a spirit of furious anti-Catholicism among the English Protestants. Just when the struggle was entering its acutest phase, a flood of English Catholic missionaries, trained abroad, made their appearance in the country;

these were soon backed by the powerful society of Jesus. Elizabeth's Government fought with every weapon, fair or foul, at its command. Dr. William Allen (afterwards a cardinal) had established a Seminary at Douay for the training of priests for the work of reconverting England. They literally poured into the country, and journeyed from house to house exciting the zeal of many who hitherto had been but lukewarm. Their enthusiasm made them formidable. Spies watched their every step, and numbers were arrested on a charge, not of heresy, but of treason. Many were put to death and endured all the horrible and prolonged sufferings of a traitor's execution. That not a few, notably the Jesuit Campian, were innocent of crime is generally admitted, but the Government, too seriously alarmed to be scrupulous, was resolved to stamp out Popery as a danger to the State. Several of the Catholic nobility suffered death. At last Elizabeth's advisers resolved to defy the whole power of Philip II and of the Catholic world by executing Mary, Queen of Scots. His reply to this extreme step was the preparation to invade England by the Spanish Armada. The failure of this expedition in 1588 was regarded as a divine interposition in favour of Protestantism, and the Romanists were thereafter a distinct religious body, existing in defiance of the laws of the land, and regarded as national enemies.

For two centuries Anglo-Romanism was the religion most abhorred by popular opinion in England, and the horror it inspired is the explanation of many facts in the national history. The last serious manifestation of mob indignation against the Catholics occurred in 1780, in the famous Gordon Riots, when London was in the hands of the mob for days. The disabilities of those who practised the religion were to be found in the statute book till 1828.

The conduct of Elizabeth's Government towards the Catholics must be condemned by all, and to plead that Protestants were being subjected to similar and even greater trials in the dominion of Philip is no excuse. As a matter of fact, in England the Puritan Separatists fared scarcely better than the Romanist recusants. The cause of their sufferings was political rather than religious. The preachers on either side felt that they were discharging a solemn duty to God in endeavouring to save the souls of those whom they deemed in error, but some of them undoubtedly preferred to die or to rot in prison rather than to abandon their religious convictions. To this degree, they were martyrs and victims of a persecution for their Faith. The only excuse which can be offered for these cruelties is that many of the Romanists were undoubtedly conspirators, with the avowed object of dethroning Elizabeth and placing their country directly or indirectly under a foreign yoke. Nor is it easy to see how a policy of toleration could have succeeded under the circumstances. The extremists on either side had no idea of "living and letting live." A Catholic triumph might have meant a renewal of the fires of the reign of Mary; a victory of the ultra-Protestants, a renewal of the anarchy under Edward VI. Either way, a civil war would have resulted. This catastrophe both the Crown and the people in Tudor times were determined to avert, even at the cost of much personal suffering and injustice. The times were most critical and no price seemed too heavy to pay to hold the nation together.

But no special pleading, even that of necessity, can justify Elizabeth's treatment of such men as Father Campian and the better class of her Romanizing subjects, who suffered, rich and poor, for their religion. Equal blame, however, must fall on Pope St. Pius V for the policy he inaugurated, for he could have obtained terms, and generous terms, for his followers, both in England and Ireland, by more conciliatory action. Had the Government and the people realised that the profession of the old religions did not mean an un-English attitude, possibly Puritanism might have gone completely out of favour. By making Protestantism and patriotism synonyms the papal action drove England to take the side of the ultra-reformers.

Nevertheless, the compromises of the Elizabethan Church saved England from civil war at a time when she was in the greatest danger from foreign interference. By being both Protestant and Catholic, it satisfied the majority of the nation, and gradually, by the end of the reign of the great Queen, inspired affection and even enthusiasm.

It is always unprofitable but it is fascinating, at times, to speculate on what might have happened had events taken another course. What England would have become, had she not departed from the old religion, or had she completely identified herself with Protestantism—who can tell? The nation refused to take either course and chose to leave the final decision open. In so doing, one may believe, the English selected the path towards a freedom and toleration which neither the chair of St. Peter at Rome nor that of Calvin at Geneva would have been disposed to grant.

XII

SEPARATISTS

THREE CLASSES OF PROTESTANTS—SECTARIANISM ILLEGAL BUT INEVITABLE—THE ANABAPTISTS—PURITANS AND SEPARATISTS—REFORMATION WITHOUT TARRYING—NORTHAMPTON—THE WANDSWORTH PRESBYTERY—SUFFERINGS OF THE INDEPENDENTS—PROPHESYINGS SUPPRESSED—SEPARATION COULD NOT BE OPEN—PRESBYTERIANISM—INDEPENDENCY—ANABAPTISM.

Schism begets schism, as is abundantly shown in every stage of Church history; for, however the new party is organised, there are sure to be some who want to go to greater extremes. Moreover, there is a type of mind which rejoices in belonging to a small society, whether ethnic or religious. This spirit of division was frequently manifested whenever new religious orders were founded; each new one meant a revolt against the supposed laxity of the parent society. The Reformation in England was a national schism. The nation, as a whole, renounced communion with the Roman Church, to which it had been united since its foundation. The inevitable result in Protestantism was the rise of three religious parties. The first desired as little of a rupture as possible; the second aimed at a complete breach between the whole nation and the ancient Church; and the third resolved that, whatever the rest of their countrymen did, they would form a community of their own. Thus arose the Anglicans, Puritans, and Separatists, who will here be dealt with in the reverse order, because the earliest manifestations of independence of Rome in England were secret, as they needs must have been; since, till the nation formally took such action, any secession must have been made in private and subject to extreme personal risk.

The Reformation which followed Luther was also national. The German princes in a body protested against the Roman Church. But it was accompanied by popular movements which engendered sects, dreaded at least as much by the Lutherans as by the Catholics. Anabaptism and the parties caused by the same spirit were regarded with terror in all civilised countries and repressed with extreme severity. In England, sects date from the days of Wyclif; but after the Reformation none became politically important till the reign of Elizabeth.

In the "Twelve Tables," the stern spirit of the Roman Law ratified a principle adopted by the Church long before Christianity, by which private religions were forbidden, in the words *Nemo privatim habessit deos nisi publice adscitos* (Let no one have gods for himself that have not been publicly recognised). But neither in pagan nor Christian religions have all men been contented with the worship recognised by the State. It is but natural for them to seek something more individual, more adapted to their private needs. Thus mystery religions arose among the Greeks, and foreign cults found their way into Rome. Ezekiel found men worshipping strange gods in the secret chambers of the Temple. In Christianity, sects arose from the very beginning, the Gnostic and other bodies, each with its own private cultus. This desire for an individualistic religion found a more legitimate outlet in the monastic and religious orders, many of which, however, failed to receive the sanction of authority. Medieval Europe was full of sects, which the Church vainly endeavoured to stamp out. Judaism and Mahommedanism have been no more exempt from the sectarian spirit than Christianity. In every instance the representatives of the dominant form of religion have deplored faction, and endeavoured, but usually in vain, to bring about uniformity; and it is not surprising that divisions multiplied at the Reformation, directly the coercive power of the Church was relaxed by the successful widespread revolt of its former subjects.

Of those who deliberately separated themselves from the rest of the Christian world at the outset of the Reformation, the chief parties were the Anabaptists and those who denied the Divinity of Christ, afterwards called Socinians. The extreme advocates of reform grouped themselves into little societies, under prophets of their choice, that endeavoured to subvert the whole existing fabric of society and were very often guilty of fanatical excesses. The Anabaptists got their name from the fact that they rebaptized their converts. Anabaptism inspired fear in the ruling classes, and both Romanists and Protestants were agreed that it must be suppressed, if need be, by violence. The same attitude was taken toward those who denied the Divinity of Christ. As heretics, the only question raised was as to the method of their death: whether it should be by burning or otherwise. There were also secret sects in England before Elizabeth, mostly of foreign origin, but for present purposes these obscure bodies may be ignored in our dealing with the result of separatism on a larger scale, as it affected the peaceful settlement of religion.

A distinction must be drawn between those who were discontented with the Elizabethan religious settlement, and those who went to extremes, refused to remain in communion with the Church, and openly renounced all part in it as a national institution. The Puritan's attitude was not that of the Separatist. His discontent with the state of the Church took the form of efforts to purify it from within of what he considered to be its abuses. In his view, the whole nation was an Israel, a visible Church, and the people were to be regarded as a Christian unit with spiritual rulers appointed for its discipline, as kings, priests, and judges had been among the ancient people of God. All, saved and lost alike, while on earth were under the care of the Church. What the Puritans desired was severe, uncompromising Protestantism and the destruction of the last remains of the ancient Popery.

The Separatists despaired of Christianising the whole people. Their cry was "Reformation without tarrying for any"; and if they could not reform the nation, they would at least reform the Church. The Church was not to them a gathering of groups of people who had been baptized in infancy, and lived in the same parish, shire, diocese, or county. It could not be regarded as a collection of believers and unbelievers, godly and profane, indiscriminately banded together. A Church in their eyes was a congregation of real Christians, associated for the purpose of worship, which had no fellowship with the ungodly. Each congregation was in itself an Israel, answerable, not to bishop, presbytery, or synod, but to God alone. This has been variously called Independency, Congregationalism, or "Brownism," from Robert Browne, who advanced the idea of separate churches. In doctrine, this sect was in agreement with most Protestants in England. Its difference in principle in regard to the form of church government greatly influenced the subsequent development of dissent in England, and dissent was the dominant religion of New England in America. It has always seemed more congenial to the English character than Presbyterianism.

The founders of Congregationalism were Robert Browne and Henry Barrow, and their sect was the first Protestant body formally to secede from the English Church, as reformed by Elizabeth and her Parliament. Secession, however, began, not by any deliberate act of separation, but in an endeavour to set up a model of what a Church should be according to the ideas of the extreme reformers. In the town of Northampton, a centre of Puritanism, it was decided to establish a drastically reformed Christianity in its churches. With the approval of the Bishop of the diocese of Peterborough, it is said, the ministers of the town formed themselves into a species of synod for the regulation of discipline, which the mayor rigidly enforced, punishing severely Sabbath-breaking, and discouraging all forms of levity. The organs in these churches were destroyed, and music excluded from the services, which were conducted with Puritan simplicity. "Prophesyings," as they were called, or meetings on the model of I Corinthians xiv, became the vogue. The ministers were allowed to "prophesy" or expound Scripture, and these exercises were followed by discussion. In a word, it may be said that the Puritan party were actually putting into practice in a single town all that they were proposing to effect throughout England. A presbytery, meeting privately, was also established in the village of Wandsworth, near London. The object of these meetings, however, was not Separatism, but to create a working Church on the model of Evangelical or Calvinistic Protestantism of the Continent which could be imposed ultimately on the English nation. Independency aimed at something different, namely, to call true believers, as opposed to the rest of the world, to form congregations of their own, each possessed of the power of self-government. It arrived at something fundamentally different from that of the other Christian bodies, Roman, Anglican, or Puritan, which wanted a national Church, and only differed as to how it should be governed, whether by Rome, by Canterbury, or by a national synod in which all ministers were equal. The Separatists believed that the Church should be kept completely apart from the State.

The records of the reign of Elizabeth show how much these Separatists had to endure. Browne, who conformed, and lived to a great, if not very creditable old age, according to his traducers, says he was confined in no less than thirty-two prisons, and in some of them could hardly see his hand at midday. Their congregations were broken up and dispersed and their preachers treated with great severity. In a word, the lot of a Protestant seceder from the Church was hardly less deplorable than that of a recusant. It is not our present purpose to expatiate on their sufferings, or to defend their persecution, but simply to inquire how it was that men like Lord Burleigh, and Elizabeth's other advisers, who were not by nature persecutors, but even sympathisers with the reformed religion, were so harsh in their dealings towards men whose convictions were generally sincere, and whose position was not wholly unreasonable. Why, it may be asked, should the wise and prudent statesmen who, with the Queen, were steadily building up the prosperity of their country, and giving England a place in Europe which she had not occupied for many a long year, have prevented harmless enthusiasts from worshipping God in private as they pleased? The explanation seems to be that the Government was alarmed, not wholly unnaturally, at the slightest symptom that might point to the growth of a secret society. To allow men to meet in private on any pretext was considered to be encouraging plots against the Government. The country was full of conspirators on the side of Spain, in support of Mary, Queen of Scots, for the overthrow of Elizabeth. Members of the dreaded Order of the Jesuits were everywhere active, posing often as Puritans in order still further to discredit the national Church and in the hope of restoring Catholicism upon its ruins. The Puritans, on the other hand, had begun about 1581 a journalistic campaign against the existing Church order, by issuing the celebrated *Marprelate Libels* from their secret presses. All political passions would be brought to a white heat if the religious preachers of every sort of extreme view were to be given free rein. Elizabeth would have favoured any religious party which would have united her people in support of her throne; the Church settlement was adopted because it seemed, at any rate, least likely to drive them into rebellion. Therefore, her Government upheld it against all factions.

The suspicion felt toward all private meetings, even for devotional purposes, is seen in Elizabeth's treatment of the "Prophesyings." They were not necessarily seditious; they were highly approved by many of the bishops, and justified themselves by producing ministers able to preach, and such recruits were sorely needed. In fact, never in the whole history of the English Church was the majority of the clergy worse in quality than in the days of Elizabeth. The landowners put anyone over whom they could domineer into the parsonages. Few of the country clergy were educated, many had been servingmen, not always of good character. It was impossible to supply some churches with a man in Holy Orders; and Archbishop Parker had to appoint lay readers. Indeed, one main source of the strength of Puritanism and Separatism was the inferiority in ability and morality of the average parson; and this also contributed to the success of the Seminary priests. They were picked men, trained for the work of propaganda; whilst the best of the Protestants were strongly inclined to disaffection. The unscrupulous rapacity of the governing classes had reduced the parish clergy to a state of abject poverty, and it is scarcely to be wondered at that they were despised and unpopular. Nor was the Elizabethan episcopate altogether a credit to the Church. Yet the clergy were compelled to exercise a sort of inquisitional authority over their flocks. Anything, therefore, which could improve the capacity of the clergy was to be welcomed; and the exercises, which the "Prophesyings" were encouraging, were certainly producing good effects. But Elizabeth feared their influence in promoting discontent more than she valued the possibility of their becoming a benefit. Accordingly, Archbishop Grindal was commanded to order their discontinuance, and because he refused, with commendable courage, to obey the royal mandate he was suspended from his episcopal functions; and the see of Canterbury was practically vacant for some years. If, therefore, semi-private meetings of the clergy, under the superintendence of the bishops, were condemned, no wonder Separatist conventicles were dispersed, and those who held them severely handled.

When it is said that the followers of Browne and Barrow separated themselves from the Church, one has to remember that it was not possible to do so in any legal or formal manner. The consequence was that most sects had no continuous history, disappearing for a while, and resuming their activities under new leaders and different guises. All congregations for worship, except in the parish Church, under the legal minister, were equally illegal, whether it was to attend Mass or to listen to a sermon; and those who attended did so at their peril, much more so than ministers who conducted them. Among the discontented Protestants there was much diversity of opinion, which such a severely repressive law prevented from crystallizing into definitely organized sects. In addition to small and unmilitant societies, there were, in the sixteenth century, besides the Romanists, three main classes of Separatists, in after years represented by the great divisions of Dissenters in England. These may be taken up for discussion in turn, if it is borne in mind that those named first can hardly yet under Elizabeth be styled Separatists.

(1) The Presbyterians, as the Puritan party may be called, not with perfect accuracy, but because the name describes their general attitude, were admirers of the Calvinistic discipline of Geneva. They were in substantial accord with most English Protestants in doctrine, holding the Augustinian view of predestination. They desired discipline to be restored in its primitive severity, and nothing to be allowed which had not Scriptural authority, whilst the moral law was to be enforced with all the ruthlessness of the old Judaic legislation. Their ideal of Church government was organization into what were called *classes,* mixed assemblies of clergy and lay elders, under a national synod. They were not yet opposed to episcopacy itself, but wished it to be divested of all worldly pomp, and reduced to primitive simplicity. Their

polity was to be national, emphatically so, and not congregational. Their schismatical tendency manifested itself in attempts to set up independent local Church governments, as at Northampton, in order that these might eventually become the model for a national Church.

(2) After Elizabeth's death the Independents reduced the opinions of Browne to a systematic form. To their sect belonged the congregation formed by men like Brewster and Robinson at Scrooby in Lincolnshire, which early in the reign of James I emigrated to Holland and afterward settled in America. Their ideal, as has been seen, was a Church consisting of independent, self-governing congregations. The strength of this sect in England was most plainly shown by its ascendency in the army of Cromwell and Fairfax.

(3) The Anabaptists were the extreme left of Protestantism, the fanatics whose excesses had caused such terror in Europe. Their socialistic doctrines exposed them to persecution, and they were often accused, and sometimes burned, for heresy, because some of them denied the Divinity of Christ. Their views gave the worst offence. One branch, the so-called *Family of Love,* held some of their heretical opinions, but condemned the factiousness of the Puritans, and generally abstained from all political intrigue. The Anabaptists of the early Reformation have survived in the Baptists of modern days.

These three formed the great sects of English nonconformity, which organised themselves openly when varieties of Protestant opinion were legally sanctioned by the Toleration Act of 1688. For if the history of Elizabethan times shows how impossible it seemed to Englishmen to allow different sects to exist in their day, the history of the next century is the history of the realisation that, in some form or other, religious differences must be recognised and permitted by law.

XIII

PURITANISM

SPIRIT OF PURITANISM—THE INFLUENCE OF GENEVA—THE VESTMENT CONTROVERSY—PARKER'S "ADVERTISEMENTS"—THE PURITANS APPROACH PARLIAMENT—NEED OF MORE DISCIPLINE—THE CHURCH OF ENGLAND A MIDDLE PATH—PURITAN PAMPHLETS—REACTION AGAINST PURITANISM—THE GOVERNMENT HARSH BUT IN THE END BENEFICIAL—THE NATION ALWAYS SUPPORTED THE TUDORS.

The exiles who came back after Mary's death combined the less amiable characteristics of Englishmen with an admiration of the polity of Genevan Protestantism. The Puritan spirit existed before the Reformation and will survive its peculiar doctrines. Harsh and uncompromising, the exiles had no sympathy with customs of life or thought different from their own. Impatient of authority, their one ambition was to exercise it over others; and, in the name of liberty, they were prepared to allow no one to be free but themselves. Taking the Scriptures, and especially those of the Old Testament, for his guide, the Puritan's object was to build in England a polity resembling an ideal Israel under the moral law, his complaint against the older Roman system being, not that it was intolerably severe, but that it was not sufficiently stern. His ideal was a godly discipline, rigidly and impartially enforced, repressive of all the natural, and, for this reason, sinful, impulses of humanity. Such men were no Separatists, nor opponents of a national Church establishment: to depart, so to speak, into the wilderness and leave the rest of mankind to go to perdition in its own way formed no part of their programme. What they had in mind was to make every Englishman submit to their government, and to remodel society as a whole on what they deemed to be a scriptural basis. They could not reconcile it to their conscience to make any allowance for those who had been under the influences of the older faith, or for the grave political necessities of the Queen and her advisers. They demanded the right to dictate their own terms without reference to their feasibility or convenience, and to refuse any compromise with what they considered to be errors in practice, let alone in faith. This was Puritanism in its worst aspect. That there was a nobler side is undeniable.

The extraordinary influence which the very name of Calvin exercised in England must always be remembered in all attempts to account for the course of events in the age of Elizabeth. The Protestant exiles in the reign of Mary, numbering about eight hundred, including most of the prominent Edwardian bishops and clergy, had been ill received on the Continent by the Lutherans, but most warmly and generously welcomed by the Calvinian party in Switzerland, Holland, and the Rhine towns. As a rule, they lived together in peace; but at Frankfort, the troubles which were to come were foreshadowed by a furious quarrel about the use of the Second Prayer Book of Edward VI. The chief disputants were Dr. Cox, afterwards a bishop under Elizabeth, and John Knox, the celebrated Scottish reformer. On their return at the accession of Elizabeth the exiled Protestants hoped completely to reform the national Church on the model of Geneva. Their strength lay, not in their numbers, but partly in their ability, and chiefly in the fact that they knew exactly what they wanted and had a definite programme, easy to be understood. This was the secret of the great influence of Calvin. While Lutheranism stressed one doctrine, that of Justification, Anglicanism wavered between Rome and reformation, and Anabaptism rushed into fanaticism, Calvin gave his followers an example of a well-thought-out scheme of ecclesiastical polity and dogma. Geneva became a sample for all Protestants to imitate with its excellent, if intolerant, government, the stern purity of its life, its orderly Church polity, its admirable educational system, and its theology, based on the Institutes of its great pastor, John Calvin. To make England into a Geneva was the ambition of the reformers who had been abroad, and they never appear to have realised that a government the size of a country, with its diversity of inhabitants, could not be assimilated to that of a single city.

The Puritans, or Precisians, as they soon came to be called, accepted the Elizabethan settlement with reservations, for they were resolved at the first opportunity to subvert it in favour of the Genevan ideal.

The first pretext for complaint against the settlement was due to Elizabeth's determination to enforce a certain standard of order in the conduct of worship. The First Prayer Book had ordered the ancient Eucharistic vestments to be used. The priest was to wear "a white albe plain, with a vestment or cope," and the deacons "albes with tunicles." In the Second Book, the surplice was ordered to be used, and in the Elizabethan revision in 1559 the rubric was altered to say that "such Ornaments of the Church and of the Ministers thereof, at the times of their Ministration, shall be retained and be in use, as it were in this Church of *England,* by authority of Parliament, in the second year of the reign of King *Edward* the Sixth." As a matter of fact, this order was widely ignored; and according to the report of the state of the Church in 1564, each and every one conducted the Service as he pleased, some without any distinctive garment whatever.

This confusion disgusted Elizabeth; and she ordered Archbishop Parker to command his clergy to wear surplice and hood at least when they ministered. Though the Primate greatly doubted the wisdom of the order, he was obliged to issue what were called *Advertisements* in his own name—for the Queen declined to support him by the royal authority—enjoining the clergy to don the surplice. This the scruples of the extreme Protestants forbade them to do, and many were deprived of their parishes in consequence. Strangely enough the surplice is not, strictly speaking, a vestment at all. It is, in Latin, the *superpelliceum,* a garment worn over a fur coat when the Office was said in a cold church. It was introduced into England about 1100, and Lyndewood, the great English canonist who died in 1446, says he never remembers reading about it in the whole body of Canon or Civil Law. Yet, it was the cause of the first overt act of disobedience on the part of the Puritans. Two Heads of Oxford Colleges, Drs. Humphreys and Sampson, refused to wear a surplice, and in Cambridge in some of the Colleges the order was disobeyed for many years. We shall encounter this same controversy in nineteenth century ritualism. Copes were to be worn in cathedrals; but even they fell into desuetude, and there are instances of the wives of the canons using the vestments to make dresses for themselves.

The first direct move on the part of the Puritans, in favour of the Reformation they desired, was in the Parliament of 1572. It was now openly suggested that the Church should be remodelled on the pattern of Geneva, as set forth in the so-called *Admonitions to Parliament,* composed by two ministers named Field and Wilcox. Such a bill was introduced into the Commons, but Elizabeth declared that it trenched on her prerogative, and commanded the House to proceed no further. The next Puritan move was to draw up another scheme of church government known as the *Holy Discipline.* Its authors were the two leading Puritans of Cambridge, Thomas Cartwright and Walter Travers. Cartwright has been called the father of English dissent. He was a Fellow of Trinity College, Cambridge, and Lady Margaret Reader in Divinity. He was the chief opponent of the Master of his College, John Whitgift, Archbishop of Canterbury in 1583. The University was a hotbed of Puritanism; and Cartwright, as its leader, felt the heavy hand of Whitgift, who had him removed from his Fellowship and Professorship. Cartwright was a very able man and a University reformer with an eye for the educational abuses of his time. He had the support of the Queen's favourite, the Earl of Leicester: for the Puritans had strong political backing from those who cared little about their principles, but desired to use them in their own plans still further to despoil the already impoverished Church.

The Puritan party were assuredly not supporters of toleration or of liberty intentionally. Their two grievances were that the government, in encouraging the Anglican settlement, was not prepared to allow the Church to put the entire nation under an iron discipline. The best excuse which they can plead is that since the Reformation, the moral state of the country had become so bad that it needed the drastic remedy of the Genevan discipline. They complained that, under the old religion, discipline had not been sufficiently active in punishing sin. To remedy this condition, they desired to retain for their Boards of Elders the right, not only of ruling the Church, but of compelling the civil powers to enforce their decrees. They hated the doctrine of Erastus that the state ought not to punish offenders at the simple command of ecclesiastical tribunals.

Sixteenth century politics turned almost entirely upon the religious issues. When these are in question three types of minds are revealed: those who want to go back to an ideal past, those who are impatient to secure an ideal future, and those who desire to realise the best of the present and to make as few changes as possible. Thus, under Elizabeth, the two extreme political factions were the Papist and the Puritan, and, midway, the third growing party of Anglicans, who neither regretted the Reformation, nor desired a millennium, but accepted a middle path, as, on the whole, best for the needs of the nation.

Puritanism

Throughout the first years of Elizabeth's reign, Papists hoped that the tide would turn in favour of the Old, and Puritans, in favour of the New religion. When it became increasingly evident that the uncompromising supporters of neither party would prevail, both resorted to excesses which disgusted the nation. Nothing helped Elizabeth more to secure support than the fact that seminary priests came from abroad, and were believed to be plotting against her life. On the other hand, nothing assisted the Church of England party more than the virulence exhibited by the Puritans in the so-called *Marprelate Libels*. Both of the extremes had their martyrs. Granting that some were unjustly condemned, there was a feeling, also, that others who were executed were disloyal, and so deserved their doom. It was also commonly felt that, if the Papists sought to deprive Elizabeth of her crown, the Puritans aimed at usurping much of her authority.

The Puritan politicians understood perfectly the modern art of influencing the public by popular literature, and they may be regarded as the parents of the press campaigns of to-day. With them began, also, the use of the political term "platform" when they embodied their views in a "Platform of a Church Reformed."

The extreme Puritans, mostly Separatists, with whom the more respectable members of the party refused to be connected, made ridicule a most formidable weapon against the Church. In 1587, Dr. Bridges, Dean of Salisbury, had brought out an enormous book of 1407 pages, entitled *A Defense of the Government of the Church of England* in answer to a short Puritan work known as *A Learned Discourse on Ecclesiastical Government,* published in 1584 and distinguished by its conciliatory tone. The ponderous onslaught of the learned doctor spurred the Puritan pamphleteers to an outburst of genuine wit and humour. They kept a private printing press at the house of a Mrs. Crane, which was subsequently moved from place to place to elude the vigilance of the authorities. It was said to be financed by "Martin,

Marprelate, gentleman." Tract after tract issued from it—seven have survived—levelled at the bishops. Their style was bright, amusing, and sarcastic. Whitgift, the Archbishop, was described as the toady of Dr. Perne of Cambridge, whose frequent change of opinions enriched the Latin language with a new word "pernare," to change one's views. Aylmer, Bishop of London, was held up to especial scorn and derision. The humour of the tracts was coarse, and even brutal, but exactly suited to the taste of the age. The churchmen attempted to counteract "Marprelate"; but they lacked his vigour and pungent satire; and their bolts fell harmless. Cooper, Bishop of Winchester, was their protagonist, and his learned refutation was answered by a work bearing as a title the popular street cry, *"Hay any work for a Cooper?"* and another, *"More work for a Cooper."* These tracts were the first manifestation of popular journalism, and the laugh was against the hierarchy. The seriousness of the attack was magnified by the fact that, as the tracts appeared in the very year of the Spanish Armada, the libellers were actually playing into the hands of the enemies of the nation and of Protestantism in every form. At last, in 1589, the pursuivants captured the press, and the publishing of the libels came to an end.

Barrow is generally supposed to be the author of "Marprelate," and a fervid Welshman by the name of Penry, of "Marprelate junior," but this was never proved.

John Penry was educated at Cambridge, and in his student days he was accustomed to attend and serve at Mass. Then he went to Oxford, and was there converted to the Puritan way of thinking. Though he refused to take episcopal Orders, he was licensed by the University to preach. He became deeply interested in the evangelisation of his native country, and drew up a scheme for that purpose which he submitted to Archbishop Whitgift. His proposals made him suspected of dangerous anti-Church views and the bishops were strongly suspicious that he was the "Marprelate of the Libels." Though nothing could be proved against him, his influence was considered a danger to the State, and he was brought to trial for a letter addressed to Elizabeth, which had neither been sent to the Queen nor published. He was condemned as a traitor and hanged. He is regarded as a martyr by the Puritans as justly as Campian is by the Catholics. Nicholas Udal, who had been Vicar of Kingston-on-Thames, from which place the libels were first issued, was also condemned to death, but was pardoned. Barrow and Greenwood, two of the extreme Puritans, were hanged in 1593, the same year as Penry.

The tide was setting against Puritanism, and in 1593 Parliament, which had once been decidedly in its favour, passed an act ordering all to resume attendance at the services of the Church, and making imprisonment the penalty if they disobeyed or tried to persuade others to impugn the Queen's authority in matters ecclesiastical. If they still remained obstinate upon their release they were to "abjure the country." If they ever ventured to return to England, the penalty was death without benefit of clergy. This severe act did much to suppress militant Puritanism, which the government regarded as a serious political danger, disuniting loyal Englishmen in the face of grave national peril from Spain.

No one who knows anything of the facts can pretend that the Church settlement was completely satisfactory to all concerned, but in justice to Archbishop Whitgift and his colleagues, it must be remembered that bishops were regarded by Elizabeth as law officers and under compulsion to enforce discipline in the interests of public order. In theology, they were in sympathy with the Puritan party, especially in respect to the doctrine of predestination, which was all important at that juncture. The better class of Puritans, who were content to wait upon events, reprobated the excesses of such people as the libellers and Separatists generally.

We may condemn the harshness of the government of Elizabeth, but its firmness at least gave the nation nearly half a century of comparative peace at home which was sorely needed. The country undoubtedly increased in wealth, and was free from the civil war between the rival factions of Catholic and Protestant, which afflicted France. The Church settlement in England created a middle party, which maintained the royal authority and was supported by the bulk of the nation. Naturally a policy of toleration would have been preferable, had it been practicable. It was not to the interest of Romanism generally for English Catholics to practise their religion in humble obscurity as a minority that could safely be ignored by the authorities because it gave no trouble. It would have suited the authorities at Rome better, by furnishing martyrs in response to rigorous persecution, to win back the whole land to the unity of the ancient faith. Neither did the Puritans really desire to worship in private. They aimed at a national reformation, which every member of the community would have to accept. Elizabeth and her sagacious advisers saw that their object was political as well as religious ascendency, and crushed them by means which were entirely unjustifiable in our eyes, but which possibly find some palliation in the circumstances of the age.

And Elizabeth's Government had, on the whole, the support of the nation. False and cruel as the Queen, like most of her family, was, there was something about her which made men enthusiastic in her cause. They felt that, with all her faults, she stood for the country; and so gave her their ungrudging support. The House of Tudor was at least feared, honoured, and respected. Its members understood their people and knew when safely to behave as despots, and when they must respect the rights of their subjects. The Stuarts who succeeded could never win the sympathy of Englishmen. When the Church stood by Elizabeth, it reflected the attitude of the nation; when it asserted the divine right of her successors, it acted against the sentiment of the country. It was then the turn of Puritanism to be recognised as representative of the nation, and to become for a while dominant, and then detested.

XIV

ANGLICANISM

THE CHURCH OF ENGLAND PROFESSES PRIMITIVE DOCTRINE OF CHRISTENDOM—THE ROYAL SUPREMACY—CONSECRATION OF BISHOPS—THE OTHER ORDERS—POSITION OF THE CLERGY—RELIGIOUS FOUNDATIONS—THE CHURCH'S YEAR—RELIGIOUS LIFE OF AN ANGLICAN—THE CALENDAR—THE EUCHARIST—OCCASIONAL OFFICES—THINGS PROHIBITED—ELEVATION OF THE HOST—PRAYERS FOR THE DEAD—ANGLICANISM A COMPROMISE.

Strictly speaking, the doctrine of the Church of England is that of the Universal Church, based on Holy Scripture, and what it rejects, though, in popular jargon, called "Catholic," cannot be proved by an appeal to Scripture or the unvarying tradition of the primitive Church. As has been shown in the introduction, no Anglican could reasonably call those whom the law of the land placed under disabilities, or punished for contumacy, by the opprobrious name of heretic. A Romanist is not a heretic because he accepts doctrines or practices which are condemned as innovations, nor can a Dissenter or Non-Conformist be so styled because he has rejected much which the primitive Church considered all-important. The dogmatic decrees of the Councils of Nicæa (325), Constantinople (381), Ephesus (431), and Chalcedon (451), are the norm of Anglican orthodoxy and are recognised as such by the law of the land.

The Church of England may as an institution, therefore, be defined as a system of government or policy, based on Scripture and the immemorial traditions of the Universal Church. As such, it will here be presented.

The royal supremacy, which was the starting point of the breach with Rome, means little to-day even to an Englishman, and less than nothing to his brother Churchman in America; but it was of immense importance in the sixteenth and seventeenth centuries. It had little or no dogmatic significance. Henry VIII in renouncing the authority of the Pope had no notion that it made him any less a Catholic in his belief and practice; and the belief and services of the Church would have corresponded exactly with those of the Middle Ages, had it been possible to continue his policy. The only difference would have been that the King would have exacted all moneys previously paid to the Pope, that the Praemunire Acts would have been more vigorously enforced, any recognition of the Pope's right to interfere being punishable by a traitor's death. The Sovereign would have been the Pope, with his Vicar-General replacing the papal legate and taking precedence over the regular hierarchy. The much detested High Commission Court in the days of Elizabeth and the Stuarts exercised the same sort of powers as a papal legate in old days in superseding the authority of the archbishop and bishops.

But the royal supremacy is still real; for, even though the Sovereign may not personally exercise it, it is vested in his ministers, and their acts are done in his name. The bishops are, as a rule, nominated in this fashion: the King issues a *congé d'élire* to the dean and chapter of the cathedral, which allows them to proceed to an election of a bishop. In this letter he mentions the man he desires, and they are bound to elect him under pain of violating the Statute of *Praemunire*. Thus, the right of the chapter to elect has become in practice a mere fiction, though the bare fact that the Crown nominee has to be even formally chosen has acted on occasion as a restraining influence.

Once appointed, a bishop is practically irremovable, and his power formerly was very extensive. When all assemblies for worship outside the Church were illegal, the bishop's duty was to search out all popish "recusants," as they were termed, and to fine and imprison them for non-attendance at Church services. All the wills made in his diocese passed through his registrary. He still appoints his own judge or chancellor for the adjudication of ecclesiastical causes. All incumbents have to be instituted by him, but he cannot refuse to induct a person, legally presented, without showing good cause for his objection. He has, as a rule, a large amount of patronage to benefices, and frequently appoints the canons of his cathedral and his archdeacons. Until 1835, he had sometimes very extensive estates, and the income of some dioceses was immense, though in others it scarcely sufficed to maintain the episcopal position. If so, the bishop usually was allowed to hold other lucrative clerical appointments. Bishops sit in the House of Lords, because they held their diocesan estates as great tenants of the Crown, but in 1661 it was declared that they only did so as Lords of Parliament, and not as peers or the equals of the hereditary members.

The spiritual authority of a bishop is bestowed by the laying on of hands of other bishops. According to Church Law, one bishop under extreme necessity is sufficient to consecrate another; and the Pope invariably acts as sole consecrator. But by general custom at least three bishops officiate and lay their hands on the head of the new prelate. In England, after his election by the Chapter, bishops have to be confirmed in Bow Church in London before consecration. The reason this is done is that each may be publicly recognised as the man chosen for the office. In recent times objections have been raised against certain men presented at this ceremony, but they have been ruled to be invalid.

Spiritually there is no difference whatever between one

bishop and another. The Pope himself is no more by consecration than a bishop. In ancient times it was irregular, if not illegal, to promote a bishop from one see to another. In Rome, only a priest or deacon was ever chosen Pope till the close of the ninth century. The archbishops have peculiar rights and privileges, but these belong to their sees, and not to them as distinguished from other bishops. A strange prerogative which the Archbishop of Canterbury still retains is the right of granting academic degrees which was originally given to him as papal legate. The right of an archbishop to decide, on his own authority, a complaint against a bishop of his province is very doubtful. A bishop should only be tried by a synod of bishops.

The other clergy are priests and deacons. Minor orders are not legally recognised, as they were in the Middle Ages. Readers, it is true, were appointed after the Reformation, in the absence of duly qualified clergy, in the sixteenth century, but they were considered to be laymen in rank. The diaconate in the English, as in the Western Church, has become less of an Order than a probation for the priesthood, to which almost all active ministers are admitted. Even the archdeacon, who was head of the deacons proper in early days, is now almost invariably in priest's orders.

The clergy are not merely members of a profession; they are one of the separate estates of the realm, the first named of the three: Clergy, Nobility, and Commons. Like the Nobles, they had very special privileges formerly, their own courts, etc. These privileges, under modern conditions, take mainly the form of disabilities. The clergy are not eligible to a seat in the House of Commons, they may not act as directors of trading companies, nor engage in certain commercial undertakings. These disabilities were at one time permanent; but now a clergyman may divest himself of his orders and so escape them. The prohibition of clerical marriage was one disability in medieval days grudgingly removed after the Reformation. The Thirty-second Article states that it is not a command of God's Law that the clergy should not marry, and that they may do so at their own discretion; but Elizabeth notoriously disliked married clergy, and after the death of Parker, Archbishop of Canterbury (1575), no married man was appointed for more than a century.

After the dissolution of the great majority of the monasteries, the cathedral chapters and a few collegiate churches, such as Manchester and Ripon, which have now become bishoprics, and Windsor, Westminster, Eton, Winchester, were the sole representatives of the monastic orders. In these, the services were conducted with more or less magnificence; the Communion was ordered to be celebrated weekly in the cathedrals, and the clergy were expected to receive it. Vestments were also to be worn at the celebration, but elsewhere were generally allowed to fall into disuse, and the surplice and hood alone were worn. The Oxford and Cambridge colleges were termed, in the technical sense, "religious" foundations, and the masters (at first) and fellows forbidden to hold their offices after marriage.

The religious course of life designed for members of the English Church differed but little from that expected in the Church of Rome. The greater festivals were practically the same, as were the days of fasting and abstinence. The Saint's days to be observed were also the red-letter days of the pre-Reformation Church, in so far as the saints and events celebrated were scriptural. All the Apostles' days and two ancient festivals of the Virgin were retained, and their observance was enforced. The Catholicism of the Anglican Church appears in these features of its life: its Protestantism in the rigid exclusion of all that was not scriptural.

The best method of ascertaining the meaning of Anglicanism is to make up one's mind by the light of the Prayer Book of what sort the religious life would be that was

Anglicanism 119

lived in strict obedience to its injunctions by a devout person, lay or clerical, who had been brought up under the old religion. It was specially provided that for private devotion he might use as his language for prayer the Latin to which he had been accustomed.

We may begin our outline of this Prayer Book religious life with the Calendar. The Christian year was much the same as it had been, so far as its holidays were concerned, and the Collects, Epistles, and Gospels were also virtually the same. A few of what are now called "days of obligation," like Corpus Christi, were no longer observed; but in every month there was at least one Saint's day, and the Holy Seasons of Lent and Advent, Ember Days, Rogation days, were duly noted for observance. In the Elizabethan Calendar, many of the Saints and Fathers of the Church were called to remembrance. In the month of March, when Lent was being kept, the Calendar provided for commemorations of David, the patron saint of Wales, of Chad, or Ceadda, the disciple of St. Aidan at Lindisfarne, of Perpetua, the Carthaginian martyr in 203, of Gregory the Great, who had sent Augustine to convert England, of Edward, King of the West Saxons, and of St. Benedict, the founder of the great monastic Order. All these were reminders of the fact that the English Church acknowledged an unbroken continuity for itself with the Catholic Church of all ages. Every priest was bound to recite the daily Morning or Evening Prayers, in which the canticles, responses, psalms, prayers, were all those he had formerly used in the Breviary. Only the legends of the Saints and the extracts from the Fathers were omitted, and in their place chapters from the Old and New Testament substituted. The suggestion that this substitution be made came from the Spanish cardinal, Quignon. Down to the time of the Rebellion of 1642 many of the Churches still retained much of their pristine splendour. True, the stone altars had been destroyed and removed, but the images of saints, the carved representation of their doings, and the matchless stained glass still remained intact. All the additions to devotion in the Middle Ages that could be, after the rejection of many that were unscriptural and superstitious, were retained in the face of bitter opposition on the part of the Protestant enthusiasts.

The irreconcilable difference between the old and the new regime lay in the theory, rather than in the doctrine, of the Eucharist, the centre of Christian devotion. Protestants, it is true, found the dogma of Transubstantiation an abomination, because it implied a priestly miracle, and connoted the adoration of the consecrated elements. But in so far as a Presence of some sort was taught in the Lord's words "This is my Body" and "This is my Blood," such extreme opponents as Cardinal Pole and Bishop Ridley were practically in agreement. As Hooker declares, there was no such fundamental difference among orthodox theologians, whether Catholic or Protestant, as might be imagined from the prominence given to the controversy about the Mass and the Lord's Supper. In the matter of the celebration of the Sacrament, one has only to place in Latin side by side the Divine Liturgy, according to the Roman and Anglican rites, omitting all the rubrics, to note their similarity. It is the ritual action, more than the words, which make them so dissimilar, as is now seen when a priest recites the words of the Prayer Book, with the actions prescribed by the Missal which the Puritans imply was also done in the days of Elizabeth.

The occasional Offices, Baptism, the Solemnization of Matrimony, Burial of the Dead, etc., kept all that had been required before the Reformation, save a few omissions: those of Exorcism and putting on of the Chrisom in Baptism, the giving of gold and silver at Matrimony, and, of course, the important omission of prayers for the dead. The Ordinal is undeniably calculated to impress the recipient and the congregation with a due sense of the importance of their Office. It is, according to Apostolic practice, bound up with the celebration of the Eucharist, and if the ceremonial handing over the instru-

Anglicanism

ment proper to deacon, priest, and bishop is omitted, the laying on of hands is carefully insisted upon. The sick are formally to be visited by the priest, absolved, if they desire, and their souls, as they pass from the body, solemnly committed by his prayer to their Heavenly Father.

In a word, the whole design of Anglicanism is to make sure that a Catholic-minded Christian shall lack nothing necessary to his spiritual satisfaction, whilst nothing which a Protestant can reasonably condemn as superstitious or unscriptural, is retained to be a just cause of offence.

Certain things, however, were undoubtedly prohibited which one accustomed to pre-Reformation religion would unquestionably notice. Of these, there may be especially mentioned (1) The elevation of the Host, and (2) prayer for the dead.

(1) According to the Roman ceremonial, the celebrant, on pronouncing the words *Hoc est corpus meum,* and *Hic est sanguis meus,* is to raise the bread and the wine for the devotion of the people. They were thus to be made to realise that their Lord was absolutely present in their midst, and to adore Him in the Sacramental Elements. Now, except the followers of Zwingli, all Christians believed that in some way or other Christ was present in the Lord's Supper. But this ritual act emphasised the doctrine of Transubstantiation in its most reprehensible form; namely that by reason of the words of Consecration the Lord actually descended to the Elements on the altar and their nature suffered a complete change. But, whatever the doctrine held regarding the Presence, and in that of the Catholic and Orthodox Church of the East it is practically the same, the elevation of the Host at the moment of Consecration is not primitive practice, and, therefore, it may legitimately be omitted from the service of the altar. It is, however, undeniable that the Anglican divines, even those of the extremest type, did repudiate the doctrine of the Mass so far as Transubstantiation was

concerned. Still, following the Elizabethan policy, private opinion for or against was not called in question, but the ceremonial act was forbidden as neither scriptural nor primitive. No one can reasonably maintain that its omission invalidates the Sacrament.

(2) The question whether it is legitimate to pray for the dead is one of the most vital points in dispute between the old Catholic and the more modern Protestant religion. It was certainly practised at an early time, and it is prompted by a natural and most pardonable human impulse. This is not the place to discuss or to pronounce upon the merits of this question, but it must have been the greatest of all sacrifices a Catholic of the old school, in accepting the Elizabethan settlement, was and could have been called upon to make. The reason why the Protestant party would not tolerate prayers for the dead in any form is plain. The sole power to offer the Mass for the deceased was one of the keystones of priestly influence, and the abuses connected with it had produced a strong reaction against the doctrine of Purgatory, as commercialising religion in the interest of the priesthood. Still, the disregard in this respect of the beloved dead, and the wishes of men dead and gone who had bequeathed money to secure regular prayers on their behalf, must have stood in the way of acceptance of the reformed settlement.

Anglicanism may be defined as an attempt to settle the prevailing religious disputes in England in such a way as to satisfy the Protestant party by its respect for Scripture, and the Catholic by its regard for tradition. It was very naturally displeasing, therefore, to extremists on both sides, and for the same reason. To neither did it approve itself as the genuine article; but a snare alike to the weak Catholic and the unenthusiastic Protestant. To the nation at large, the mass of whom were not so decided in their views, it was on the whole satisfactory. They accepted it, each in accordance with his own predilections. The Catholic Anglican saw in it a reasonable continuation of the old Faith: the Protestant, a formidable barrier against Rome and the Mass. Yet a third section welcomed it as allowing more liberty of thought than any form of Christianity hitherto had provided.

XV

THE HIGH CHURCH PARTY

HOW CHURCH CONTINUITY HAD BEEN MAINTAINED—
CHURCH SETTLEMENT ENGLAND, AT FIRST DISTRUSTED,
GREW IN FAVOR—EARLY HIGH CHURCHMEN ANTI-ROMAN—
ANDREWES—LAUD—PRINCIPLES OF CAROLINE DIVINES—
PREDESTINATION A POPULAR DOCTRINE—REACTION AGAINST
IT—HIGH CHURCHMEN AFTER THE RESTORATION—HIGH
CHURCH SYMPATHISERS AT THE REVOLUTION OF 1688—
HIGH CHURCH ASCENDANCY UNDER ANNE—INTOLERANCE,
THE CAUSE OF A REACTION AGAINST THE CHURCH.

Anglicanism, treated in the preceding section as a system of Church order, appealed to two types of men: to those who were attached to the old system and found that the Church of England, in rejecting the abuses of the Middle Ages, had retained all that was necessary to the maintenance of its right to be called a branch of the Catholic Church; and to those who were devoted to the scriptural teaching of the reformers, yet found nothing inconsistent with it in the Anglican settlement. To the first named attention must now be directed.

In the seventeenth century, Protestant and Catholic Churchmen differed markedly as to the links in the chain of continuity between the contemporary Church and primitive times. The Protestant party held that the true succession was, as it were, a narrow thread of devout people, who, like the Waldenses, had never consented to the superstitions and abuses of Rome. The Catholic-minded, on the contrary, maintained that the visible Church had been a constant witness to the teaching of the

The High Church Party

Lord and his Apostles, and had never, despite the abuses which had crept in, relaxed its hold on certain fundamental truths. To the Protestant Anglican, therefore, the Reformation was a revelation of truth after centuries of apostasy and darkness; to the Catholic it was the continuance of the old Church purified from its corruptions. Rome to the one was utterly accursed, to the other it was a branch of the Church which needed only to be purged of certain abuses for a re-union to take place with those who had already cast it off. In Laud's memorable words, the religion before and after the Reformation was like Naaman before and after his cure. But it was "the same Naaman, leprous with them (the Romanists), cleansed with us (the Anglicans)."

From the days of Elizabeth to the Restoration, the Anglican Church passed through the following stages. Till about 1590 it was regarded as a makeshift that might at any time come to an end, swept away by a wave of Popery or of Puritanism. Then it began to be regarded with increasing enthusiasm by its supporters, as, with the help of the Crown, it brought the Puritans to their knees. It lost the support of the nation when it identified itself with arbitrary power, as exercised by Charles I. It endured real persecution during the Commonwealth, only to be welcomed back with enthusiasm when the gloomy tyranny of Puritanism ended with the coming of Charles II. Our object here is to indicate the standpoint of those who upheld the position, during this period, that the reformed Church was the legitimate successor of the unreformed. But these men had not the slightest desire to return to communion with an unreformed Romanism. They differed from the Puritans in regarding the adherents of the old religion as fellow Christians, and strenuously maintained that their errors had not excluded them from all hope of salvation. They acknowledged that many good things had been retained which the ultra-Protestants had rejected; but they did not regret their separation from Rome, nor entertain any doubt whatever as to the validity of their sacraments. They were sure that their Church was a return to the primitive Christianity of the first five centuries, and that it was based on Scripture, the Creeds, and the first four Councils. Various practices which were said to be marks of catholicity they indignantly denied were Catholic at all. They were ready to accept the sacrificial doctrine of the Eucharist, but not at the price of acknowledging the comparatively modern dogma of Transubstantiation. Episcopacy they declared to be primitive, apostolic, and scriptural, and it was to be retained by the Church of England at all costs, but they were not prepared to unchurch other Christians who had not the same privilege as they enjoyed. Nor did they, in their insistence on the catholicity of their Church, refuse the name of Protestant; and even Laud, as Archbishop, interested himself in the reconciliation of the Lutheran and Evangelical sections of continental Protestantism.

The first High Churchmen were prevented by loyalty to their own position from any tendency Rome-wards. Because the Roman controversialists, headed by Cardinal Bellarmine, denied that the English Church was Catholic, and maintained that the Sovereign might be deposed by his subjects, Churchmen under the Stuarts became almost fanatically loyal. In James I and Charles I they found kings who understood and appreciated their position, and proved ready to defend them against their enemies, the Puritans. They repaid these sovereigns with boundless gratitude and denounced all who desired to limit their authority, whether they were Popes, Parliaments, or Puritans. The divine right of the King of England was asserted in order to destroy the claims of the Pope to rule in God' s name. The mark of High Churchmanship throughout the seventeenth century was loyalty to the King, who ruled by hereditary right. It was carried to surprising lengths, and the most servile doctrines were preached by men, showed anything but an abject spirit in days of trial. Churchmanship, in taking the side of the King against the people, made Puritanism, for a time at least, popular.

The first great High Churchman, Launcelot Andrewes, was successively Master of Pembroke College, Cambridge, Dean of Westminster, Bishop of Chester, Ely, and finally of Winchester; for Richard Hooker, the greatest of Anglican divines, was too balanced in his judgment to be confined to any party. The saintliness of Andrewes, which would have adorned any cause, prevented his becoming a conspicuous figure in the ecclesiastical politics of his age. At the same time, his proved a more abiding influence than that of any of his more active colleagues, for Andrewes was the real inspirer of the revival in Laud's time and its far-reaching results. Quietly and unostentatiously, he set the example of restoring the churches to their former comeliness. In the name of spirituality, Puritanism had made worship hideous and frequently irreverent. The churches were falling into decay, the Prayer Book services were raced through with indecent haste before the preacher appeared—for nothing seemed to matter but the sermon. Andrewes, as dean, made the service at Westminster an example of what decent worship should be, and as a bishop he did the same in his cathedrals and private chapels. He inaugurated the reforms on which Laud subsequently insisted; but even in the eyes of the Puritans, his gentle character and his profuse liberality partially atoned for his ritualistic proclivities, especially as he did not harass those under his jurisdiction. All acknowledged his great learning and his gifts as a preacher.

Very different in character was Andrewes's friend and admirer, William Laud, the celebrated Archbishop of Canterbury, who shared his Church views and liberality in acts of benevolence, but was a man of affairs, ungracious in manner, harsh in his judgments, and unfeeling in his dealing with individuals. Yet he differed from his predecessor Abbot in being very sympathetic to the needs of his clergy, and did his utmost to relieve the grinding poverty by which many were oppressed. He combined an unflinching Protestantism, which resisted all the Romeward influences of the court of Charles I, with an intense belief in the continuity and catholicity of the Church of England. As a contemporary of such great Saints as St. Francis of Sales, St. Charles Borromeo, and St. Teresa, Laud was not blind to the devotional merits of continental Catholicism, though he firmly resisted the Queen and the Roman party in England in their efforts to destroy the Church Settlement. Realising that it was necessary not to alienate those who were Catholic at heart by a Puritan insistence on a bald Protestant form of worship, Laud provided a decent and dignified ceremonial. He placed the Holy Table altarwise and railed it in to prevent desecration; he insisted on the custom of bowing at the name of Jesus, and on entering the church; and he repressed as illegal all attempts to Puritanise the worship. On this account he drew down upon himself the undying hatred, not only of Puritans, but also of the more moderate Churchmen; especially when he went so far as to identify his form of Churchmanship with the support of royal absolutism, as interpreted by his trusted friend, Lord Strafford, thereby bringing about the failure of the revived Anglicanism of the first period of the Stuart dynasty. But its spirit did not perish with the executions of its chief supporters, Strafford, the Archbishop, and Charles I.

The main tenets of the Laudian school were the insistence on the divine right of Kings, to which allusion has already been made, and the opposition to the Calvinist doctrine of predestination.

It is not easy for us to realise how the entire Christian world was distracted after the Reformation by a question which can never be answered; namely, "If God has perfect foreknowledge, how can man be responsible for his actions in this life, and his salvation in the next?" In the early Church, the followers of astrology, who taught that all was determined by Fate, were opposed by Christian preachers, who insisted that men were given freedom to choose good and evil and that their fate depended on their own actions. Free Will was the keynote of early theology till the time of St. Augustine. This great example of conversion was led, partly by his own personal experience, and partly by his study of St. Paul, to lay especial stress on the doctrine that we are saved only by divine grace, without which we cannot do anything pleasing to God. He was led to infer with St. Paul that this divine grace was bestowed only on those whom God had, from all eternity, designed to save; and he also followed the Apostle in maintaining that the entire human race, as the descendants of Adam, deserved the wrath of God. Calvin taught the Augustinian doctrine in its extremest form and most of the reformers held it. Nor was it a novelty. It is characteristic of Western Christianity. It appears markedly in the ancient collects preserved in the Prayer Book: it was taught by the most famous of the schoolmen, Archbishop Bradwardine, for example. And it can be abundantly justified by an appeal to Scripture.

But a tide of reaction has always set in against the idea of such arbitrariness on the part of God, and irresponsibility on that of man. The heresy of Pelagius was due to his emphasis on Free Will in opposition to what he considered the immoral influence which might flow from the doctrine of Grace as taught by Augustine. There was a powerful school of Semi-Pelagians, and even Church Councils condemned extreme Augustinians. After the Reformation the Romans as well as the Protestants became divided among themselves on the same momentous question. The Jansenists in France were the counterpart of the English Puritans in this respect, and their opponents, the Jesuits, answered to the High Churchmen. The Puritans had no graver charge to bring against the bishops of Laud's party than that they favoured the opinions of Arminius, who had denied the infallibility of Calvin's doctrines of election and reprobation. This explains why the controversy grew so bitter when Charles I was under Laud's influence. James I, a staunch supporter of Episcopacy, was theologically with the Puritans in their abhorrence of Arminian doctrine.

After the Restoration in 1660, on account of the enthusiasm which the overthrow of Puritanism had inspired and the universal delight at welcoming back the King and the Church which had been faithful to him in all his troubles, the High Church party was naturally in the ascendant. A careful comparison between the Elizabethan Prayer Book and the one sanctioned in 1662 shows how little consideration it was determined to show the Puritans. The alterations are slight, but significant: "Priest" is substituted here and there for "Minister"; the manual directions are added to the Prayer of Consecration; more Apocrypha is inserted into the Lectionary. But the clergy of Charles II did not enjoy the same power as under his father; nor did they make any rash attempts at innovations in the services. Their High Churchmanship expressed itself in an extreme loyalty to the Crown and opposition to all forms of dissent. So strong was the belief of most clergy in non-resistance and passive obedience to the hereditary monarch, that not even the peril of a bigoted Roman Catholic on the throne, at a time when the nation was almost in a frenzy of fear over real or alleged Popish plots, could shake their fidelity to James II as successor to his brother; nor could his persecution of the Church when he became King permanently alienate many of the clergy, who remembered that St. Paul had ordered his converts to be subject even to Nero.

At the Revolution of 1688, the bishops and higher ecclesiastics began to side with the Low, and the inferior clergy with the High Church. The bishops, after the withdrawal of the Non-jurors, were naturally disposed to the side of the new Government, and inclined to favour the Dissenters, and, if possible, to make it easy for them to rejoin the Church by making the Prayer Book more

The High Church Party

acceptable to them. This policy the majority of the clergy resisted vigorously; and though they could not prevent the Toleration Act of 1689, they effectually killed the Comprehension Bill and the Revision of the Prayer Book. Provoked by the liberalising tendencies of the bishops, many clergy secretly favoured the return of the Stuarts, and fought any attempt to alter the doctrine or discipline of the Church.

The death of William III brought general relief; for the Church could rally to Anne as a real Stuart, famed for her devotion to its principles, and sincerely religious. The immense influence of High Church sentiment was seen when Dr. Sacheverell, a Fellow of Magdalen College, Oxford, a man of no importance, preached a sermon against the Revolution of 1688 before the Lord Mayor of London. The text was "In perils among false brethren." The sermon was delivered on Nov. 5, 1709, the day kept in honour of the deliverance of King and Parliament from the Gunpowder Plot, and of the landing of William of Orange to save the country from Popery. It was full of covert attacks on the Government of the day, as false to the Church, and contained this sentence, "In what moving characters does the holy Psalmist point out the crafty insidiousness of our modern *volpones.*" "Volpone" was the nickname of Lord Godolphin, the Queen's chief minister, who had the incredible folly to have Dr. Sacheverell impeached to the Lords by the House of Commons. Public interest was aroused, and feeling ran high in favour of the persecuted doctor. He was declared guilty by the Lords, and suspended from preaching for three years, as a punishment. His sermon was ordered to be burned by the common hangman. As he was not debarred from preferment, his friends gave him a rich living, and he retired into his proper obscurity.

The elections for Parliament went overwhelmingly against the Government, and for four years the Tories and the High Churchmen were in power. It was a period of much religious earnestness and of a real revival of devotional life; but the intolerance of the successful Churchmen, shown by their legislation regarding "Occasional Conformity"; that is, receiving the Communion in obedience to the Test Act, but continuing to attend dissenting chapels, and in the Schism Act, prohibiting dissenting schools, as well as by their partiality for the exiled Stuarts, made High Churchmanship suspect to the advisers of the Hanoverian dynasty; and after the death of Queen Anne in 1714, little is heard of it as a power in the nation. But its same spirit revived in a surprising way in the Oxford Movement a century later; and even in the dreariest period of Anglican Church History, though little in evidence, it was always alive.

XVI

LOW CHURCHMANSHIP

TYPICAL HIGH CHURCH LEADERS—LOW CHURCH HARD TO DEFINE—GEORGE ABBOTT—ABBOTT'S PROMOTION—WILLIAMS—BURNET—TILLOTSON—DOWNFALL OF THE WHIG SPIRIT—THE CHURCH AND THE LEISURED CLASS—HOADLEY—OPPOSITION TO DEISM—TOLERANT SPIRIT ENCOURAGED.

The term High Church can be applied to persons of most various views throughout at least three centuries with complete suitability. Bishop Andrewes in the early days of the Stuarts was emphatically a High Churchman, as was Laud, his spiritual successor. At the Restoration Sheldon was a representative of the party, and at the Revolution, Ken. In the eighteenth century typical figures belonging to it are Bishop Atterbury, Edmund Law, the mystic, and the active Non-jurors. In like manner in the nineteenth century, we have no difficulty in thus describing Pusey, Keble, and their successors down to Bishop Gore. It would be absurd to say that all these men would have been in complete agreement had it been possible for them to meet on earth; but they would all recognise each other as representing the same temper of Churchmanship.

The words Low Church are of a different and more fluctuating character. Their meaning must always depend on the period of which they are used. The Evangelicals, who are often thus described, have little in common with the Low Churchmen of the Revolution or early Georgian days. It is true that in approaching nonconformists in a more friendly manner than the High

Churchmen they agreed; but the motives in doing so of the Low Church and of the Evangelical party were not the same. In the earlier period the reason was chiefly political. The Dissenter was courted because he supported the Protestant succession and the House of Hanover. It was not so with the Evangelicals, who were in real sympathy with the religious and charitable aims of those outside the pale of the Established Church, and therefore well disposed to work with them. Our present object is to discuss the Protestantising portion of the Church, especially in the seventeenth century, and to stop short with the rise of Evangelicalism which will be dealt with elsewhere.

If the first real High Churchman was Andrewes, the first Low Churchman was his contemporary, Abbott, provided a Low Churchman may be defined as one to whom it is of the first importance that the Church shall be an institution more in sympathy with Protestantism than Catholicism, while its dignity and antiquity is to him a matter of indifference. Upon this definition, Low Churchmen are the least attractive religious representatives of the Anglican Church. They lack the chivalry of the High Churchmen, the intellectuality of the Latitudinarians, and the undoubted spiritual fervour of the later Evangelicals. There are, it is true, remarkable exceptions, like the eloquent and amiable Archbishop Tillotson, and the generous and impulsive Burnet; but as a rule Low Churchmen represent the Whig party in its least attractive aspects: its grasping propensities, its encouragement of nepotism, and its complete lack of idealism. They are responsible for the deadness of the Church and its isolation during the eighteenth century, and for the growing severance of comradeship between the highly placed clergy and their less fortunate brethren. Abbott, who was a Whig, long before the term was invented, is thoroughly representative of this worst phase of Low Churchmanship. In theology he regarded as heretical all that was not to be found in the Scriptures and the *Institutes* of Calvin. At Oxford he was distinguished for his learning and his unrelenting hatred of William Laud, then a young Fellow of St. John's College, the rising hope of the party in the Church which maintained the divine authority of the episcopate. Abbott attracted the favourable attention of James I by his attack on one Sprot, who had expressed his doubts as to the reality of the Gowrie Conspiracy, which had so terrified the timid monarch in his youth, when he was King of Scotland. Sprot was hanged, and Abbott became sure of the royal patronage. His severe predestinarianism further endeared him to the King, who saw in Abbott a theologian after his own heart, as well as a man likely to support the royal authority untrammelled by any scruples as to what was required of him by the commission entrusted to him as a bishop.

The King made him successively Dean of Winchester, Bishop of Coventry and Lichfield, of London, and in 1611 Archbishop of Canterbury. His appointment as primate was unpopular even with Puritans. He had no parochial experience and he was totally out of sympathy with the clergy, whose poverty he did nothing to relieve or even alleviate in face of the demands of James on their slender incomes. He preferred the society of wealthy laymen who could advance his interests to that of his clerical brethren. His very virtues made him repellent; for, like his enemy, Chief Justice Coke, who was at constant war with the ecclesiastical courts, he had a sort of brutal honesty which entitled him to respect, but never to affection. His conduct in resisting the King by refusing to assent to the suit for nullity of marriage, brought by the fascinating but infamous Lady Frances Howard against her husband, the Earl of Essex, deserves praise, and Carlyle gives him much credit for it. The event justified the conduct of the Archbishop. The divorced Countess and the King's favourite, Robert Ker, connived at the poisoning of Sir Thomas Overbury in the Tower and were convicted, but received a pardon. This denouement served to increase the King's respect for Abbott. A strange accident made Abbott's primacy remarkable. Whilst a guest of Lord Zouche, he accidentally shot a gamekeeper. The four bishops-elect, Laud among them, refused to be consecrated by a primate who had shed blood; and an attempt was made to deprive him of his office, which failed owing to the defence made for him by Andrewes, who might well have been chosen to succeed him as Archbishop. With the accession of Charles I, Abbott was virtually deprived of all authority, and his place in 1633 was filled by Laud, who, as Bishop of London, had long virtually ruled the Church. Abbott left no successor to carry on his policy, which was to devitalise the Church of England by making it such a copy of Continental Protestantism as to divest it of every claim to represent the pre-Reformation Church.

A younger contemporary of Archbishop Abbott was another enemy of Laud, John Williams, the last great English ecclesiastical lawyer, and one of those rare combinations of political with legal ability. Curiously enough he was a fellow of St. John's College, Cambridge, when Laud was a fellow of St. John's College, Oxford, and the two contended in noble enthusiasm in striving each to be the greatest benefactor of his respective college and university. Williams had been chaplain to the eminent jurist, Sir Thomas Egerton, afterward Lord Ellesmere, and his ability had so impressed his patron that he bequeathed his legal treatises to his chaplain. Although clerical lawyers and courts were specially detested, as a rule, by the civilians, Williams was honoured by a still greater man than Ellesmere, as he was made executor of Francis Bacon, Lord Verulam. James I made Williams Lord Keeper, as the substitute for a Lord Chancellor was called, when he was Dean of Westminster, and promoted him to be Bishop of Lincoln without requiring him to resign the deanery. During the first days of the Civil War he was elected Archbishop of York.

The long strife between Laud and Williams may be

considered a contest between Cavalier Oxford and Puritan Cambridge, the romance being entirely with the older University. Laud dreamed of a restored Catholicism, purified by reformation, but with all the glory, dignity, and beauty of the old, medieval English Church. He allied himself with Lord Strafford, the one man—as Laud acknowledged—who could have made Charles I great had he been capable of greatness, but whose policy of "Through" led the monarchy to ruin. Blind to the consequences of his actions, Laud pushed his ideals forward, regardless of the Puritans of the land and the papists of the court. The end saw the reversal of all he had striven for, and Laud's life was crowned by a martyr's death. Yet he infused a spirit into the Church which it never lost. In this respect he is typical of Oxford. Williams, on the contrary, was eminently cautious and sensible. He knew well what he was doing and always brought his knowledge to bear on his actions. Had he occupied Laud's place, the Church might have been saved, and Charles I might have died in his bed. But the Church directed by him might have lacked inspiration and lofty ideas. To do Williams justice, he would not allow himself, when the great crisis came, to be used as a tool by the Puritans.

Low Churchmanship had existed, therefore, long before the name; but we now come to two typical men branded with this appellation: Tillotson, Archbishop of Canterbury, and Burnet, Bishop of Salisbury, who both played a great part in the Revolution of 1688. Few men were more detested by the High Church party than Gilbert Burnet, a native of Aberdeenshire in Scotland, who had accepted episcopal orders when his country was compelled, against the will of the people, to endure the bishops. But though he had to suffer the displeasure of his family for renouncing Presbyterianism, Burnet was in favour of an episcopacy willing to conciliate the ultra-Protestantism of the Scotch. He was a friend of the saintly Archbishop Leighton of Glasgow, and was offered a bishopric in Scotland, which he prudently refused. He was at first favoured by the Duke of York, afterward James II, but he had offended the court before his accession and taken refuge in Holland. There he became attached to the Prince of Orange, and acted as spiritual adviser of his wife, Mary, daughter of James II. At the Revolution he was active in bringing over the Prince and in inducing Mary to decline the Crown unless her husband could be associated with her in the monarchy. Burnet was a strong supporter of schemes to include Dissenters within the Church and would readily have parted with most of the distinctive marks of Anglicanism to include them in a comprehensive church. This willingness to surrender church principles and his conspicuous lack of tact—he actually declared that the English ought to accept William of Orange as King by right of conquest—made him very unpopular; and not even his literary services to the Church, and the fact that it was to him that the clergy owed the surrender by the Crown of the tithes and first-fruits, and the creation of Queen Anne's Bounty, could cause the High Church party to relent in his favour. He was made Bishop of Salisbury and, unlike many Low Churchmen, took the duties of his position very seriously, visiting every part of his diocese, establishing a school for clergy, and showing the liberality characteristic of the best Caroline divines in the disposition of his fortune.

As the supplanter of Sancroft in the Archbishopric of Canterbury, Tillotson was, if less ridiculed, as much detested by the extremists as Burnet himself; yet it is generally agreed that the admiration of his friends was deserved. He was more of a Low Churchman than a Latitudinarian and his general attitude is revealed in the Comprehension Bill which he and his friends desired to add to the Toleration Act of 1689. The Act, as its name implied, gave those Protestants who dissented from the Church of England the right, subject to severe limitation, to worship in their own way. The object was to frame a bill so as to make it almost impossible for any

Low Churchmanship 139

dissenter to remain outside the Church. The Prayer Book was to be remodelled; the services were to be conducted in practically Puritan fashion; the surplice was to be optional, and the musical services in the cathedrals were to be abolished. The collects were to be "improved" and become almost unrecognisable by translation into the florid prose fashionable in the pulpit of the age. But these proposals satisfied nobody. The Churchmen were furious at the emasculation of the Church, which would remove all its cherished Catholicism; and the dissenter (the Puritan had virtually disappeared) preferred his independence and the generous patronage of the middle class with whom his ministrations found special favour. So this well-meaning but ill-judged scheme of comprehension found no genuine support.

The great period of Low Churchman life began with the accession of George I and ended with the defeat of the Whig aristocracy by George III. Four men, three of them of the laity, brought about its downfall: William Pitt, not as Earl of Chatham, but as the Great Commoner; John Wesley, George III, and Samuel Johnson. Pitt was not in any sense a religious leader, but he reintroduced into the sordid politics of the day an idealism which had been repressed by the materialism of the governing class of his age. His elevated conception of the greatness of his beloved country infused a new spirit into the national life. John Wesley and those who shared his zeal with the same warmth as his followers, although opposed to his religious views, called forth and cultivated a new spirituality which ended the vogue of the notion that the function of the Church was to maintain the *status quo* and assist the government in maintaining order by keeping down all enthusiasm. George III by his sincere personal religion and the purity of his life, and Johnson by throwing his immense literary prestige and his sound common sense on the side of the religion which he practised with so much honesty and simplicity, gave people a nobler ideal of Christianity which put infidelity to shame.

Throughout the middle years of the eighteenth century the intense hatred of Popery, the dread of the renewal of a "Church in Danger" cry which had proved so formidable in the trial of Sacheverell, and the fear of Jacobism, combined, with the long period of national prosperity under Walpole, to dispose men to be content with a religion which preached morality and left the State undisturbed. The higher ranks of the Church were found to afford respectable provisions for the needier members of the upper classes, and quiet leisurely retreats for the devotees of scholarship and literature. The inferior clergy were left in obscurity, often in humble dependence on the landed classes. Those who rose to places of dignity were expected to support the government and not to give trouble by any excess of zeal.

Hoadley, but for his Latitudinarian opinions, would have been the perfect model of a Low Churchman. His zeal for the Hanoverian Government and his readiness to let the Church be reduced to a tool in its hands marked him out for high honours—an opulent and splendid prelate, enjoying the temporal pomp and repudiating the spiritual responsibilities of his high office.

Nevertheless, in this period of ecclesiastical depression and deadness, a good work was being accomplished. If the Low Church Bishops were not men of energy, they were at any rate men of learning who devoted their time to refuting what was to them error. The Deists of the time were not persecuted as they would have been in the previous century but crushed under the ponderous force of the controversial literature which the orthodox produced; and it is very noteworthy that those of the laity who had least reason to admire the bishops joined them in condemnation of the rising infidelity of the day. Swift, Addison, Steele, and even Pope, a Romanist by education and a friend of the skeptical Lord Bolingbroke, all helped to hold the Deist writers up to scorn. Despite the repeated assertion that unbelief was fashionable, it does not appear, after all, to have been very deep-seated in England.

In one respect the religious apathy of the century assisted the cause of progress. It made for toleration, though of a characteristically illogical English type. According to law, the position of a Romanist in the eighteenth century was absolutely untenable in England, as the penal laws deprived him of all rights as a citizen, and placed him at the mercy of every petty magistrate. But, as a matter of fact, these laws were very rarely enforced; for when such cases were brought into court they were commonly dismissed without a hearing, usually on some alleged informality. Before the law, the Dissenter was, despite the Toleration Act, in scarcely a better plight. All the Acts of Charles II were unrepealed; but they, too, were regarded as dead letter, and an Act of Indemnity was generally passed to relieve people of the penalties they had incurred. Thus practical toleration coexisted with legal intolerance; and no one cared to attack the anomaly because few were inconvenienced by it. The superstitions of earlier times, as well as the spirit of intolerance, were passing away. Astrology and witchcraft, which had been believed in by the most intelligent a century before, were fading out in an age of reason, which, with all its defects, was one of common sense.

But Low Churchmanship, according to the old definition of the term, was not an attractive type of Christianity. It lacked the stern righteousness of Puritanism, and the romantic piety of the churchmen of the Jacobean age. Its virtues were eminently those of common-sense politicians, with practical rather than spiritual ends in view, and its one achievement was it gave to England the period of materialistic peace that the country so much needed after the distracting clash of factions in the Great Rebellion, the Restoration, and the Revolution.

XVII

LATITUDINARIANISM

MEANING OF LATITUDINARIANISM—JEREMY TAYLOR—THE CAMBRIDGE PLATONISTS—THE NEW NATIONAL PHILOSOPHY—THE IMPORTANCE OF "REASON"—PROFLIGACY OF THE RESTORATION—TILLOTSON—TRINITARIAN CONTROVERSIES—BANGORIAN CONTROVERSIES—SUBSCRIPTION TO THE ARTICLES—GOOD WORK OF ENGLISH DIVINES—WEAKNESS OF DEISM.

The word Latitudinarianism describes a habit of mind due in part to an indifference to religion and a distrust of the supernatural, and on the other hand to a more justifiable dislike of the intense dogmatism of the Reformation and post-Reformation period; to a desire for a more comprehensive religion; and to a reaction against the unreasoning acceptance of many Christian dogmas. One result was a certain coldness of religious temper, and a tendency to regard Christianity as a useful means of maintaining civil authority; and another, the destruction of many superstitions, which, by reason of their alleged support in Scripture, had caused much misery and injustice. It has survived in a much modified form in what is now known as Broad Churchmanship, represented by men as a rule abhorred by their own generation and blessed by posterity. Some few men of this type have been men of remarkable piety; others have stepped outside the limits of the Church and denied the Faith; a few have occupied high places to their own temporal advantage—scarcely any of them have been men of commonplace ability. Except when the Latitudinarians supported the house of Hanover

Latitudinarianism

and the Revolution Settlement, they have never been a coherent party, because their members have represented many shades of opinion, and displayed more independence of mind than capacity to coöperate.

When the majority of Englishmen, divided into Roundheads and Cavaliers, Churchmen and Puritans, were flying at one another's throats, a few, mentally, stood aloof, caring but little which party triumphed, provided peace was restored. The University of Cambridge produced men of this type, more interested in their studies than in the ecclesiastical questions of the hour. Representatives of this type of men are best found among those who revolted against the intense dogmatism of the age. Two examples may be taken—Bishop Jeremy Taylor, author of the "Liberty of Prophesying," and Ralph Cudworth, the Puritan Platonist. Jeremy Taylor was a royalist and a sufferer in the cause of Charles I, a strong churchman, a devotional writer, and a profound scholar. He was a Fellow of Caius College, Cambridge, and of All Souls', Oxford, and in his retirement, during the civil war, at Golden Grove in Wales, he composed *"The Liberty of Prophesying,"* the earliest plea of conspicuous merit for Toleration. In this work, he points out that men in the early Church differed on many points of discipline and practice, but this never caused them to renounce communion with one another, since such divergences do not touch the fundamentals of Christianity, which alone are important. One is surprised to find how liberal a man of strong convictions could be on subjects which many considered to be vital points, distracting the Church itself as well as causing a fatal breach between Cavaliers and Puritans. When Taylor died, in 1667, he was Bishop of Down, in Ireland.

Almost contemporary with Taylor was the famous school of Cambridge Platonists, chief of whom were Cudworth, Whitchcote, Henry Moore, and John Smith. Like many movements from that University, this was individual rather than coöperative, and produced less sensation at the time than subsequent influence. The power of Puritanism in the University was very great; and these Platonists were educated in the Calvinistic circle. After the restoration they conformed and took little part in the political and religious disputes of the time. Cudworth, for example, was Master of Christ's College from 1652 to 1688. Their central interest was not in controversial theology, but in Platonic idealism; and they devoted themselves to the study of Plotinus, the great Neo-platonist and mystic of the third century A. D. Cudworth protests strongly against the exclusive pursuit of theology and urges that more attention be paid to the other sciences which are her handmaids. Moore highly commends the new philosophy of Des Cartes. But the most important contribution of the school is Cudworth's "Immutable Morality," which shows that morality is not, as many Calvinists supposed it to be, simply due to the arbitrary will of a God whom we do not understand, but that it resembles the *ideas* of Plato, which are immutable. The broad and liberal spirit of these Cambridge philosophers was paving the way toward a more humane and broader theology than the dogmatism of the Calvinist or the ecclesiasticism of the clerical party.

The Cambridge Platonists had recommended the study of the natural sciences; and this advice was enthusiastically followed in the seventeenth century. After Bacon had indicated the path which the new philosophy should pursue, men of the most different tastes early in the reign of Charles II were attracted by it. The King himself was deeply interested in natural philosophy; his kinsman, the gallant Prince Rupert, was a chemist of ability, and the Court naturally followed the pursuits of royalty. The Royal Society was founded at this time: Newton was beginning his marvellous researches. The age marked the dawn of modern science in England, the study of nature and the further knowledge of the laws of the Universe, which was then as always to have its effect on religion. The immediate result was, however, not that which we should expect; instead of an opponent, science was looked upon as a fresh aid to faith, because it appeared to confirm the teaching of Scripture, and to reveal in a new way the goodness and benevolence of God. Some went so far as to conclude that true religion had been disclosed in Nature, and that far less depended on revelation than had been assumed; in fact, that much of what was pronounced to be of divine authority was actually the work of priests, deceivers belonging to all religions, who had for ages conspired to enslave the human race. In this way a method of thought arose, for it gave rise to no party, called Deism, which sought by unaided human reason to find a simple belief in God and more or less to eliminate all that was mysterious or supernatural. It was against Deism that the defences of Christianity in the eighteenth century were mainly directed. The most famous survivals from this interminable and somewhat dreary controversy were Bishop Butler's *Analogy* and, much later, Paley's *Evidences* and *Natural Religion*.

If Cambridge helped, by the scientific work of Sir Isaac Newton, to change the direction of the thought of the age, Oxford did its share through the philosophy of Locke. The strength of Christianity was to be due, henceforth, not only to its confirmation by science, but to its corroboration by reason. The theological disputes and hairsplittings which followed the Reformation had produced an intense disgust, and in reaction came a determined demand for something which would not, perhaps, satisfy the aspiration of fanatics, but would the reason of thoughtful men. Religion must, it was felt, be so presented as to appeal to common-sense people, and tend to make them, not so much pilgrims seeking the heavenly Jerusalem, as decent, God-fearing men and women here on earth.

There was need for this shifting of emphasis. Public morality was never at a lower ebb than after the Restoration. Puritan repression had compelled wickedness to assume the cloak of hypocrisy; and, when that was laid aside, vice reappeared in multiplied forms of shamefulness. Charles II was not by any means a moral man or monarch; but the cynical wickedness of the statesmen of his time make him by contrast almost respectable. The horrible wickedness of the judges at the time of the Popish Plot, and the judicial murders which followed the suppression of the Rye House Plot, show that the new Whig and Tory parties rivalled one another in unscrupulousness. The literature of the time, and especially that for the stage, revelled in obscenity; and the general tone of the nation had sunk to its lowest depth. No wonder, therefore, that people, wearied by controversies as to the relative merits of Presbyterianism and Episcopacy, asked for instruction in the elementary truths of morality. The days of the Revolution of 1688 in England were not unlike our own in this impatience for something practical, instead of the dry bones of arid controversies about obscure mysteries, or the necessity of certain ceremonial acts.

The chief representative of this new temper of mind which prevailed throughout the eighteenth century is Archbishop Tillotson, the great London preacher, who was raised to the primacy when Sancroft refused to take the oath of allegiance to William and Mary. Tillotson's much-admired sermons show the reasonableness of the Christian religion and its utility in persuading men to lead moral lives. The Jacobite party, indignant at his usurpation of Sancroft's see, accused Tillotson of being a Latitudinarian, and even an atheist: they asserted that he had never been baptized and nicknamed him "undipped John." But his amiable character made him generally respected and his views reflected the general tendency of the men of his age, who, though terribly shocked by the publication of a book with the title, *"Christianity Not Mysterious,"* were mostly in their hearts of that same opinion. This very common-sense view of the Christian religion made it somewhat commonplace. Its excessive reliance on reason unsupported by evidence is less scientific than it at first appears; for that which appears improbable to us with our limited experience may be confirmed by overwhelming later evidence.

The Deistical controversy led to one on the mysterious doctrine of the Trinity, which by a strict law of the land was subject to no dispute whatever, and any who depraved it were expressly excluded from immunity in the Toleration Act of 1689. Nevertheless the issue drawn was too burning a one to be neglected either by the Church or non-conformity. One of the strongest exponents of heretical doctrine was William Whiston, the successor of Sir Isaac Newton in the Chair of Mathematics at Cambridge. His abiding title to fame is his translation of the Jewish historian, Josephus, which has never been superseded. Whiston was a man of great attainments and his scientific work was highly approved by his great predecessor for whom he acted as deputy. But Whiston's learning was strangely perverse; as Gibbon says, he seems to have believed in everything except St. Athanasius. He held that the *Apostolical Constitutions*, which speak in the name of the Apostles, but patently belong in the fourth century, were second only in importance to the Scriptures; he maintained that Eusebius of Cæsarea, the historian (fl. 330), was the champion of true Christianity, and St. Athanasius, by his insistence on the Creed of Nicea, a corrupter of the faith. Whiston lives in fiction as Dr. Primrose, the Vicar of Wakefield, who was convinced of the special wickedness of second marriage. In 1711, after trial, he was deprived of his professorship for his Arian opinions. He founded no school, but on all sides strenuous efforts were made to allow more latitude in the interpretation of the Creed and to adapt the services of the Book of Common Prayer generally to Unitarian views.

Attention was turned in the first twenty years of the eighteenth century to the nature of the Church and Sacraments and it gave rise to one of the greatest pamphlet controversies in the history of the English Church. The protagonists were Benjamin Hoadley, Bishop of Bangor, and Francis Atterbury, the Jacobite Bishop of Rochester, who for his devotion to the exiled Stuarts was banished and died abroad in the reign of George I. Hoadley is the typical Hanoverian bishop. He was a man of great intellectual power, a skillful if not always honest controversialist, negligent in his episcopal duties, but industrious as a writer, and never neglectful of his own profit or advancement. His view of religion was as lukewarm as his notion of his episcopal duties; to him the Church was a human ordinance with little of mystery even in its Sacraments. He stood high in the favour of the government and died at an advanced age, Bishop of Winchester, then the most lucrative see in England. Hoadley's book on the Church roused the dying embers of High Churchmanship in the reign of George I, and it was condemned by Convocation. So bitter was the spirit displayed in this debate that Convocation was never allowed to assemble between 1717 and 1854.

Men of the type of Dr. Hoadley could mount the ladder of preferment with undisturbed consciences, and the general temper of the age was acquiescent to abuses and true to the motto of Walpole, its greatest statesman, *Quieta non movere;* but there were some men who felt much difficulty in interpreting the Thirty-Nine Articles in such a way as to be able on accepting clerical office to sign them conscientiously, not only as a Trinitarian pronouncement, but also because they committed those who subscribed to the Calvinistic view of God's economy. A serious attempt was made to modify the rules of subscription to the Articles and meetings were held in London at the Feathers Tavern to petition Parliament to that effect. One of the leaders was Archdeacon Blackburne, whose father had been Archbishop of York. The proposal excited violent opposition, especially from the clergy who were influenced by the spirit of the Wesleys. The matter was debated in the House of Commons and it is said that Charles Fox fully intended to support the petition, but as he happened to be intoxicated that night, he was compelled to be absent. But it was vain to expect that Parliament would exert itself to remove such a grievance. Ever since the Tory outburst in the days of Sacheverell, statesmen had fought shy of ecclesiastical disturbances; and they drew the rough conclusion that clergymen who desired to receive the emoluments of the Church ought to be able to subscribe to its articles.

The bishops and leading clergy of the eighteenth century have been subjected to much abuse, which is deserved, because of the worldliness and laxity of certain individuals among them. But they certainly deserve also credit for their victory for orthodox Christianity over opponents of no little controversial ability. The objections raised to the accepted religion of the day were not such as proved formidable in the nineteenth century, nor are they troubling Christians to-day. The present objection that the Church is a failure as a social reformer caused little trouble. In eighteenth century England, people were at times discontented with their rulers, but few cared seriously for political, much less social reform. Englishmen desired chiefly to be let alone and lightly taxed, and approved the general idea that it was a just Providence which gave money to the deserving, and poverty, the pillory, and the gallows to those whose idleness had merited them. In many respects a sentimental age, it was also distinguished for practical common sense of a somewhat harsh type. Dr. Johnson is an admirable example of a layman deeply religious and for his age remarkably humane, but the thought never entered his head that the inequalities of society were an objection to Christianity as a religion. The difficulties of the nineteenth century were scientific and critical, but neither of these troubled the eighteenth. A close analogy between the God of nature and of revelation was stoutly believed and most ably upheld, and the optimism of the time delighted to see in the world not a "nature red in tooth and claw," but a benevolent God who consulted the comfort of His creatures. Critical difficulties as to the date and authenticity of the Scriptures hardly existed then for the English theologian. The authority of the Bible was undisputed, and the only ground for difference was how it should be interpreted.

The appeal to reason, characteristic of Deism in all its varieties, could be more easily answered than objections against the Article on the Trinity, because nothing more than a conflict of opinions was involved. Facts were not in question. The learned refused, for example, to accept the doctrine of the Trinity because it seemed to them, much as it does to the man in the street to-day—absurd. They declined to accept miracles "because they do not come into our personal experience." In his debating, the Deist based his arguments on his own interpretation of the words of Scripture as opposed to that of the Church. His theories of the origin of religion and of human society were derived from an anthropology evolved out of his own consciousness, not from observation. He asserted that "priests" had invented religion and that the free and noble savage had at some unknown period entered upon a social contract much as stockholders form a trading company. Such assaults could be met and overthrown by highly educated men, as some of the leading Church controversialists undoubtedly were. Since it was not confronted with the facts of later science and archeological discovery, the skepticism of the eighteenth century had little in common with that of more modern times. The spirit alone was the same.

XVIII

THE NON-JURORS

IMPORTANCE OF THE NON-JURORS—THE STRENGTH OF THEIR ANGLICANISM—ORIGIN OF THE SCHISM—OATH OF ALLEGIANCE—NON-JURORS EJECTED—PERPETUATION OF THE SCHISM—ABILITY OF THE NON-JURORS—NO ROMEWARD LEANINGS—KEN AND NELSON—SANCROFT—HICKES—BRETT—HICKES—DODWELL—JEREMY COLLIER—IDEAL OF THE NON-JURORS—THE NON-JURORS' OVERTURES TO SCOTLAND AND THE EASTERN CHURCH.

A sect which broke off from the Church, for reasons which we must now consider entirely wrong, which entertained scruples that we must now pronounce ridiculous, and never numbered more than a few adherents at any time, must appear to the reader quite unworthy of consideration. Yet to dismiss it from attention would be a grave mistake, because it would deprive us of a clue to the understanding of the subsequent history of Anglicanism. The appearance and career of the Non-jurors was a proof that latent in the Church was a spirit as earnest as Puritanism, and as romantic as that displayed by the saints of the Church of Rome. A generation after the last Non-juror had passed away, their principles were revived in another form among the Tractarians. The successors of Ken and Hickes were the followers of Keble and Pusey.

The uncompromising spirit of the Non-jurors was equally displayed in its refusal to accept the Revolution of 1688, and in its unflinching resistance to Rome. These men, true Anglicans before the word came into use, resolved to maintain the Catholic position of their Church against both Protestant and Papist. They might have purchased comfort and ease by compromising with Protestantism of the Revolution or gained the favour of the monarch, for whom they had sacrificed everything, by conforming to the Roman Church; but they preferred to remain in isolation and to endure the discomforts it entailed. They stood out staunchly for their principles, and remained free of the reproach of worldliness. Their position may be condemned as absurd but it cannot be refused the praise of disinterestedness.

Their history can be told in a few words. The protest of Sancroft and his six suffragans against the order of James II, that the Declaration of Indulgence be read in the churches, was an immediate cause of the Revolution which drove that monarch from his throne. No sooner was James II deposed than the bishops, who had protested against his illegal acts, protested against his illegal deposition. The loyalty of Churchmen to the House of Stuart in the seventeenth century was proof against all the provocations to desert its standard which they endured at its hands; for it was due not only to a real affection but to a profound conviction that hereditary monarchy was established, not by man, but by God Himself, and so the worst tyranny would not justify resistance to the will of a lawful sovereign. They could not forget that the constitutional opposition to Charles I had brought about the Civil War, the ruin of the Church, the death of the King, and years of Puritan tyranny. But apart from every consideration of this kind the duty of passive obedience was to them a matter of principle based on the Scriptural injunction to be subject to the higher power, even if it were committed to a Nero. Consequently when James II began deliberately to seek to subvert the Protestantism of England and to destroy the Church itself in his mad attempt to subject the country to Rome, many of them considered that it was their duty to suffer the extremity of persecution, but not under any circumstances to resist the royal authority. They had preached passive obedience to the lawful king for almost a century. They had declared such obedience to be characteristic of the Church of England. They had taught on every thirtieth of January that in the execution of Charles I the nation had been guilty of as great a sin as the Jews had been on Good Friday, and with much less excuse; for Jesus was not actually King, and Charles was, when he suffered. Now, not forty years after the execution of the Martyr King, they were being called upon to repudiate his heir, who with all his mistakes was the son of one who had laid down his life for the Church. No wonder, therefore, that the clergy found it almost impossible to abandon James II and to deny his right to their obedience.

There was also the matter to be considered of the oath they had taken to be loyal to James. Oaths were constantly demanded in the seventeenth century, and were often taken with no intention of being kept. In an age of political changes, men transferred their allegiance back and forth without scruple and almost gloried in their fickleness. But these more scrupulous Churchmen could not thus easily throw off their allegiance in view of their high doctrines of kingship; and though they might go so far as to resist misgovernment or to connive at another, or others, acting in the King's name, they could not violate their oath to him and transfer their vow of fidelity to someone else. Nor could they refuse publicly to pray for their lawful King, even though the present occupant of the throne were unfit to rule.

It was the seven bishops who really caused the downfall of James II. Their respectful petition to be excused from reading his Declaration of Indulgence till it had been sanctioned by Parliament was followed by the famous trial which ended in their acquittal. It thus became evident that James was totally unfit to reign in a Protestant country, and his flight was regarded by those who had frightened him away as an abdication which vacated the throne. Archbishop Sancroft was quite prepared to admit that James was unfit to reign, and even tacitly to acknowledge William III and Mary as sovereigns *de facto,* but not as *de jure.* But when the clergy were ordered to abjure James and swear allegiance to the new monarchs as lawful occupants of the throne, he, with six out of the seven bishops, refused, and were all deprived of their sees. The primacy was declared vacated by Sancroft's refusal; Tillotson was put in his place, and the other sees were filled. Here were all the makings of a schism: six men of blameless life, including the Archbishop, who had proved their zeal for the Protestant religion and perhaps put their lives in peril by resisting the Popish tyrant, were thrust out of their legal position as bishops of the Church solely because they would not take an oath against their conscience. They were guilty of no act of rebellion and were under no suspicion of plotting against William and Mary. One of them, Bishop Ken of Bath and Wells, was considered almost a saint in his lifetime: all were ready to face poverty for principle.

The deprived bishops numbered in all ten, with about 400 clergy. The Non-juror schism was not precipitated by Ken, the best of those bishops who had been deprived of office for their loyalty to James II. Archbishop Sancroft withdrew from all public affairs, and died on November 24, 1693, at Fressingfield, in Suffolk, after living for some time on £50 a year. James was too bigoted to recognise the sacrifices his Primate had made on his behalf and the exiles at the Court of St. Germains referred to him as a second Judas Iscariot. Nevertheless the Archbishop, determined to continue the schism, had delegated his authority to Lloyd, the deprived Bishop of Norwich. Exactly a year after the death of Sancroft, in 1694, Lloyd and two other deprived bishops, Turner of Ely and White of Peterborough, consecrated two prelates to insure what they considered to be the continuity of the true Church of England. Bishop Turner was an active Jacobite who shortly after became involved in a plot to restore James, and fled for his life to France.

The succession of Non-juring bishops only ended with the death of the last of them in 1804. In 1713 Hickes, who had been consecrated by Lloyd and his colleagues, called in the aid of the Scottish bishops to consecrate three other Non-jurors, and two more were appointed in 1716. In 1718, a schism occurred in the tiny church on the subject of the adoption of the First Prayer Book of Edward VI and of what were called the *Usages,* four points of Catholic practice neglected by the established Church. After that, the Non-juring church became the shadow of a shade and faded into complete obscurity.

But the failure to continue a schism does not lessen the importance of the original movement nor of the ideas of the men who originated it. Individually, many Non-jurors were among the very ablest clergymen of the Church of England, and their contributions to learning rivalled the work of their predecessors, the great Caroline divines, and surpassed the product of their brethren who had sworn allegiance to William of Orange and the Hanoverian dynasty.

The Non-jurors may be classified under two heads: those who refused to break with the rest of the Church of England, kept outside only by the requirement to pray for the *de facto* sovereign, and those who broke completely with what they pronounced to be an apostate national Church.

It is well, however, to remember that even the most extreme Non-jurors, whose zeal for Catholic practices led them into great excesses, had nothing in common with those Anglo-Catholics to-day who turn a longing eye upon the Church of Rome. Their loyalty to the House of Stuart, for whom they had sacrificed everything, never impaired their devotion to what they believed to be the true Church of England. Upon the scaffold even some declared that they belonged to the same church as Archbishop Cranmer; and in the overtures they made to the Church of the East, they never forgot that they were

Protestants, nor had the slightest doubt as to the validity of their orders as bishops, priests, and deacons.

The Non-juring laity were fully the equal of their clergy. The most respected of the non-schismatical Nonjurors, if not of all of them, were a bishop and a layman, Thomas Ken, Bishop of Bath and Wells, and Robert Nelson, who seems to have been the friend of every good man irrespective of his party or opinions. In the second generation an equally devout, and far abler man, William Law, refused the oaths. He was one of the few theologians who rank among the masters of English literature.

Among those who broke with the Church and set up altar against altar, the highest in rank was Sancroft; but in ability he takes a lower place than most of his colleagues. His literary fame rests on a satire on Calvinism called the *Fur prædestinatus,* a dialogue between a thief about to be hanged and a Calvinistic chaplain. It has, however, been pronounced too witty to have been written by a man of his type, as well as too uncharitable to come from a future archbishop. The other bishops to whom Sancroft bequeathed the schism were of no particular note; but two of their successors, Hickes and Collier, would have been remarkable anywhere. Bishop Brett was a great liturgiologist, and Dodwell, though a layman, eclipsed the clergy in his vast range of ecclesiastical learning. Nelson occupies a place among the Non-juring priests like that of Ken among the bishops.

Most of those here mentioned were eccentric men of genius. Hickes was one of the most learned men in the country, famed for his knowledge of the languages of Northern Europe and a controversialist of extraordinary vigour and ferocity, who managed to retain the friendship of some of his strongest opponents. Dodwell resigned his readership at Oxford because he could not bring himself to take the oaths to William and Mary. He is held up to ridicule by Macaulay for the argument of his book that the effect of Baptism is to give immortality to the human soul. The heathen, therefore, simply perish and are not tormented after death; not so dissenters and schismatics, on whom Baptism confers an immortality which will mean for them an eternity of suffering in hell. This is scarcely a just description of Dodwell's work, which is intended to limit damnation to those willful men deserving it and to reject the idea that those who, through no fault of their own are ignorant of Christ, are tortured for all eternity. Strangely enough the Non-jurors adopted the opinion, generally condemned in the West, that only Baptism by a properly ordained priest was valid, whereas the Catholic Church has since St. Cyprian's day, in the middle of the third century, declared that all Baptism in the name of the Trinity by whomsoever administered is valid.

Collier will always be famous, not as a Non-juring bishop but as the reformer of the impurity of the English stage, which he attacked with unsparing severity. The wits, headed by Dryden, tried to defend themselves, but were put to rout, not because Collier had the better cause, but because he excelled them in their own specialty. It is hardly too much to say that the reformation of the stage was largely due to Collier and that he drove the vile comedies of the Restoration into the obscurity they merited. In connection with the Assassination Plot of 1696, Collier incurred much not undeserved odium. Two knights of the city of London, Parkyn and Field, suffered the extreme penalty for their share in the conspiracy, and Collier and two Non-juring priests attended them on the scaffold and solemnly pronounced the absolution provided in the Visitation of the Sick. All the bishops protested at this act, because it seemed to condone the sin of men who died without penitence for the crime of plotting to murder the king.

The perversity of the Non-jurors must not blind us to the importance of their movement. Theirs is the one and only schism in the history of the Church of England. Others have left its communion altogether for various forms of Christianity. The Non-jurors declared that they alone were the true representatives of Anglicanism. Able and pious as their leaders were, they tried to restore an impossible condition of things which the nation had repudiated. Their ideal was a king like Charles I, or even James I, guiding a church with which he was wholly in sympathy, and in return receiving its support against common enemies whether Papist or Puritan. Their wishes were granted after the restoration of Charles II, who, if he did not believe that the Church of England was powerful to secure his salvation hereafter, at least was wise enough to see that it was his most useful ally on earth. James II was the antithesis of his brother, who concealed great ability under a cloak of frivolity and much natural kindness of heart under a humorous cynicism. James on the contrary was solemn, pompous, arrogant, business-like, utterly devoid of humour and, in his later days, only wicked because of his intense stupidity. Sancroft was as ready as anyone to entrust the government to William and Mary if only they would have consented to exercise it in the name of James II, and have forced no oath on the clergy. But when the innocent son of James II was excluded from the succession in favour of the Elector of Hanover, an uncouth foreigner, whose native religion was more repulsive to a churchman than Romanism itself, there can be little wonder that some joined the ranks of the Non-jurors. But the movement died down for want of additions in any numbers from the laity and became little more than a body of clergymen disputing among themselves on points which excited slight general interest. The exiled Stuarts were in fact little regretted by anyone in England, and the northern rebellions of 1715 and 1745 emphasised this indifference, for these uprisings identified their cause with Popery and foreign interference, the two things most unpopular in the country, which connected with Protestantism the prosperity it enjoyed under the peaceful administration of Sir Robert Walpole.

The Non-jurors accomplished things out of all proportion to their insignificant size and lack of sympathy with their age. They allied themselves to the Episcopal Church of Scotland, which maintained a struggling existence in the face of deep poverty and the intolerance of the Presbyterian ministers, and naturally was Jacobite till the cause of the Stuarts became entirely hopeless. Like the Non-jurors, the Scottish Churchmen resisted all inducement to join the Roman Communion.

They turned, instead, to the orthodox church of the East with proposals for a church union which would comprehend East and West, something that churchmen had desired throughout the seventeenth century, when England, Holland, and France were rivalling one another for the trade of the East, and Catholics and Protestants were seeking a way to unite with the Christian subjects of the Turkish Empire. The Non-jurors approached the orthodox church through the Metropolitan of the Thebaid, who had come to visit England in hopes of raising money for his flock. They addressed him as members of the church of Anglo-Britannia headed by Collier, who wrote as *Jeremias Princeps Anglo-Britanniæ Episcopus*. Some of their proposals for reunion were fantastic in the extreme and displayed lack of common sense characteristic of the Non-juror movement. They suggested, for example, that Constantinople should yield its primacy in the reunited church to the ancient church of Jerusalem. But as regards the worship of pictures, the doctrine of Transubstantiation and other things of the kind which they deemed superstitious, the Non-jurors adopted as uncompromising an attitude as they did to Rome or Canterbury.

Their importance for us is all due to the one fact that in an age of cold and unimaginative Protestantism they kept alive the old Laudian feeling that their Church was an apostolic institution, the only true representative of primitive antiquity. Their temper was that of the Frenchman, Isaac Basire, who joined the English Church in the eighteenth century and travelled far and wide as its "Apostle," to use Evelyn's word, in the East. "I have surveyed most churches Eastern and Western in an ecclesiastical pilgrimage of fifteen years, and I dare pronounce of the Church of England what David said of Goliath's sword, 'There is none like it both for primitive doctrine, worship, discipline, and government.' "

XIX

THE WESLEYS

THE WESLEY FAMILY—SAMUEL WESLEY, THE YOUNGER—JOHN AND CHARLES AT OXFORD—JOHN—THE TWO WESLEYS GO TO GEORGIA—WHITEFIELD AS A PREACHER—DISLIKE OF "ENTHUSIASM"—CONDITION OF ENGLAND—THE METHODISTS—WESLEY AND THE BISHOPS—MACAULAY'S CRITICISM—ACTIVITY OF THE WESLEYS—METHODISM CONSIDERED POPISH—WIDE SPREAD OF METHODISM—CHURCHMANSHIP OF JOHN WESLEY.

After the restoration of Charles II, there were two Puritan divines who suffered deprivation for their opinions. They were a father and his son, and their name was Wesley. Both had been distinguished at Oxford, the son especially. They were of good family, though scantily furnished with this world's store. Because he was forbidden to preach, the younger of these two Wesleys practised as a physician. His son Samuel did not maintain the Puritan tradition. He too was an Oxford man and made a reputation as a man of learning and a sound Churchman. At one time he held the chaplaincy of a regiment, but finally settled down at Epworth, a fairly comfortable living in the gift of the Crown. He married Susanna Annesley, related to a peer of that name, and a most remarkable lady. She had an almost incredibly large family, which she ruled with a rod of iron. As her husband had to go to London to sit in Convocation, Mrs. Wesley ran the parish as far as the curate would permit. For three years she and her husband separated because she would not pray with him for King William

III. When Queen Anne, for whom Mrs. Wesley could pray, succeeded, she and her husband were reconciled, and in 1703 another child was born, the famous John Wesley. At this time there was an elder brother, called after his father, Samuel, who was the good angel of the family, as he contributed liberally to the education of his brothers, John and Charles.

It is customary to depict Samuel the younger as a dull fellow without the genius of his brothers. It is doubtful if this is correct. Samuel was a student of Christ Church, Oxford, and Second Master of Westminster School. In the days of the wits he ranked as one, and was a friend of Bishop Atterbury, who was not the man to associate with fools. The High Church principles of Samuel interfered with his preferment and he never rose higher than Head Master of Blundell's School in Devonshire. He made an unforgettable remark about his more famous brother—"I am not afraid that the Church of England will excommunicate John; my fear is that John will excommunicate the Church of England." The fame of the elder brother is small indeed compared to that of his two juniors, yet they owed much to the unselfishness which he displayed in assisting their education. His Churchmanship was that of the whole family, High and not out of sympathy with the best Non-jurors. Like his father, the younger Samuel Wesley was a man of some mark in his generation as a man of letters and a devout and useful clergyman. The home at Epworth was very remote and isolated, the household was in constant money difficulties, but both father and mother were well educated and came of good parentage and its influence is manifest throughout the long lives of the two younger sons, John and Charles.

They received the best education of their day and at Oxford were markedly distinguished as men promising alike for their piety and ability. They gathered round them a devout society of young men, who visited the prisons, communicated weekly, and were nicknamed

"Methodists," a name they assumed and retained. The society received an unexpected accession of strength in a humble adherent named Whitefield, who was a college "servitor" working his way by menial service to a degree at the University. He was the son of a small innkeeper at Bristol and had in his boyhood won some distinction for his dramatic talent. These three men, John and Charles Wesley and George Whitefield, may be said to have changed the religious history of England. John was the guide and organizer, a stronger character and brain than either of his colleagues; Charles, the hymn writer, one of the best England has produced; and Whitefield, the pulpit orator. It is a curious fact that the two Wesleys, who were cultured gentlemen and highly educated, were not nearly as successful with the upper classes as Whitefield.

John Wesley passed through numerous spiritual experiences. He was a man of wide interests and very impressionable. At the same time he was of a masterful disposition and maintained his views with great pertinacity. His home was a school of religion, but neither that of his family, nor his own practice of it at Oxford, satisfied him. He sought advice on his troubles of William Law, the Non-juror, but his mystical religion did not come up to Wesley's anticipation and he repudiated him as a spiritual guide.

John and Charles then accepted chaplaincies in General Oglethorpe's proposed Colony of Georgia. This was a philanthropic scheme to give people who had failed at home a fresh start in America. On the long and tempestuous voyage, the two brothers came into close contact with some Moravians, who had been driven out of their own country and were going as settlers in the new colony. The calmness of these exiles produced a deep impression on the Wesleys, who learned that the secret of it all was a serene trust in God and the assurance of their own salvation. For some time the two brothers were almost entirely under the religious influence of the sect and shared in its quietism.

On their arrival in Georgia, however, the Wesleys endeavoured to enforce the discipline of the Church of England with a primitive severity unknown at home. They soon became embroiled with the other colonists. John had an unfortunate love affair, which, if it left his character unstained, did not improve his reputation for sound judgment. Charles made himself very unpopular, and in 1738 they returned to England.

In the meantime the eloquence of their friend Whitefield was making a great impression at home and arousing no little opposition. Driven from the churches, he began to preach in the fields, an example gradually followed by the Wesleys. They preached in Moorfields, then an open space near the city of London, used for bull fighting, bear baiting, and other cruel sports of the age. They produced an extraordinary effect on the wild mining population of Kingswood, near Bristol. They began missionary tours and inaugurated the Methodist revival.

Both the Church of England and the dissenting bodies were out of sympathy with the new preaching, which was emotional and touched men's deepest feelings, whereas those who were in authority desired a religion which would encourage a well-ordered life and make its appeal for adoption to man's reason. The Methodists encouraged an enthusiasm which produced violent convulsions and other extreme spiritual manifestations and not unnaturally disgusted those whose chief desire was to avoid undue excitement in religion. The Church was decorous, somnolent and thoroughly parochial. If a popular orator overcrowded a church he disturbed the comfort of the regular parishioners. Not that the Church was intolerant. The fierce passions of a previous age had so far cooled that a new movement would not be regarded as dangerous unless it promised to cause open political trouble. There was no great dislike to Dissent on the part of the higher placed clergy. Their besetting sin assuredly was not sacerdotal pretension. All gloried in being Protestant. Except for the beauty of the Prayer Book, the service of an ordinary parish church was as drab and dreary as that of a non-conformist chapel. The privileges of the clergy were so assured that they had no apprehensions; and there does not seem to have been much difference as far as doctrines were concerned. Both Church and Dissent united in their dread and detestation of Popery— of which the famous Bishop Butler was accused when he recommended in his charge to the clergy of Durham the churches to their care, and suggested that they should be kept from falling into decay. As for non-conformists, they had no serious grievances. They belonged, as a rule, to the commercial class, which was daily increasing in prosperity. Their ministers were often in a better position socially than the average clergyman. Though nothing was done for the repeal of their legal disabilities, the majority of them were on the whole fairly contented.

The material condition of England was indeed prosperous when compared with that of Europe, but morally it was profoundly unsatisfactory. The old parochial system was breaking down and no proper Church provision was made for people who were crowding into the towns or around the coal mines. It was a time of coarse brutality, and the law was administered with no little cruelty, whilst the police were ludicrously inefficient. Intemperance was more prevalent than it had been, owing to the introduction of spirits, which had formerly been almost unknown, but were now becoming common and cheap. The profligacy of the upper classes was notorious, and the spiritual destitution of the masses, together with the prevalence of gin-drinking, was a danger to the community.

Under such circumstances the missionary labors of the Methodists began. The churches were often closed against them, and then they preached in the open air or hired halls or rooms for the purpose. Lay preaching was also adopted; and at last John formed his followers into a society. His power of organising and disciplining men was as remarkable as his zeal for the saving of souls. He permitted no interference from without or within his society. "My brother and I" constituted the paramount authority. His preachers were subjected to the strictest regulations; his converts assigned to classes each under its own leader. The Conference, under the Wesleys, controlled the whole body. Yet neither John nor Charles had any desire to separate from the Church. True, they admitted Dissenters without much regard to their church principles; but in the eighteenth century the line of demarcation was not as clearly defined as in the present day. The idea still was that Methodism should be a society, as Franciscanism had been an order, for the practice of a stricter religious life within the Church.

The question now arises how far the bishops and ecclesiastical authorities and how far circumstances beyond their control were to blame for their attitude to the movement. The popular notion shared by the Churchmen and non-conformists of to-day is that the Methodists were driven out of the Church by the bigotry and intolerance of its ecclesiastics. Macaulay's contrast between the wisdom of the Church of Rome and the folly of the Church of England is generally admitted to be true. In his essay on Von Ranke's History of the Popes there is a long and brilliant passage which begins: "We will therefore, at present, advert to one important part of the policy of Rome. She thoroughly understands what no other church has ever understood: how to deal with enthusiasts," and ends, "Place John Wesley at Rome. He is certain to be the first General of a new society devoted to the interests and honour of the Church."

Macaulay is obviously thinking here of St. Francis, whose enthusiasm was utilised by some of the ablest ecclesiastical statesmen of the thirteenth century. He does not mention that those who followed St. Francis literally were subjected to savage persecution and even to the fires of the Inquisition. But let us compare John and Charles Wesley with St. Francis. St. Francis was always at heart a layman, and his charm lay in his untutored piety. His movement was under the control of an ecclesiastical organisation which could have crushed it any time had it shown any symptom of insubordination. Francis, it is true, could be as firm about his principles as Wesley; but even before he died he had ceased to be the real guide of the destinies of his order. John and Charles Wesley, on the contrary, lived in an age and country without any real ecclesiastical discipline: they were not even as beneficed clergymen dependent on any bishop. Moreover, both socially and intellectually they were among the very foremost Churchmen of their day. Like Wyclif, they were highly distinguished Oxford men, whom no bishop could regard as ignorant enthusiasts. Also, even if he had the will, no bishop had the power to persecute them. On the whole the episcopate appears to have shown as much consideration to the Methodists as was consistent toward a movement which, like that of the friars, was subversive of the parochial system which was then considered indispensable.

The activity of the Wesleys, especially of John, was almost incredible, and the opposition to them and their followers only increased their zeal. For a time the arrival of the Methodists in a town was a signal for a furious mob to assemble against them. The magistrates, some of whom were clergymen, were occasionally inclined to take the part of the turbulent populace; but so novel a procedure of evangelisation as they adopted made the disturbances inevitable for a time, and they gradually passed away. Another not wholly illegitimate grievance against the Methodists was that their preaching threw the minds of their hearers into disorder. Violent convulsions accompanied much of the preaching and people indulged in excessively unrestrained spiritual emotion, something very repellent to the staid respectability of the age. Constant complaint against this "enthusiasm" of the Methodists, comparing it to that of the Papists, was heard.

Far the most serious objection to Methodism in the eyes of the majority of Englishmen was, not that it was opposed to the principles of the Church or that it was a revival of the old Puritanism, but that it was Popish and Jacobite. John Wesley's linguistic abilities were considered a sure proof that he was a Popish agent of the exiled Stuarts, and he had repeatedly to deny that he was a Jacobite in disguise, one cause for suspicion being that he spoke Spanish.

But Wesley's bitterest opponents were not all Churchmen, and of the clergy who denounced his views not all by any means were devoted to the Catholic aspect of Anglicanism. In fact, the "heresy" laid to his charge was the same one Laud was accused of by the Puritans. He denied the Calvinistic doctrine of Election and maintained that God desired the salvation of all men who would accept it. His old friend and associate Whitefield broke with him on this score, as did the Countess of Huntingdon and her clergy. The attack on the Arminianism of the Wesleys and Fletcher of Madeley was carried on with extraordinary animosity. It divided the Methodists themselves into hostile parties.

To the last John Wesley maintained that he was in full communion with the Church; and Charles, who had retired from active life a few years before his death, did not approve of many of the actions of his brother because they appeared to him schismatical. In his famous "Korah" Sermon, however, at the end of his life, John warned the Methodists not to forsake the Church of England; and he protested vigorously against the insistence of the clergy that the Methodist meeting houses should be registered as dissenting chapels. To the last he opposed the demand of his unordained preachers that they be allowed to administer the Lord's Supper. Still, the fact cannot be denied that John Wesley had of his own authority ordained "superintendents" for America who ultimately became bishops of the Methodist Episcopal Church, and this act had widened the breach with the Church of England. After his death, in 1791, his preachers insisted on exercising the full rights of a Methodist ministry and on becoming practically an independent Church.

Methodism is the most widespread of Protestant bodies in the English world; and, if it does not faithfully reproduce all the ecclesiastical views of the great man who founded it, at least it has preserved much of his evangelistic enthusiasm, and owes a debt to his marvellous power of organisation. But John Wesley cannot be claimed as the sole property of any religious denomination; least of all can the Church of England forego the honour of having nurtured him in her bosom and retained his affection till the end of his long life.

Here it is not possible to relate in full the story of Methodism, but only to dwell on how the movement affected the Church of England. The Wesleys as a family were people of remarkable ability, living in uncongenial surroundings at Epworth, one of the most isolated market towns in England. The father was a scholar and even a poet; the mother was one of the most remarkable women of her time; the three sons were all men of mark; the daughters, if unfortunate in their marriages, were by no means ordinary. Although, therefore, the family was brought up in poverty, the home was not lacking in refinement and there is an air of distinction about the careers of all three brothers. The musical genius of the Wesleys was long perpetuated.

Though of Puritan ancestry, the Wesleys had a decidedly High Church upbringing. They were free of the unreasoning hatred of Popery, so common in their day, and they had no sympathy with the hard Calvinism of doctrine or the bald and dreary worship of the older non-conformists. Nor did the High Church party, as in after days, regard them as disloyal to the Church. Dr. Johnson, for all his unbending principles, looked on John Wesley as a friend and spiritual guide, and only complained that Wesley never had leisure for a long talk with him. The Churchmanship the Wesleys contended against was the placid worldliness on the part of the clergy and neglect of duty of the Hanoverian age. It was that which made them revolt against the Church of their time. The original Methodists were a survival of the active religious spirit of the days of the Revolution, of the reign of Queen Anne, and of the best of the Non-jurors. They were carrying on the work of such men as Beveridge, Collier, Bray, and of laymen like Boyle and Nelson, and even of the great Caroline divines of an earlier generation. That it should end in the greatest of all secessions from the English Church is one of the ironies of history and one is tempted to ask if the breach even now is irreparable.

XX

EVANGELICALISM

SKEPTICISM OF THE AGE—ABUSES TOLERATED—STRENGTH OF CALVINISM—EVANGELICALISM NOT FAVOURED BY AUTHORITY—EVANGELICAL CLERGY SCORNED—THE CLAPHAM SECT—LIFE AT CLAPHAM—THE CAMBRIDGE EVANGELICALS—ISAAC MILNER—CHARLES SIMEON—EVANGELICALS SENTIMENTAL BUT PRACTICAL—HUMANITARIAN REFORM—PRISON REFORM—MISERY OF THE POOR—NATIONAL EDUCATION—CRIMINAL LAW REFORM—BIBLE SOCIETY—MISSIONS.

In the eighteenth century the characteristic mark of English Churchmanship was a reasonable piety crossed with a tinge of worldliness. The Christian religion was admired for its benevolence, and its inculcation of practical morality. That it discouraged enthusiasm was a great merit in the Gospel. Virtue was manifested by a steady application to business, and rewarded by affluence and prosperity. Vice began with Sabbath-breaking and ended with the gallows. Side by side with this eminently respectable religion went much well-bred infidelity. The cultured few sneered, rather than scoffed, at the infatuation of the "vulgar," and Christianity was considered a negligible factor in the life of an educated man. Methodism did not touch the evil. In the first place, it prevailed mainly in the lower middle class, and repelled many of the more serious clergy by its avowed Arminianism; and in the second, it rendered itself suspect by the excesses of its adherents, especially in the early days of the preaching of the Wesleys. The religious ecstasies, the convulsions of the converts, the excitement manifested during the sermons were repugnant to the strong sense of decorum of a formal age. At the same time it was undeniable that the profligacy of high society and the ferocity of the masses demanded a stronger antidote than that which the sober religion of the average Churchman provided.

One of the most shocking features of eighteenth century society was the apathetic way it acquiesced in abuses. The most dreadful cruelties, if only they were legal, or even customary, were accepted without protest. The penal laws, which were scandalously severe; the prisons, which were a disgrace; the slave trade and the horrors of the "middle passage"—none of them called forth remonstrances, any more than the corruptions in political life. The privileges of the Church were conditional on observing silence and repressing all manifestations of enthusiasm. But dead as the Church appeared to be, Wesley had shown there was no lack of religion in the country; and the Methodist movement had had a great effect on those who were naturally opposed to its dogmatic teaching.

It is a curious fact that in Christianity a belief in predestination and election is often accompanied, not by a comfortable acquiescence in things as they are determined by the will of God, but in energetic labours for the furtherance of the work of the Gospel. The Calvinistic clergy who opposed Methodism most vigorously, vied with it in activity and benevolence, and in combat with the worst evils of the age. Their religion was intensely personal, but also practical: they had no objection to the established Church, or to its ordinances, nor had they any enthusiasm for it. In fact, the necessity of the Church as a divine institution carried hardly any weight with them; and in their missionary and benevolent activities they were so successful as individuals, often in coöperation with Dissenters, that it seemed a hindrance rather than a help. As regards doctrine, they preferred the cautious Calvinism allowed by the Articles, to the

Catholicism of the Book of Common Prayer, and they attached the highest importance to the Atonement in the scheme of salvation. They were not theologians in the sense that either the Puritan or Churchmen of the seventeenth century had been, nor were they interested in questions of scholarship or learning; their piety was prayerful, practical, and above all businesslike. No form of Anglicanism appeals less to romance than the Evangelical Movement, and none proved so rich in achievement. It was directed by men successful in business, it worked through committees of benevolent philanthropists, its language was affected and its methods commonplace: it can only be justly judged nevertheless by what it accomplished.

Despite their Protestantism, the conservatism of their religious opinions, their wealth, their great liberality where money was concerned, and their genuine desire for the moral improvement of the country, the Evangelicals found no more favour with the Church authorities than the Methodists. The Church was a profession, like the English bar, rather than a vocation, with many blanks, but a few great prizes. The fact was appreciated by the aristocracy, and many took Holy Orders. But the rich benefices were never exclusively the monopoly of birth, and men reached the highest positions in the Church through learning or ability. But promotion whether attained by high birth, patronage, or merit, was always regarded as a prize rather than as entailing responsibilities, and the one condition on which they could be won was to give the Government no trouble, but to live comfortable lives of decorous respectability instead. It is not necessary here to dwell on the abuses of the Church, the pluralities, the neglect of clerical duty, and the comparatively low view of the ministry. The greatest condemnation of the eighteenth century Church lies in the simple fact that, whereas in 1700 it was estimated that there was one dissenter to every twenty-five Englishmen, in 1800 a quarter of the population were non-conformists.

Dignitaries in such a condition of affairs were not

likely to look with favour on the activities of the evangelical party, and most positions of dignity were closed to those clergy who were attached to its tenets. At a later time they were in high favour with the authorities but at first they were suspected of being disloyal to the Church and embarrassing to the government. Even now the record of their somewhat unctuous piety is distasteful to most people, and it was subjected to merciless ridicule by the satirists of the manners of their day. The Evangelicals produced no striking writer nor thinker; they are not picturesque figures in ecclesiastical history. Forgotten or discredited now, their achievements for humanity, nevertheless, changed the world for the better.

Clapham and Cambridge were the two centres of Evangelicalism. Clapham was a pleasant village within easy driving distance of the city of London. It was the home of wealthy merchants and bankers, who formed what is known as the Clapham Sect. The leaders were Henry Thornton (1760–1815), Member of Parliament for Southwark, Wilberforce, Lord Teignmouth, Zachary Macaulay, father of the historian, James Stephen and the Venns. Those who decry the ability of the Evangelicals would find it difficult to name a group of men whose descendants became more distinguished. The lives of the Clapham band of friends were well ordered, deeply religious, beneficent, and charitable to a degree, not entirely neglectful of material comfort. The tone of the society was serious, "not exhilarating," to quote the words of James Stephens, "except when Wilberforce was present."

In his novel of *"The Newcomes,"* Thackeray draws an imaginary, but not inaccurate, picture of the life at Clapham and a few extracts may not be out of place. Of Mrs. Newcome, he says, "To manage the great house of Hobson Bros. and Newcome; to attend to the interests of the enslaved negro; to awaken the benighted Hottentot to a sense of the truth; to convert Jews, Turks, infidels, and Papists . . . to head all the public charities of her sect, and to do a thousand secret kindnesses that none knew of, etc." Her house was "surrounded by lawns and gardens, pineries, graperies, aviaries, luxuries of all kinds. The paradise, five miles from the Standard at Cornhill, was separated from the outer world by a thick hedge. . . . It was a serious paradise. As you entered the gate, gravity fell on you; and decorum wrapped you in a garment of starch." Young Thomas Newcome, her step-son, repeated religious poems to his step-mother after dinner "before a great, shining, mahogany table, covered with grapes, pineapples, plum cake, port wine, and Madeira." No better picture could be given of the combination of lavish charity and material comfort, of energy often misdirected and good sense, of severity and real kindness of heart, of unctuous righteousness and sincere religion, which characterised the wealthy and serious world at the beginning of the nineteenth century.

The Cambridge Evangelicals naturally were better educated and less wealthy than the city magnates of Clapham. The University had always been inclined to Puritanism, and its piety naturally displayed itself in that direction. Not that at the close of the eighteenth century there was any danger there from excessive Puritanism. The intellectual life of Cambridge was more vigorous than that of Oxford at this time, owing to the severity of the examination system, which fostered the competitive spirit; but the moral standard was low, a strong rationalism prevailed and the general tone was Whig. Most of the great statesmen of the century were educated at Cambridge, Sir Robert Walpole, the Duke of Newcastle and the younger Pitt. The hardest-headed bishops, Watson of Llandaff, the one adversary Gibbon did not despise, Pretyman of Winchester, Sparke, and Allen of Ely, all of whom proved that godliness was indeed great riches, were highly placed among the Cambridge Wranglers. Archdeacon Paley, like Bishop Pretyman, was the Senior Wrangler of his year. These worthy, but worldly, men were not likely to create an enthusiasm for religion, but their promotion is a proof that care was taken to select men of ability as leaders of the English Church.

Isaac Milner, a man intellectually fitted to rank among the best of these men, was noted as an Evangelical. Senior Wrangler in 1774, he was long regarded as the best judge of mathematical ability in the University. He consistently favoured the evangelically minded students; and virtually ruled Cambridge by his masterful character as the President of Queens College, and as Dean of the Cathedral the Diocese of Carlisle. It is surprising to us to learn that, despite the austerity of his views, and the masterfulness of his character, he was beloved in the University for his geniality and the extremely convivial character of his entertainments.

A greater, if less able man, was Charles Simeon, a Fellow of Kings College, who for many years attracted the most devout among undergraduates. Simeon's influence was mainly exercised by his preaching in Trinity Church, and by the receptions he held in his college. He was exposed to persecution, ridicule, and unpopularity, but by his saintly character he drew around him several brilliant, and many devoted men; and at the time of his death in 1836 he was regarded with an almost excessive veneration. He it was who sent the most distinguished Cambridge men, headed by Henry Martyn, to the mission field in India; and the outlines of sermons provided by him for his admirers influenced evangelical piety for future generations. He was distinguished by great liberality of view toward every form of Protestantism, and his influence over the young men of his day gave the Evangelical party a supply of able clergy to oppose the growing popularity of the Oxford Movement, which began just before Simeon's death at Cambridge.

It is on the achievements of Evangelicalism that one must dwell in order to estimate its true value. The eighteenth century was an age of sentiment. It was the fashion to display emotion and to be deeply moved by the woes of others, especially if they existed only in

Evangelicalism

imagination. There was a good deal of the Rev. Lawrence Sterne in the well bred man or woman of the closing years of the period. But though people could shed tears, as an eloquent testimony to their "exquisite sensibility," over Werther's Sorrows or Clarissa's perils, they could also act imperviously complacent about a savage penal code and the horrors of the Middle Passage to which the slaves were exposed. To its glory, the religious world of the day used its sentiment in a practical way and endeavoured to remedy real evils.

It would not be just to attribute the great humanitarian reforms that were accomplished entirely, or even chiefly, to the Church of England, because some were actually initiated, and others largely aided, by those outside its pale. Indeed, the Evangelicals themselves, though they stood by the Prayer Book and Articles, acted more as individual Christians than as Churchmen. The fields of their activities were:

(1) The suppression of the slave trade.
(2) Prison reform.
(3) The improvement of the condition of the poor.
(4) The education of the poor.
(5) Reform of the criminal law.
(6) The circulation of the Bible.
(7) Christian missions.

Within the first thirty years of the nineteenth century, that is before the passing of Parliamentary Reform, all these subjects had at least attracted public attention, and all of them enlisted the active sympathy of the Evangelical Party.

(1) The traffic in slaves, who were regularly exported from Africa to work in the West Indies and America, had been too profitable to be abandoned on account of the occasional discomfort it had caused the Christian conscience, and the arguments in its favour had thus far outweighed the scruples against it. As early as 1765, Granville Sharp brought up a case of exceptional barbarity to a negro slave; and in 1771 Lord Mansfield declared that

a man landed on English soil was thereby free and could not be regarded as a slave and demanded back by his owners. But in 1783 the master of a ship named the Zong, who had, on the plea of safety, drowned an hundred sickly negroes in order to throw the loss on the underwriters, was pronounced by the same judge, "though it shocks me very much," to have acted within the law. The cruelty connected with the slave trade was exposed by the labours of Thomas Clarkson, whose attention had been turned to the subject in his preparation for a prize essay at Cambridge; and after most violent opposition, the slave traffic was abolished by Act of Parliament in 1807. Slavery in the British colonies was ended in 1833 by the Reformed Parliament.

(2) The state of the prisons in England in the eighteenth century and first years of the nineteenth century was almost incredible for neglect, disorder, exactions on the part of the gaolers, and even actual cruelty. The work of reform began with Howard and was continued by the untiring labours of Mrs. Elizabeth Fry, who belonged to the Society of Friends. It is hardly too much to say that the sufferings of English prisoners through mere negligence exceeded those of the African negroes who were sold into slavery.

(3) The English poor after the Napoleonic wars were in some respects far more miserable than most plantation slaves, who were at least looked on as valuable property, worth keeping alive. The squalor and misery of some parts of London, the destitution in many parishes, the harshness of the workhouse system, the worse than slavery to which pauper apprentices were subjected, the horrors of child labour, were beginning to arouse the conscience of Christian people. One of the leading Evangelicals, Anthony Ashley Cowper, Earl of Shaftesbury, was the greatest champion of the poor.

(4) The need of making education national had begun to be felt but progress in devising the requisite machinery was hampered by a variety of causes. Rivalry existed

between Church and Non-conformity, and distrust of the possible evils which a too general diffusion of knowledges might produce. The Evangelicals were more desirous for spiritual than for intellectual development. Still the Sunday Schools, founded by Raikes of Gloucester, 1781, certainly furthered education generally as they taught reading and writing. The two educational societies, the National and the British, were founded early in the nineteenth century.

(5) The ferocious criminal laws of England were exposed and denounced by Sir Samuel Romilly who, though not an Evangelical, was akin to them in his blameless life and spirit; and their amelioration was a sign of the growing humanitarianism of the age. Romilly was strongly opposed by those who feared that a mistaken leniency might foster the dreaded spirit of the French Revolution.

(6) The Evangelicals combined with the Dissenters to found the British and Foreign Bible Society in 1804.

(7) They also followed the lead of the Baptist, Carey, and showed much enthusiasm for foreign missions. One result was the foundation of the Church Missionary Society.

XXI

THE OXFORD MOVEMENT

APATHY OF OXFORD AND CAMBRIDGE—THE HIGH AND DRYS—OLDER HIGH CHURCHMEN—GOTHIC REVIVAL—LIBERALISM MATERIALISTIC—THE "NOETICS" OF ORIEL—JOHN KEBLE—HURRELL FROUDE—FROUDE AND NEWMAN ABROAD—THE ASSIZE SERMON—TRACTS OF THE TIMES—DR. PUSEY—TRACT 90—TRACTARIANS CONDEMNED—THE HIGH CHURCHMEN DO NOT SECEDE.

The close of the Napoleonic wars was marked by a revival of intellectual activity in Oxford and Cambridge, the only two Universities in England and Wales. These great seats of learning sank to their lowest ebb during the Hanoverian period, and if they produced great men, these generally won their distinction away from, and often in spite of, their University. "To the University of Oxford," said one of the greatest scholars and men of letters she can boast, "I acknowledge no obligation; and she will as cheerfully renounce me as a son, as I am willing to disclaim her for a mother. I spent fourteen months at Magdalen College; they proved to be the most idle and unprofitable fourteen months of my whole life." So wrote Edward Gibbon, the historian, of his undergraduate career, 1752–3. The poet Gray, who was Regius Professor of History in the sister University, was not a whit more complimentary to its intellectual atmosphere. Here, he said, Scripture seemed to be fulfilled when it prophesies "The houses shall be full of doleful creatures."

The High Churchmanship of the eighteenth century

had been largely political, inclining to Jacobitism. When the Stuarts disappeared it tended to become orthodox and acquiescent in the doctrine of the Church of England, as expressed in the Prayer Book, and opposed to all forms of religious excitement. It distrusted emotionalism and showed no disposition to make worship more attractive by rendering the services of the Church more beautiful or dignified. The adherents of the school are not unfairly described as "high and dry."

Curiously, the seeds of the new movement were sown by Alexander Knox (1757–1831), an Irish layman, a friend and correspondent of John Wesley, and admired by Bishop Jebb of Limerick who brought his views into prominence. It was Knox who laid emphasis on the saying of Vicentius of Lerinum, that Catholicism is the concurrent judgment or tradition of the Church, the common consent to what all Christians have always and everywhere believed, the *quod ubique, quod semper quod ab omnibus*. Almost contemporary with Knox was a country rector, Thomas Sikes of Guilsborough, who declared the belief in the Holy Catholic Church to be the neglected article of the Creed. Another layman, Joshua Watson, a rich London wine merchant, retired from business early in the nineteenth century, and lived at Hackney in the north of London to be near his brother, the Archdeacon of St. Albans, devoting himself to good works. There gathered round the Watsons a set of Churchmen known as the "Hackney phalanx" or "Clapton sect," who held views diametrically opposed to the "Clapham sect," south of the Thames. They thought little of evangelical preaching, and much of orthodoxy and the discipline of the Church. Less fervid, but more learned, less energetic, but with better balanced minds, the coterie at Hackney upheld an ideal of Christian life, which made the Church as central to piety, at least, as the Scripture.

Another factor was changing the religious atmosphere. The classical revival lasted long into the eighteenth century. Architecture and poetry borrowed inspiration from Greece and Rome. That influence was on the wane. A new poetic impulse was coming in which was leading men to set more store by the beauties of nature and the romantic side of life. Men turned from their worship of the severely correct art of classicism to admire Gothic richness of decoration, which their immediate ancestors had despised, and in so doing felt once more the charm of medieval life. The architects were endeavouring to imitate the cathedral and baronial castle, the poets with far greater skill to draw inspiration from the thoughts of the age of chivalry. It was impossible to disregard the fact that the days when knights were bold were those of the ascendancy of the ancient Church. Rome and Popery were still hated; but it was recognised that they had a good side at least in byegone days, and they began to appear less forbidding than the drabness of Evangelicalism and dissenting piety. As good Protestants, Englishmen abhorred Rome, but as men of taste they were forced to admit that it was often attractive. Wordsworth, Coleridge, Southey, and Scott, were all paving the way for a new order of thought.

The Liberalism of the early nineteenth century was antipathetic to the new religious aspirations. It was hard, crude, commercial, and materialistic. Its prophet was Henry Brougham, with his famous phrase "the schoolmaster is abroad." Professing a certain respect for religion, it had little or no use for it. The Church was at heart Tory, and could hope for little from the new school of Reformers; even its political supporters had little heart to stand firm in its defence. Never in its history, since the days of Elizabeth, did the Church of England inspire less enthusiasm than in the age which ushered in the Reform Bill of 1832. Those who were devoted to it were compelled to ask the question: For what does the national Church really stand?

Oriel College, a small and by no means wealthy foundation, now became the centre of an intellectual revival at

Oxford and the University began to shake off the lethargy of the eighteenth century.

One of the worst parts of the system of unreformed Oxford was the restriction of many college fellowships to certain counties, schools, and even families. This reduced the incentive to study, and the teaching was mainly in the hands of not always competent resident Fellows. Oriel College had thrown open its fellowships to competition, and consequently they were more eagerly sought than many richer emoluments; and it was regarded as a high distinction to be elected to one. The Fellows of Oriel formed a society which virtually led the intellect of Oxford; at first in the direction of Liberalism. The intellectuals of the college were called "noetics," and the most prominent were Whateley, afterwards Archbishop of Dublin, and Arnold, the famous headmaster of Rugby; John Henry Newman also was reckoned as one of them. Both Whateley and Arnold desired to create a truly national Protestant Church, Arnold's plan being designed to include Dissenters on somewhat the lines of the old Comprehension Bill of 1689.

But there was another Fellow of Oriel who had been trained by a devout and scholarly father, and had surprised Oxford by the brilliant degree he took as a mere boy. John Keble, the author of the *Christian Year,* retired from the University to act as curate to his father, taking with him as pupils, Hurrell Froude, Isaac Williams (like his tutor—a poet), and Robert Wilberforce.

Of these men, who all had their part in the new movement, by far the most brilliant was Froude. The three pupils were devoted to Keble, whose saintly character made a deep impression on their minds, but Froude's impulsive nature and trenchant intellect swept the elder man on. Brilliant and sarcastic, Froude was relentless in exposing the intellectual fallacies and the specious hypocrisy of the religion of the day. He had no mercy for smug respectability, and scoffed at what he called "the gentleman heresy"; that is, that the clergy was valuable simply as a well-bred caste. He had as little mercy toward himself as toward others, and practised to the full the asceticism he preached. Unlike the earlier Anglicans, he admired Rome and loathed the reformers and "the Deformation," as he styled their great achievement. Though stern in self-discipline, unsparing in his wit, intolerant in his views, Hurrell Froude possessed all the attractive qualities of an English gentleman and scholar. Those who loved him called him "bright and beautiful."

Froude returned to Oxford, gained a fellowship at Oriel, was tutor with Newman; and a strong friendship arose between the two colleagues, so united in aim, and different in disposition. They made their famous tour in the Mediterranean together in 1832–33; and then the Movement began. In the words of Dean Church, "Keble had given the inspiration, Froude had given the impulse, Newman took up the work, and the impulse henceforward and the direction were his."

The keynote was struck by Keble's Assize Sermon, preached in the University pulpit on July 14, 1833. It was published under the title of *National Apostasy*. The reformed Parliament had inaugurated a policy of Liberalism which to the preacher appeared "a direct disavowal of the sovereignty of God." The Church was in danger of being regarded as little more than a pawn on the political chessboard. Parliament was about to deal with its dioceses in Ireland and its revenues in England, and might at any time claim the power to alter its doctrines. The publication of the sermon aroused Churchmen to action. A new adherent of Keble's party now appeared in a Cambridge man, Hugh James Rose, who had been Christian Advocate in the University, and was now Rector in a little town in Suffolk, called Hadleigh. Rose had put the true position of the Church boldly forward at Cambridge, and now invited some friends to meet him and discuss what course was to be pursued. The conference at Hadleigh resulted in the *Tracts for the Times*.

These were at first literally "Tracts"; that is, short

leaflets, setting forth the dangers of a Church discredited by the nation and robbed by Parliament; and of a clergy, no longer in a position of comfort and honour, but poor and persecuted, and asking the question, "On what could the bishops and ministers of religion then rely for support?" The answer was on their Apostolic Succession. In other words, the fundamental basis on which the Church of England rested was not that it was "by law established," but that it was and had always been part of the One Holy Catholic and Apostolic Church.

Before the death of Hurrell Froude in 1836, and of Rose in 1833, a new recruit had joined the movement in Dr. Pusey, Regius Professor of Hebrew, from whom the party ultimately took the name of Puseyite. Pusey proved a tower of strength. He had a great reputation in the University for his learning and the sanctity of his life. His position as a scholar, a man of family, and a professor, gave the party he supported importance in Oxford. Though only two years older than Newman, Pusey ranked in public estimation, and even in the mind of Newman himself, as almost immeasurably his senior. His great reputation, enhanced by a certain lack of brilliancy, especially as a preacher, gave weight to all he said or did. Under him the Tracts ceased to be leaflets and became learned treatises; the *Library of the Fathers* was started and the prestige of solid learning began to attach itself to the movement.

The Tractarians had declared themselves uncompromising enemies of the Roman Church. In this they had followed the Caroline and even the Non-juring divines. But the old hostility to Rome was abating. The Papacy appeared to be a political danger no longer. As the Continent was more visited and better known, the virtues of the Catholic clergy were recognised, and many of their doctrines seemed no longer dangerous. At least they had the same creed as the Church of England, and held the fundamentals of the same faith. Definite accusations of Roman tendencies were launched against the

Tractarians, and not wholly without show of reason; for some were undoubtedly inclined in that direction. But three of the Tracts which produced the final explosion were by men who remained Anglicans to the end; whilst Newman, when he wrote the last of the series, the famous Tract, 90, was genuinely anxious to save the Anglican position. The four Tracts which caused the greatest uproar were one by Keble on *Mysticism,* two by Isaac Williams on *Reserve in Communicating Religious Knowledge;* and finally Newman's famous *Remarks on Certain Passages in the Thirty-nine Articles* published on February 27, 1841. These were numbered, in the order used above, 89, 80, 87, and 90.

The University was in a fever of excitement. To most of its leaders the Tractarians were declared Papists, only remaining in the Church of England in order to betray it to Rome. Newman and his friends retired to Littlemore, a village just outside Oxford, where they lived in monastic seclusion. He believed that by the publication of Tract 90 he had averted the threatened secession to Rome; and certainly he had made it possible for a Catholic-minded man to stay inside the pale of the Church of England. For, after all, most people who signed the Thirty-nine Articles did so with certain reservations, and few indeed fully comprehended exactly what those who framed them intended. They certainly meant to condemn Popery or the errors imputed to Rome in the sixteenth century; but does their language, taken in its simple and grammatical sense, condemn what Newman and his friends thought "Catholic" truth? Take for example Article XXII "Of Purgatory." The "Romish" doctrine is condemned. But what does "Romish" signify? Not Catholic, but the perversion of the true doctrine at the time the article was issued. A belief therefore in Purgatory is allowable: but the abuse of it is condemned.

Argument of this description was regarded by the Protestant party of the University as Jesuitical in the extreme; and a wild outcry arose that Newman should be condemned. The heads of the colleges were up in arms. Four college tutors, including Dr. Tait, later the famous Archbishop of Canterbury, entered into the fray, though Tait a little later showed his usual wisdom by a protest against a definition of the sense in which Oxford men should accept the Articles. "It would operate to the exclusion of the best, because the most conscientious men." It was now a strife between dull, and not always learned, Heads of Houses, heavy, if learned, professors like Hampden, whose fame rests on the controversies he provoked, and some of the most intelligent and active minds in Oxford, men of burning zeal and strong convictions, determined to infuse a real spirit of religion into the University. It lasted for four years, and ended in the triumph of authority. The Roman proclivities of some Tractarians became more marked: their language became more aggressive. The triumphant party of Oxford orthodoxy attacked Pusey for a sermon on the Eucharist, and suspended him from preaching within the University for two years. Then followed the publication by W. G. Ward, a Fellow of Balliol, of his *Ideal of a Christian Church* and his condemnation by Convocation, which deprived him of his University degrees. This drove him into the Church of Rome, and on October 8, 1845, Newman and some of his friends were also received into its communion. The Oxford Movement was at an end, but its effects were only beginning.

It is a remarkable fact that those High Churchmen who remained faithful had been from the first brought up in loyal allegiance to the English Church, and remained firm in their trust in the ultimate triumph of their cause. To do so required no little courage, for it meant charges of dishonesty against them from those within their Church, and at least the silent reproach of those whom they had refused to accompany within the Roman fold. But it is no discredit for a man who has lived his life in the atmosphere of a Church, a country, or even a party, to see and lament its defects and not show any desire for that reason to desert it. Pusey, Keble, Isaac Williams, and the older Tractarians loved their Church and were under no illusions as to its present imperfections. They had never "discovered" the Church of England, but had always known it. Newman on the contrary first idealised Anglicanism and then found it wanting: he paid excessive deference to the authority of bishops who were unwilling to exercise or even claim it. W. G. Ward was never really attached to the Church, and good humoredly left it when Oxford condemned him. But whether they went or stayed, the work of the Tractarians was done. They had made Churchmen realise that they belonged to a divine society and were inheritors, not of a Church established at the Reformation, but of the one Catholic and Apostolic Church. They founded their principles on the severe learning of an ancient University. Henceforward work of a more public character had to be done.

XXII

RITUALISM

TRACTARIANISM ACADEMIC—AN EIGHTEENTH CENTURY CHURCH—OBJECT OF RITUALISM—SYMPTOMS OF RITUALISM—FIRST RITUALISTIC CHURCHES—THE VESTMENTS—ACTION TAKEN IN THE COURTS—MEANING OF THE ROYAL SUPREMACY—COURT OF DELEGATES ABOLISHED IN 1833—THE LINCOLN JUDGMENT—WIDESPREAD EFFECTS OF RITUALISM—ACTIVITIES OF RITUALISTS—DANGERS: INTOLERANCE; SUBMISSION TO ROME.

The Oxford Movement was an academic one. The leaders who strove to restore the primitive Church by a learned investigation into its principles were inaugurators of a new scholasticism in the University. They were, like the Non-jurors, devoted to the abstract theories of an ideal polity, and their devotion to the Church resembled that of their predecessors to the Stuart monarchy. They had no sympathy with modern conditions, and were relentlessly opposed to the spirit of the age. The defection of Newman and his friends meant to the majority of Englishmen that they were willing to submit to a foreign yoke, rather than abandon their cherished principles and theories of Church government; and there was little in their teaching which could be appreciated by the public.

It soon became evident that, to make the principles of Tractarianism intelligible to the majority, more must be done than to give the world translations from the fathers and reprints from dry Anglican divines. The Church service of an old-fashioned High Churchman was conducted on precisely the same lines as had been customary for generations. To understand ritualism it is necessary to have a mental picture of a Church in the later part of the eighteenth and in the early nineteenth century. At the East-end was a small table covered with a blue or red cloth, generally moth-eaten; it was railed in and served as the altar, over which occasionally a picture was hung; but the usual decorations of the eastern wall were the Creed and Commandments. The chief ornament was the pulpit, often called "a three decker." From the uppermost tier the sermon was delivered; below the preacher, if there were two clergy, sat the reader of the service, and below him the parish clerk. If the church were a fine Gothic building, the arches at the nave were broken by a gallery, and the floor was filled with square pews, some of them the private property of individual parishioners, secured by lock and key. The Squire had a large pew, sometimes with a retiring room at the back. The chief ornament was the Royal Arms, more or less elaborately carved and painted. Those who could afford it were buried inside the Church, and the presence of the dead was consequently brought to the attention of the living. Large wall panels, usually at the West-end, reminded the worshippers of past benefactions to the parish, and sometimes the date of some "beautification" of the church was recorded with the names of the rector and churchwardens. A favourite text was "And Jacob said, How dreadful is this place." Frequently the churches were allowed to fall into decay, the walls were crumbling and mildewed, and windows often broken. Bishop Butler complained of this neglect in his charge to the clergy of Durham in 1752, and drew upon himself the reproach of being a Papist. The service was long if the officiant were not in a hurry to ride off to conduct another in a neighbouring Church. The responses were given by the parish clerk. Sometimes the village band led the music, but later barrel-organs with a very limited number of tunes were substituted. Metrical psalms were sung from the collections of Sternhold and Hopkins, which John Wesley called "scandalous doggrel," or of Tate and Brady. Hymns were long unknown, and their use condemned as Methodistical. The one "ritualistic" ceremony was the retirement of the clergyman to the vestry to divest himself of his surplice and don a black gown to preach in. In some churches cake and wine were provided to fortify him for the task. In city churches the preacher wore a silk gown and band, and preached in black kid gloves. In the country, where there was no vestry, the parson sometimes changed his surplice in the pulpit. Three or at most four times a year the communion was celebrated. It was not possible to tell the party views of the clergyman except from his pulpit utterances. The conduct of the worship was much the same everywhere. It must never be forgotten that the Puseys and Kebles were accustomed to this sort of service well on into the nineteenth century.

The term ritualism is apt to be misleading unless carefully defined. It is often taken to imply an elaborate method of conducting the services of the Church, calculated to appeal to the artistic sense of the congregation and to gratify the hierarchical pride of the priesthood, whereas those who suffered deeply rather than abandon their convictions were aiming at something more definite. They adhered to principles which were those of the Tractarians who had remained loyal to Anglicanism, carried to their logical conclusions. If some ritualistic clergymen appeared to be absurd or frivolous in their insistence on externals, the object of their party was to insist that the Reformation of the Church of England was intended to be, not a triumph of continental Protestantism, but an assertion of the continuance of its existence as a branch of the Church Catholic, and the right of its members to all the spiritual privileges of their ancestors. Comparatively few ritualists have gone over to the Roman obedience, though under much provocation to do so. Rather have they endured actual persecution from the mob, financial ruin in the law courts, and constant reproach for dishonesty for maintaining what they believed to be the rights of the English Church. Their views, their opinions, and their methods may be more easily condemned than their motives.

The beginnings of ritualism were seen in the foundation of the "Architectural Society" of Oxford in 1838, and the "Camden Society" at Cambridge in 1839, both founded to advocate and encourage the restoration of the fine but decayed churches and cathedrals of the country. It was noticed that most of the members were High Churchmen. In 1842, Bishop Blomfield of London charged his clergy, whom he warned against Tractarianism, to be more careful about the conduct of the services, and to conform to the rubrics. Perhaps he suggested the retention of the surplice in the pulpit, which became a mark of ritualism. "He used to preach his sermons in a surplice. He's a Puseyite, Mr. Snob"—to quote Thackeray. Many clergy went further than the Bishop intended. Others refused to obey him and the injunctions were withdrawn. Still, as early as 1843, superstitious innovations were condemned in Churches, but vestments and incense are not mentioned. Ritualism, as then interpreted, consisted in surpliced choirs, walking in procession, chanting the services, decorating the altars, celebrating the communion not at the North-end, but in the centre of the altar, using the Eastward position, preaching in a surplice, and turning to the East when repeating the Creed. One of the complaints of the bishops was that the service of a Cathedral was not intended for imitation in a parish Church. In fact, the ceremonial used to-day in many a Protestant Church outside Anglicanism would have aroused a no-Popery agitation in the "fifties."

The first truly ritualistic Churches were St. Paul's, Knightsbridge, and St. Barnabas Pimlico, in West London, and St. George's in the East. The display of a full Catholic ritual was the occasion of furious manifestations of mob indignation, unparalleled disorder, and often insults to the clergy, with which the police and the magistrates were often in partial sympathy. It is unnecessary to dwell on these scenes. Let us rather indicate the principles underlying ritualism and the consequences involved: (1) The ritualistic clergy claimed the right to restore the ancient Eucharistic vestments, and (2) the legal action which this claim caused to be taken.

(1) The balancing policy of Elizabeth had ordered the continuance of the Eucharistic vestments used in the first years of Edward VI. By the canons of 1604, copes were ordered to be used in Cathedrals. But as a general rule these garments had long ceased to be worn and the surplice alone was adopted at the altar. The ritualistic clergy claimed that the legal vestment of the celebrant at the Holy Communion was the "Cope," and of the deacons assisting, "Albes with Tunicles." This connoted that the English Communion Office permitted the celebration to be performed with all the splendour of the Mass of the ancient Church of England, according to the ritual of Sarum, which is even more elaborate than that of Rome. They began, further, to use all the genuflections, crossings, and ceremonial acts of the ancient priesthood; incense, altar lights, the mixed chalice, were all reintroduced, and in appearance the service was altogether similar to the Mass. The claim put forth was that nothing had been really altered at the Reformation, and that the faithful had lost none of the spiritual rights they enjoyed before the breach with the Papacy. The Church, like some Churches of the East, might have the liturgy in the vernacular; but otherwise nothing was changed.

(2) This open proclamation of Catholic and Romeward sympathy expressed, not in tract or treatise, but so that all could witness what it meant, naturally provoked an outburst of Protestant zeal. The bishops remonstrated in vain and in some instances the parishioners objected; but the clergy of the new school only passed on to further excesses in the matter of ritual. The result was that the

legality of what was being done was tested by actions in the different courts, and as this brought on a crisis between Church and State in England, it is necessary to inquire into the question of the royal supremacy in matters ecclesiastical, and the rights of the bishops to legislate in purely spiritual matters. The ritual disputes involved these most complicated legal questions.

When Henry VIII broke off relations with the Roman see, the Crown became the final court of appeal in all matters ecclesiastical It was, however, declared that the Sovereign claimed no spiritual functions; that is, the King could exercise no sacerdotal ministry, and that in any cause "of the law divine happening to come into question, or of spiritual learning," the body spiritual was "to declare, interpret it, and show it." But, as the Act of Supremacy gave the Crown the power to "visit, repress, redress, reform, and amend all heresies, etc.," and since all ecclesiastical jurisdiction was derived from it, it virtually meant that all spiritual powers, short of administration of the Sacraments, belonged to the king.

To administer this law, two courts were created: (1) The Court of Delegates, a civil court, created by Henry VIII to hear appeals, and (2) the Court of High Commission, called into being by Elizabeth, and abolished under Charles I. The Court of Delegates continued in existence till 1833, when appeals were transferred from it to the Judicial Committee of the Privy Council. Other Acts were passed, the Church Discipline Act of 1840, the Public Worship Regulation Act of 1874, and the Clergy Discipline Act of 1892. The bishops, when consulted, raised no objection to the Judicial Committee of the Privy Council acting as the final Court of Appeal from the Archbishop's Court.

For nearly fifty years ritual questions were a subject of litigation, the most contradictory judgments were delivered, and appeals were carried from one court to another. Some clergy absolutely refused to accept the decisions of the Judicial Committee on the ground that it was a secular court, and to obey it was Erastian. Several were imprisoned for contumacy, with the result that public opinion veered round in their favour, disgusted at the virulence displayed by the ultra-Protestant Church Association. At last, in 1888, the Association selected the Bishop of Lincoln, Dr. King, for prosecution; and, with the consent of the Judicial Commission, Archbishop Benson, with other bishops as assessors, tried the case. The Bishop of Lincoln was accused of seven illegal acts. He admitted all the facts, but said that his acts were allowed by the law of the English Church. These are the charges and the decisions:

(1) Mixing water and wine.—May not be done ceremonially.

(2) The Eastward position.—Allowed.

(3) Standing at the west side of the table, and so hindering the congregation from seeing the manual acts of Consecration.—The manual acts must be seen by the communicants present and not deliberately concealed.

(4) Causing the Agnus Dei to be sung.—Not illegal.

(5) Ablution of the vessels after the service.—Not a ceremonial act, and, therefore, not illegal.

(6) Use of lights on the altar, not for purpose of giving light.—Legal, but must not be lit ceremonially.

(7) Making the sign of the Cross in benediction and absolution.—Illegal.

Since this decision, confirmed by the Judicial Committee in 1892, there have been no more ritual prosecutions, and the extremists have gone on almost unrestrained to still further extremes.

But to judge ritualism by its methods of conducting worship is to take an unjust and superficial view of the movement. It has transformed, not only the Anglican Church, but the whole conception of worship in the Anglo-Saxon world. Almost every church recently built by Christians in the English-speaking world bears the marks of its influence. Worship has almost unconsciously become more dignified and calculated to appeal to the æsthetic sense. The old feeling that the more hideous the building, the more discordant the music, the drearier the services, the more acceptable the worship, because more spiritual, has entirely disappeared. The very bitterest opponents of an ornate form of service have adopted some of the principles of ritualism, if not its spirit.

It is, however, hardly fair to give the Catholic movement in Anglicanism its popular name, for its best fruits are not found in attractive services or decorated altars. Nor is it to be judged by the stress, often indiscreet, laid upon apparent trifles of ceremonial. The work of such leaders as Mackonochie, Lowder, Dolling, and Stanton among the poor, the sisterhoods and houses of mercy, the institution of religious communities, and orders for men are its fruits. At present, the clergy of this party are by far the most active in Anglicanism.

Whether its success will be enduring is a serious question. The greater its progress is now, the more conspicuous are the dangers which it will encounter in the future. It has hitherto done good service in stopping the secession of Anglicans to Rome; but the fascination of the Romanist type of piety is great; and the way in which it is often mis-presented, both by its admirers and its detractors, exercises influence over a certain type of mind. As long as the Anglican clergy are clearly understood to be opposed to all foreign interference with religion, they will have the confidence of their flocks, and they can advance the cause they have at heart; but they cannot ignore with impunity the intense national antipathy to the political aspirations of the Roman See inherent in the Anglo-Saxon race in all parts of the world. Some may regret this is so, but it is a fact which they are bound to face.

There is also a danger that intolerance on their part of all non-Catholic Christianity may hinder the reunion which is most to be desired, namely, that of all English-speaking peoples and those of kindred race in one religious communion. In justice to the most saintly Anglo-Catholics, it must be said that this intolerance has not usually been displayed, and they have recognised good Christian work outside their own body whilst holding rigidly to their opinions. By this means, they may hope to secure adherents from without as well as within the Church.

But most serious is the peril that æsthetic ritualism may lead to a formalism in religion, and this the most earnest Anglo-Catholics themselves are the first to recognise. The Romanists reproach them both with aping Catholicism, and neglecting the true spirit of sacramental Christianity. If they succeed in avoiding this dilemma they will be able to present their faith to the world in an attractive form. But Anglo-Catholicism will fall the moment it ceases to follow in the steps of the Caroline divines, the Non-jurors, and the Tractarians, who did not fail their Church in the hour of trial, but stood staunch in opposition to every Roman claim to dictate to Englishmen.

XXIII

THE NEW THEOLOGY

LITTLE ESSENTIAL DIFFERENCE OF BELIEF BEFORE THE NEW SCIENCE AND CRITICISM—EVOLUTION—INERRANCY OF SCRIPTURE—LEGAL QUESTIONS INVOLVED—"THE ORIGIN OF SPECIES"—"ESSAYS AND REVIEWS"—COLENSO AND THE PENTATEUCH—THE NEW LIBERALISM—ITS OPPONENTS—RELIGIOUS BELIEF MATERIALLY AFFECTED—THE OLD TESTAMENT—DANGER OF THE HIGHER CRITICISM OF THE OLD TESTAMENT—THE NEW TESTAMENT BELIEVED TO BE SECURE—PRESENT INDIFFERENCE TO THEOLOGY—SUBSTITUTES: MYSTICISM; SENTIMENT; ATTRACTIVE WORSHIP; SOCIAL SERVICE.

In 1859 *The Origin of Species,* by Charles Darwin, was published; and in 1862–63 *The Pentateuch and Book of Joshua Critically Examined,* by John William Colenso, Bishop of Natal, appeared. Two years before Colenso, in 1861, seven eminent Liberals had laid *Essays and Reviews* before the public. A movement more momentous than that of 1833 was thus inaugurated. Science and criticism called into question the inerrancy of Scripture, on which the very foundation of the Church rested, and forced men to reconsider their entire position in regard to religious belief.

It is not always easy to realise how little difference in creed there was between Christians in England before the appearance of these books. Catholics, Roman as well as Anglican, and also Protestants of every variety, including even Unitarians, were in far more substantial agreement than they imagined. Suppose, for example, a devout Unitarian of that earlier day passed over to the

Roman obedience. He had always believed that God had revealed Himself through Jesus Christ, and that the record of this revelation had been given in an infallible manner through Scripture. He did not deny that Jesus had been miraculously born of a Virgin, that He had died to save mankind, that He had risen from the grave on the first Easter morning. It is true that he refused to believe in the Divinity of Christ: but why? Because he considered that the Scripture did not teach it. Jesus said Himself, "The Father is greater than I." He had said, "The Son can do nothing without the Father," and other like things. All that was necessary to convert him on any point was to prove that he had misunderstood the Bible. He refused to accept the Roman doctrine of the Church, the Sacraments, tradition, etc. Again the most effective appeal must be to Scripture. Even if he had been so bold as to teach or hold that God did not condemn the wicked to eternal punishment, he used the Scripture to confirm the view which his reason had induced him to take. He would have made an outwardly immense change in his religious opinions before becoming Roman Catholic, but really he had done little more than accept another interpretation of a Book he had always acknowledged to be an infallible record.

This, however, is an extreme example. All Christian Churches, Protestant as well as Catholic, professed a belief in common in the doctrine of the Trinity, the saving power of Christ, the inspiration of Scripture, the miracles in the Bible, eternal life in heaven, and everlasting torment in hell.

And now it was openly declared in *The Origin of Species* that the human race was the result, not of creative act, as related in Scripture, but of an age-long evolution from lower forms of life, with the result that Creation, the Fall, and the scheme of Redemption were in need of fresh explanation.

Bishop Colenso had expressed his belief that the Pentateuch was not the work of Moses, that it abounded in numerical impossibilities, and could not be regarded as in any sense literally true, thus striking at the authority of the Bible as our infallible guide. In *Essays and Reviews,* a single sentence of Jowett's is enough to account for the turmoil produced, "Interpret the Bible as any other book."

It requires as much historical imagination to transport our minds to the early sixties of the last century as it does to the days of the schoolmen, so greatly have our ideas in regard to Science and Biblical criticism as applied to religion changed, so completely have we outlived an age which has only just vanished.

As in ritualism, the history of the controversy has to be studied more in the law courts than anywhere else. The question was how far could the new opinions legally be held by Churchmen. In a new form, moreover, the burning problem of *Tract 90* came to the fore. In what sense ought a man to subscribe to the Articles? Thus the very people who had denounced Newman for saying that the Articles could be taken in a Roman Catholic sense, now almost tearfully pleaded the right to interpret them to mean what their framers could never have intended, and to countenance views which at the time of the Reformation would have united all, Catholic and Protestant, in demanding the execution as heretics of those who held them. The story of the legal proceedings must be omitted here; but as an illustration of the temper of the time, the complaint of Dr. Pusey may be quoted that "The radical evil of law judges is their bias to acquit the accused."

Darwin's *The Origin of Species* only indirectly affected religion; and as a layman the author was not amenable to the law of the Church, nor could he be made to retract as Galileo had been. The leader of the attack on the book was Samuel Wilberforce, Bishop of Oxford, and Professor Huxley was the defender of the theory of evolution, who came forward as the foe of the theologians. Mr. Gladstone was one of the champions of Orthodoxy against Science. The fight was long and bitter; but the amateur science of the defenders of the Mosaic cosmogony was no match for the trained intellects of the Victorian naturalists, supported by the facts of geology and physiology. It became evident that the Churchmen had strayed outside their province and had damaged their cause by their rashness. Wilberforce, by his readiness and eloquence, gained several imaginary triumphs and the admiration of his supporters; but educated men were forced to acknowledge that his conclusions were wrong. With the advance of knowledge, however, Science became less assertive and Religion more acquiescent toward unpalatable facts.

Essays and Reviews were different: the writers were all, except two, clergymen, and as such were responsible to the authorities of the Church. Dealing with theories rather than facts, they were more open to criticism. The three most prominent of the seven Essayists were Frederick Temple, then Headmaster of Rugby School, who died Archbishop of Canterbury. His essay on *The Education of the World* appeared to make conscience, rather than the Bible, the supreme arbiter. Mark Pattison, on *Tendencies of English Religious Thought, 1688–1720*, and Jowett, on the *Interpretation of the Bible*, were men of learning and authority in Oxford. The one later became the famous Master of Balliol College, and the other Rector of Lincoln College and one of the acutest thinkers of the day. Temple's and Pattison's essays excited little indignation, but Jowett's was furiously attacked, as was one on *The National Church* by Wilson, who was one of the four tutors who had complained of Newman's Tract 90, and another by Roland Williams on *Bunsen's Biblical Researches*.

The essays are long forgotten; not so Colenso's attack on the Pentateuch. Colenso, a Cambridge mathematician of distinction, was appointed Bishop of Natal in 1853. He was known as a friend and champion of the Zulus, whose cause he made his own, and it was while engaged in translating the Bible with the aid of a native that his attention was drawn to the impossibility of accepting the numbers of the Israelites mentioned in Exodus in a literal sense. This led him to a complete and thorough critical examination of the Pentateuch and the Book of Joshua, resulting in a rejection of the Mosaic authorship of the first five books. His Metropolitan, Bishop Gray of Capetown, on his own authority deposed Bishop Colenso and excommunicated him, and a vast amount of litigation ensued. As the Bishop of Natal had been appointed by the Crown, he was irremovable, and he retained his see despite his unanimous condemnation by the clerical authorities in Africa and at home.

Colenso's criticism bore no fruits. The real attack on the Mosaic authorship had come from Germany and was continued on other lines. The Old Testament story had been told in a more familiar way than hitherto in Dean Milman's *History of the Jews;* and later, Stanley's *Jewish Church* was written under the influence of Ewald's *History of the People of Israel*. But the Higher Criticism exerted little influence on English thought till nearly twenty years after Colenso's book had been published.

All that has just been related was a presage of the greater change which was about to come over religious thought, and to differentiate it from all that had gone before. The new Science and the new Criticism were so transforming the ideas of the Christian world that the old controversies were becoming meaningless. The old apologetics were no longer convincing and the religious opinions held by a generation which had hardly yet died out had been rendered almost unintelligible. A new liberalism in Christian thought, not by any means entirely or necessarily Anglican, had forced itself into notice. Whether they liked it or not, Christian teachers had now to explain their position to men who believed that the world had come into being by evolution and not creation, and that the Scriptures were the work of fallible men.

Those who opposed the new tendencies have been subjected to more blame than they deserve. Because they endeavoured to stem the influence of the new scientific views of the immense antiquity of the earth and the gradual evolution of man, they are condemned for injuring the cause of religion. But the theories in question were not as familiar then as they are to-day, and to many they seemed to rest on slender foundations. Opposition to a dogma, whether scientific or religious, is not always a disservice. If it proves to be false, those responsible for the attack have deserved well of mankind. If, on the contrary, it is finally demonstrated to be sound, criticism has only given its champions the opportunity of vindicating their position. Nor must it be forgotten that there was as much tendency on the part of the scientist to assert his supremacy over religion as the reverse. Each was inclined to proclaim the bankruptcy of the other. It was only when religion began to listen to the voice of science, and science to acknowledge the part religion had to play in the development of the world, that the acute phase of the controversy was passed.

But at the same time it must not be forgotten that religious belief was seriously shaken by the revelations of the scientists. It is futile to try to maintain that whether the world was created or evolved was a matter of no importance. It made all the difference; and the theologians were right in perceiving this to be so. They failed, as their predecessors a century earlier had not failed in the Deist controversies, because unlike them they were opposed by indisputable facts. The Christian scheme of redemption had been so bound up with the earlier chapters of Genesis, that if the accuracy of their account of the origin of humanity be disproved, a considerable revision of preconceived ideas is absolutely necessary.

The biblical question was even more acute than the scientific. To write the history of Israel before the new criticism came into vogue was comparatively an easy task. The story then was consistent and continuous from the call of Abraham to Malachi. The family called by God became the ancestors of the Chosen People who received the Law at Sinai, wandered in the wilderness, possessed the Promised Land, became a powerful kingdom, forsook the Lord and disobeyed the Law, were punished by Captivity and Exile, and returned to rebuild the Temple, and to practise a purer worship. A series of prophets had foretold the coming of a Messiah who would save this people, and Israel waited for four centuries till He came. The Scriptures which recorded these events grew gradually for a thousand years and were based upon the revelation given by the God of Israel to His servant Moses, embodied in the Law. The whole Old Testament —Law, History, Wisdom, Literature, and the language of devotion—was acknowledged in its entirety to be the inspired word of God.

It was no small sacrifice to ask Churchmen, even in the cause of demonstrated truth, to revise their entire conception of the Scriptures of the Old Testament. To realise that the Law as we now have it dates from the very end of the old Dispensation, that the prophets spoke more of their own age than of a coming Messiah, that David did not write most of the Psalms, and that Proverbs and Ecclesiastes were not Solomon's, was not easy for men who had all their lives accepted them as self-evident facts. But on this point the strife was carried on mostly outside the pale of Anglicanism, because the English Church, with all its reverence for Scripture, was less committed to the defense of the Old Testament than were some Protestant bodies. Thus, there was little excitement when Dr. Gore's Essay in *Lux Mundi* appeared, in which the Oxford school of High Churchmen acknowledged that there was much to be said in favour of the German Higher Criticism, compared with the stir in Presbyterian circles both in Scotland and in America.

The Anglicans had been comparatively indifferent to the question of the Old Testament, because they were convinced that the New was safe from attack. A vigorous counter-assault on those who attacked the credibility of the whole story of the Christian revelation in a book called *Supernatural Religion,* by Dr. Lightfoot, afterwards Bishop of Durham, encouraged many to believe that the authority of the New Testament was unassailable. Even really learned men could not believe that the problem of the Synoptic Gospels needed further investigation. Recently, however, the criticism of the books of the New Testament has become as startling in its results as that of the Old.

For various reasons the interest in theological problems has waned. The War turned men's minds into more practical channels than abstract points of sacred scholarship. Though the most fundamental doctrines of Christianity are now the subject of attack, there are few attempts to justify them, nor do the rulers of the Church appear as capable as were their predecessors in defending its beliefs. Theology languishes as in the days before the Reformation. Then the first requisite for preferment was to be a good lawyer, and now the demand is for energetic and more or less capable men of affairs. The result of this conspiracy of silence in regard to the problems of the New Testament is deplorable. Only half-educated, religiously speaking, the mass of Christians have a vague belief that there is something wrong with the current theology and have no clear conception of the reason for it. The result is they have abandoned, or jettisoned as worthless, many doctrines once regarded as all-important to Christianity, without any attempt to investigate whether they are meaningless, or misleading, or vital. Controversy may be deplored as hateful; but the present apathy is even more fatal to clear thinking.

Since dogma, which is no more than an endeavour to define with special care what is actually believed, has been relegated to the background, various substitutes have been put in its place. Four of these are of chief influence in the theology of the present: (1) Mysticism, (2) Sentiment, (3) Ritual, and (4) Social Service. They will be taken up in turn.

(1) Mysticism is not essentially Christian, but has been magnified in many, especially oriental, religions. Its aim is an interior union with God by entire merging of all personality in His. In the West, mysticism is to be found in Neo-Platonism, Mohammedanism, Catholicism, and Protestantism. By it the soul rises from this world and even from the visible Church into unthinkably intimate communion with God, and a full present realisation of His Being. Mysticism flourishes best in the cloister or the sheltered life. But beautiful as is its ideal and valuable as the thoughts of the great mystics, something less detached and more social is needed for the healthy life of a Christian community. It cannot supply the place of a more active Christianity, and is too often recommended or followed by those who have retired in despair from even the sight of the evil around them to the consolations of a private philosophical devotion.

(2) Religion has also a tendency to resolve itself into a sentiment. Older generations believed with all their hearts in a future life and a coming judgment. This attitude gave a touch of severity to the faith of the whole Tractarian party, and of their opponents in the Evangelical ranks. Both united in denouncing any attempt to mitigate the accepted doctrine of heaven and hell, and both taught unflinchingly the eternity of the punishment of the wicked. With the disappearance of the terrible anxiety as to the future and the gloom it entailed, religion has tended to become, not only amiable, but anæmic. The denunciation of sinners, of the scribes and Pharisees and the unmerciful by Christ is now being attributed not to Him but later polemics on the part of His followers; and the sterner side of Christianity is thus thrown so much into the background that some belated Calvinist might say that the principal business now of the Christian religion seems to be to administer soothing syrup to troubled consciences.

(3) The introduction of ceremonial, designed to make the churches attractive, is very marked in Protestantism to-day, as if the extremists thought that art could supply the place of definite belief. But art will not vivify or inspire religion. It would be contrary to human experience for art to begin now to evoke religion. The reverse is the case: it is religion which must call the art which ministers to it into being.

(4) The most practical and energetic form of modern religion exerts itself in the direction of the social improvement of the human race. Here much can be effected by emphasising the moral duties not only of capital but also of labour, and denouncing the class spirit which is breaking up modern society. But nothing can be effected till the ethical principles of Christianity take the lead again as of yore. The work of the theologian and philosopher is more needed now than hitherto and cannot long be disregarded.

XXIV

THE EXPANSION OF THE ANGLICAN CHURCH

LITTLE DESIRE FOR EXPANSION BOTH AT HOME AND ABROAD—ROMANISM IN ENGLAND—NATURAL TENDENCY OF THE BRITISH TO KEEP THEMSELVES SEPARATE—THE EXPANSION OF THE BRITISH OF RECENT DATE—ENGLISH-SPEAKING PROTESTANTISM REPRODUCED—EXTENSION OF THE ANGLICAN EPISCOPATE: (1) IRISH, (2) SCOTTISH, (3) IN UNITED STATES OF AMERICA, (4) COLONIAL, (5) INDIA, (6) MISSIONARIES—G. A. SELWYN—MISSION TO CENTRAL AFRICA—CHINA AND JAPAN, (7) NATIVE EPISCOPATE.

In the Thirteen Colonies of America, and in other British possessions, the clergy of the established Church of England was under the jurisdiction of the Bishop of London; and every child born on an English ship was supposed to have been born in the Parish of Stepney. The Church enjoyed extraordinary privileges at home, and all who dissented from it were refused full legal recognition and merely tolerated. They were allowed to exist, that was all. The price the Church had to pay for its favoured position was that the clergy should give no trouble but support the Government and the existing state of affairs. Any attempt at expansion was regarded with disfavour at home, and usually with suspicion in the Colonies. Priests with episcopal ordination were welcomed and respected, but a bishop was looked upon as undesirable, as that office was considered inseparable from aristocratic privilege. Till the beginning of the nineteenth century there was hardly any missionary enterprise or activity shown, and the Church outside England was

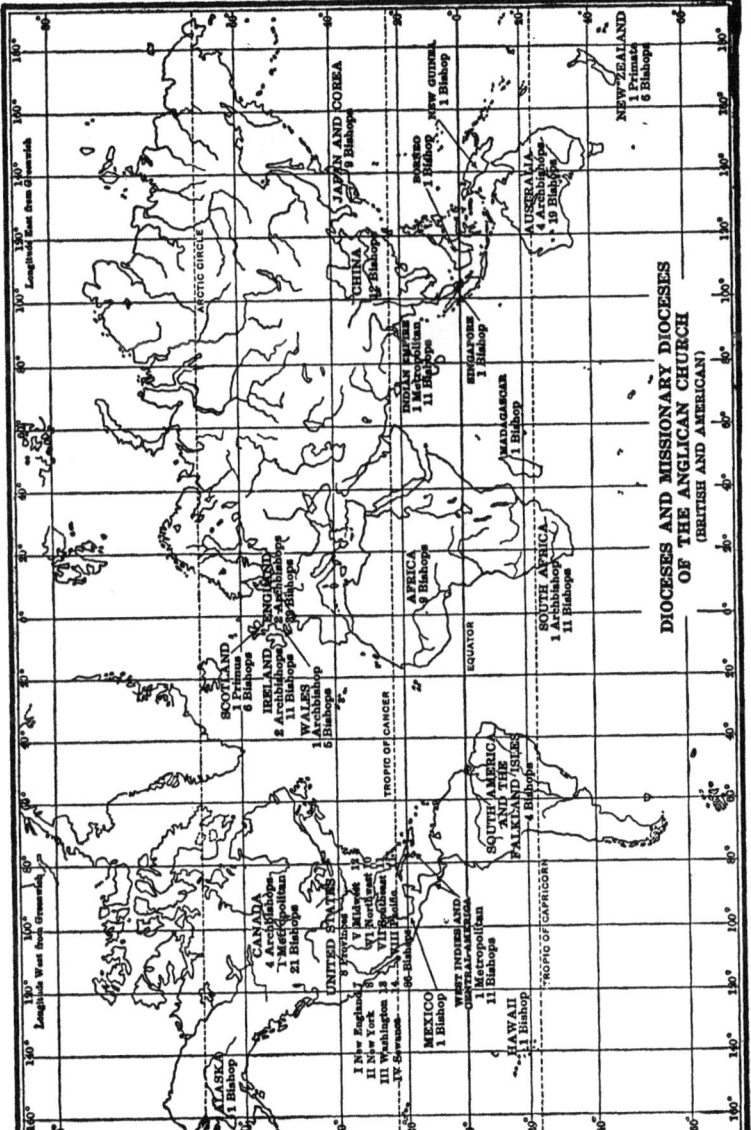

virtually the "Society for the Propagation of Christian Knowledge, and of the Gospel," founded in the reign of William III. In a word, the Church was commonly thought to be a purely national affair and Englishmen were not wholly displeased to think that it was an article which could not be exported. The Scottish Church and its bishops were obscure and suspected of disloyalty to the Hanoverian Government, and the Irish episcopate was often valued as providing English divines with rewards which could not suitably be given them in their own country. The expansion of Anglicanism throughout the world is one of the achievements of the nineteenth century.

But outside the shores of England the Anglican community is not the most numerous religious body among the English-speaking race. Nor is the Church of Rome there what it is in England. In controversy it is more opposed to the Anglican Church than to any other body, because the Church of England claims to be the Catholic Church in the country, and it appears to the Romanist in its orders, its ceremonies, and its service books to "ape" the true Church. But in the ordinary intercourse of life, the Roman and Anglican Englishman have much in common. They at least understand each other's position. On certain points, notably the educational question, they are in the main agreed. Neither in England nor in Presbyterian Scotland is it forgotten that the Romanist represents the old religion, and a certain respect is paid to those families who have never bowed to the Reformation. In addition, the loyalty of the English Roman Catholics is beyond question; and they have shown no sympathy with their coreligionists who are anti-English at heart. It is not so beyond the seas, where the Roman Church as a rule stands for something antagonistic to "British" ideals, and, with the exception of the Irish, represents the less energetic races of the human family. With these races no part of the inhabitants of the British Isles easily amalgamates; and in North America the Irish Catholic intermingles as slowly with the French-Canadian and the Italian and the Portuguese immigrant as does the English, Scotch, or Scotch-Irish Protestant.

The tendency of the English-speaking and indeed the Nordic peoples generally is to stand apart. Up to the present time they have taken the chief share in the development of the modern world, and the pioneers among them have been without question the English-speaking Protestants, of whom those who are in full communion with the Anglican Church are not the majority. All these elements must be considered in this connection as representatives of English and Scottish Christianity.

A study of maps of the world till the middle of the nineteenth century will show what a small proportion of it was Europeanized and what an insignificant part the British race had played in its development. At the beginning of the eighteenth century the foreign possessions of Great Britain consisted of a narrow strip of the coast of North America, extending from what is now the State of Maine to Georgia and bounded by the Allegheny Mountains. The Bermudas, the Bahamas, and Jamaica, and a few trading forts on the West Coast of Africa and in India made up the rest of the Empire. The colonial possessions of the Netherlands, France, and above all Portugal and Spain were far more extensive. The American Revolution extended the extreme boundary of the new United States to the Mississippi; and even then the actual settlement of the country and formation of new States did not take place, with the exception of Kentucky and Tennessee, till the nineteenth century, when a very rapid expansion of the United States set in through a westward thrust of its surplus population, largely recruited from England, Scotland, and later, Ireland. Of the other great settlements of the English-speaking peoples which are now developing from colonies into sovereign states, hardly any existed before the close of the Napoleonic Wars. Canada, Australia, New Zealand, the Cape, British Columbia, the Northwest provinces of

The Expansion of the Anglican Church 211

Canada are all comparatively modern. India and the Asiatic portions of the British Empire come under a different category, for they were not colonies in the sense of new settlements, but were alien peoples almost unconsciously incorporated by the commercial establishments of a great trading company, which felt compelled by circumstances to take the government over from those who had proved incapable of ruling their people or protecting themselves from foreign aggression.

Wherever English-speaking Protestants have settled they have reproduced the sects and parties which divided them at home. In America still newer forms of Protestantism have appeared, partly owing to the circumstances and to the disposition of the people in that direction, and partly to other European influences. Roughly speaking, however, Methodism has proved most enterprising, Presbyterianism the most educated, Congregationalism the most democratic in theory, if conservative in practice, and Anglicanism the least emotional and with little tendency to schism. To the Baptists belong the glory of sending pioneer missionaries to the heathen.

Our present task is to trace the increase of an Anglican Episcopate outside England and the growth of its churches as self-governing communities in the different Episcopates: (1) the Irish, (2) the Scottish, (3) the American, (4) the Colonial, (5) the Indian, (6) the missionary, (7) the native.

(1) The Irish ecclesiastical difficulties began long before the Reformation. The Normans had been invited to settle the intestine disputes and to regulate the Church in Ireland. When English settlements were made, the two nations, though of the same faith, worshipped apart and had separate monasteries, and no native Irishman was allowed to occupy a bishopric wherever the English could prevent it. By the statute of Kilkenny, 1377, the Anglo-Irish were forbidden, under the penalty of high treason, to hold any intercourse with the natives. At the Reformation, Protestants were placed in the Irish sees,

and the Church became the symbol of the English ascendancy. Despite many scandalous appointments, two of the most famous divines in the seventeenth and eighteenth centuries were Irish bishops. Archbishop Usher, though his biblical chronology is now discredited, was one of the most learned bishops in any Church, and George Berkeley, Bishop of Cloyne, by his philosophy and the masterly language in which it is expounded, is almost entitled to rank with Plato. Berkeley is as honourably distinguished a Christian as he was a philosopher, and unique in his day for the zeal with which he urged the diffusion of the Gospel in the Colonies and in the West Indies. Disestablished in 1869, the Irish Church has showed marvellous vitality and powers of recuperation in the face of great difficulties.

(2) The Episcopal Church of Scotland, ruined and oppressed by the intolerance of the triumphant Presbyterians at the Revolution, maintained a precarious existence, "the shadow of a shade," as Sir Walter Scott calls it. Yet this apparently barren and proscribed Church was the means of giving the Episcopal Succession to the Protestant Episcopal Church of America.

(3) The English Church had a varied career in the Colonies. In New England it naturally made slow progress among a population mainly Puritan in sympathy: in Virginia, it was the established Church. But even its clergy were as a rule agreed that it was preferable to go to England to be ordained than to have a bishop on the spot. When, however, the Revolution broke out, Episcopalians, though Washington himself was one, were suspected of disloyalty and many of the clergy left the country. But when the separation from the mother country was finally accomplished, a desire for bishops was felt and a small body of Connecticut clergy sent one of their number, Samuel Seabury, to England to seek consecration. The English episcopate felt legally prohibited from acceding to his request, and he was consecrated by the Scottish bishops at Aberdeen in 1784.

Three years later the Archbishop of Canterbury was empowered to consecrate American bishops without requiring them to take the oath of allegiance to the British Sovereign. The consecrations both at Aberdeen and in Lambeth Palace were most unimposing ceremonies and gave but little promise of being the beginning of a Church of first-rate importance, a Church of an influence far in excess of its numerical strength, which has covered the whole country with its dioceses, and in addition has a growing missionary episcopate. It still retains the name of Protestant, a title treasured by the established Church in England at the time of the consecration of its first bishops: but it has never identified itself with the revivalism which in the past was a characteristic mark of American Protestants.

(4) The first colonial bishopric was that of Nova Scotia, founded in 1787, and in 1793 another was established at Quebec, but before 1850 there were only twelve bishops in the entire British Empire, excluding India. There are now about ninety, including missionary sees. In justice to those responsible for the administration of the colonies, notably the Bishops of London and the officials of the Society for the Propagation of the Gospel, it is worth noting that there had been a strong desire throughout the eighteenth century to appoint resident bishops. Indeed, just before Queen Anne's death (1714) it seemed probable there would be a Colonial episcopate; but, as the idea found no favour abroad and had little support from the home government, nothing was done till after the American Revolution. This may account in part for the comparative weakness of the Colonial Church; but a stronger reason is the fact that when emigration from England was at its height Non-conformists were in the great majority. But at the present time many of the Churches beyond the seas are self-supporting and already capable of self-expansion. In the different dominions the Anglican Churches are evolving their own

government as independent provinces under their respective metropolitans.

(5) India is not in the same class as the colonies or dominions thus far treated. As far as the Anglican Church entered it at all, it was the religion of the members of a trading company who came out to make a fortune and return home, and had no desire whatever to introduce their religion among the natives. The chaplains of the East India Company were not expected to be missionaries but to minister solely to its European officials. Indeed, where the Company had authority, it was considered most dangerous to its security to preach the Gospel to the Hindoos, and nothing was definitely attempted in that line till the close of the eighteenth century. Missions to India had long been carried on by the Roman Catholic Church, but English Protestants did not begin till the foundation of the Baptist Missionary Society. So strong was the prejudice against missionaries after the Vellore Mutiny in 1806 that they were all ordered to leave India by the Governor-General, Lord Hastings. But Christian interest in missions to India was already too strong in England for a policy of exclusion to become permanent, and the Church Missionary Society had the support of Lord Teignmouth, who had been himself Governor General. In 1814, Thomas Fanshaw Middleton, a Cambridge scholar of some distinction, author of a work on the *Greek Article* which is described as "a landmark in New Testament criticism," was appointed Bishop of Calcutta. In the same year the Church Missionary Society, which had previously employed German Lutherans, dispatched the first English clergymen as missionaries to India. Bishops were sent to Madras in 1835 and to Bombay in 1837. But the earlier bishops were for the English Colony in India and missionary work went on under the superintendence of the societies at home. Missionary bishops came later.

(6) It is impossible in a short space to do justice to the work of the Missions of the Church of England out-

side the British Empire. Mention only can be made here of the establishment of the principal dioceses or spheres of work entrusted to bishops, because these indicate the permanent establishment of centres of Anglican influence. It must, however, be remembered that noble work in this direction has been done to spread the Christian influence of the English-speaking world by the Presbyterians of Scotland, the Protestants of America and other missionary organizations outside the Church of England.

Of the most important missions organised under Episcopal supervision, three may be selected—Borneo, 1855; Melanesia, 1861, and Central Africa, in the same year. With the diocese of Central Africa is connected the later establishment of the Church in Uganda. One of the most romantic episodes in British enterprise is the story of how James Brooke, an Englishman, became Rajah of Sarawak in Borneo. The first missionary, F. T. McDougall, went out to the Straits in 1847 and was consecrated Bishop of Singapore and Labuan in 1855. As Borneo was outside the empire, this was the first organised Anglican community among a heathen people not subject to Britain. The success of Christianity here has been very marked. The administration of these British Rajahs has done a very great deal to civilise the Dyak population of their dominions.

The greatest of Anglican missionaries was George Augustus Selwyn, who in 1841 was sent out to be Bishop of New Zealand. His work among the native Maoris was marked by unusual sympathy and broad-mindedness, and on his return to England he took with him John Coleridge Patteson and left him to labour in the islands of the South Sea, where he afterward consecrated him Bishop of Melanesia. Patteson was murdered in 1871 by the natives in revenge for the kidnapping of five men by traders. It was a martyrdom so far as its fruits were concerned, for it drew hostile attention to the South Sea slave trade that ended in drastic reforms.

The last of the three missions mentioned above was

inspired by a visit of the great Scottish explorer and missionary, David Livingstone, to the Universities of Oxford and Cambridge in 1857, which resulted in the establishment of the Universities Mission to Central Africa under Bishop Mackenzie, a distinguished Cambridge mathematician. It finally set up headquarters at Zanzibar, once the headquarters of the slave trade. The personnel of the Universities Mission has been mainly of the High Church party; the work has been conspicuous for its wisdom and devotion and several have given their lives for the cause. The Low Church Mission to Uganda was the scene of a real martyrdom, that of Bishop Hannington in 1885, which was followed by a persecution of native Christians that proved to be the training school of a strong and self-supporting Christianity.

The Anglican Church is represented by bishops both from England and America in China and Japan and its missionary posts are numerous throughout the world. Though there are serious points still that remain to be negotiated, it is becoming evident upon the whole that all non-Roman Christian missions must coöperate, because rival Churches cannot afford to place undue emphasis upon their domestic differences while millions of heathen remain unevangelised.

(7) As yet few of the newly converted peoples have contributed bishops to the Church, but a beginning has been made and their number will undoubtedly increase. The time must come, if Christianity is to become indigenous among people at present non-Christian, that these Churches must have, like our own, a national existence and be served by a native ministry and not by missionaries.

As the survey of a map of the Anglican dioceses must not encourage undue optimism as to the extent and predominance of the communion, so there is no need to be depressed by the modest statistics as to the number of its adherents. If we consider the shortness of the period of modern mission work and of colonial expansion, we must be rather astonished at the progress made, and regard the generous plans for the future sketched by the various organisations of our Church as an evidence of its desire to give the world the best it has to offer.

XXV

THE PRESENT SITUATION

NATIONAL SENTIMENT ALWAYS STRONG—INDIVIDUALITY—UNITY WITH DIVERSITY—RELIGION NOT NOW A SERIOUS CAUSE OF DISUNION AMONG ANGLO-SAXON PEOPLES—UNION WITH ROME—THE FUTURE—THE TASK OF CIVILISATION—ADAPTABILITY OF ANGLICAN CHURCH—COMPREHENSIVENESS—RECUPERATIVE POWER—PERIODS OF REACTION—SUBSERVIENCE TO PARTY IN POWER—POLITICAL COMPLICATIONS—DANGERS OF DISRUPTION—NON-JURORS: A WARNING—DOGMATIC DIFFERENCES—NEED OF A MESSAGE TO THE WORLD.

A survey has now been made of Anglicanism from the first appearance of Christianity in Britain to the present day. The parallel in gradual development between the English State and the Church is very noticeable. In both there was constant change and yet unbroken continuity. Even when drastic alterations were seen to be necessary, tradition remained powerful and precedent was revered. Curiously enough, despite the fact that so many strains have been introduced into the making of the English race, the same characteristics have always manifested themselves in its history, both in State and Church; and St. Wilfrid's opposition, alike to dictation from the Celtic bishops of the north, and from Theodore of Tarsus, as Archbishop of the southern province, is typical of an Englishman standing out for his just rights. When Tennyson sang:

"Saxon and Norman and Danes are we,"

he practically acknowledged the unity of the race; for all

three came to Britain, adventurers from the north, in search of a new home.

The chief characteristic of the English as a race is intense individuality. Its greatest exploits are not so much national as personal. In modern times its best colonists have been religious enthusiasts, traders, discontented subjects, and victims of the game laws. Its greatest conquerors were also employes of a trading company. But wherever an Englishman has settled, whether he has retained or renounced his native country, he has shown fundamentally the same characteristics, a respect for law and order, no tendency to identify himself with alien races, and no desire for interference from his home government. Wherever he goes the Englishman desires to conserve his nationality and independence.

This intense individualism is responsible for so much religious difference among men of the English race who show the same kind of aptitude in organising a sect as in establishing a colony. At the same time there are Englishmen who thoroughly understand there must be mutual give and take in this world and that friendly relations can be maintained despite serious differences of opinion. It is this spirit, perhaps the most valuable heritage of the race, which has kept the loosely connected members of the Empire in a unity which seems in constant danger in prosperous times, but unbreakable in days of adversity. Nowhere else, however, is this spirit more powerful than in the Church of England. It has often been plausibly maintained that the Establishment has kept such apparently discordant elements as the Anglo-Catholic, the Evangelical, and the Broad-Church in one community. Few would be inclined to dispute the statement but for the fatal argument of actual fact. There is no established Church in any British colony, and yet those Churchmen who have officially broken with the parent body are as insignificant in number in the colonies as at home. Yet even here the fact that it is the established Church in the home country might operate as a potent influence in maintaining unity, but this argument cannot apply to the United States of America. Even after the severance of the colonies from the mother country, the clergy of the Church in America resolved to remain in communion with that of England, though the English bishops showed no marked anxiety to retain the allegiance of the newly constituted body. Under these entirely different circumstances, there are exactly the same parties in the Church, the same varieties in ritual, the same differences of opinion, and the same unity of discordant elements. Further, the American Civil War, which caused most Protestant communities to divide into Northern and Southern, proved as powerless to create any division in the Anglican as it was in the Roman communion.

Thus, in the Anglican Church there is a unifying power at work which is not easy to account for or explain, but is at the same time undeniable. Along with it there has always been another side of English religion which delights in maintaining certain doctrines at the expense of unity. In these separatist bodies it may safely be said there is far less hostility to the Anglican Church than formerly, and that, as the English race is drawing closer together throughout the world, owing to the growing influx of foreigners into its territories, religion is less than ever a cause of disunion. It is, indeed, quite conceivable that if a discreet silence were maintained as to how reunion might be brought about, there might come a merging of English Christianity in the bosom of a Catholic, but comprehensive Church.

But it must never be overlooked that the common Christianity of the entire English race was born in the ancient Western Church, and the question is whether the Church of England will ever again be merged in the Roman Communion. At the present time it would appear as though there was in England a party of earnest clergy for whom such union has an attraction; but it is not conceivable that the Roman authorities would receive them on any terms short of complete submission. The real point at issue, raised by the preceding discussion, is whether the Anglican Church does not stand of itself for much which would be lost to the Christianity of the world if it were merged in modern Protestantism or surrendered at discretion to modern Romanism. The approaches made to the ancient Churches of the East hold out some prospect of an understanding, but so far as anything practical is concerned the best result to be hoped for is mutual good will and coöperation: an actual corporate reunion is almost incredible.

As regards its future prospects, the only sound optimism must be derived from a philosophic study of the past. Christianity has at the present time either to save civilisation or to perish with it. This was not so evident a few years ago, when it was generally assumed that society could continue to endure by the aid of such a morality as reason and expediency would supply. But now an active propaganda among the class which is endeavouring to seize the entire power over the community, exhorts them to use it wholly and solely for their own advantage and not only to deprive all others of the property they now possess, but to take vengeance on them for the prosperity which they have enjoyed in the past. Recognising that every form of Christianity will always protest against such ruthlessness, fanatics of this description propose to destroy it utterly in order to carry out their schemes. For anyone to have written thus ten years ago might have seemed sheer insanity; but to-day it is an indisputable truth, and not only Christians who are opposed to a social revolution, but even those who are most keenly in favour of it are aware of the danger that human society shall be overwhelmed by the absolutely anti-religious leaders of a triumphant proletariat. It is now no question of Roman, or Protestant, or even Jewish ascendancy, but of a new barbarism which has thrown off all moral restraint. The problem of every association of religious men of whatever description is how to play its part in staving off such a calamity as has overtaken Russia. It is for Churchmen to consider what part the Anglican community is to take in the inevitable struggle.

Its long history shows that it has an unusual capacity to alter with altered circumstances and still retain its true identity; that it is capable of reform without revolution and that it is prepared to acknowledge and try to remedy mistakes. Throughout its history it has avoided some mistakes into which other Churches have fallen. Despite all that has been said to the contrary, its clergy, even in the highest places, have at no time represented an aristocratic caste. It never had abbeys or chapters as on the Continent, to which nobility was an essential qualification for admission, and at no time, not even during the Norman tyranny, nor the fifteenth century when the feudal nobility were in power, nor in the days of the ascendancy of the great Whig aristocracy, did men fail to rise from the humblest rank in society to the highest in the Church. From the early days of the Middle Ages to the present day the poverty of the country clergy has been a just cause of reproach to the Church, and they have been constantly subject to contempt, on account of their lowly station. Exclusiveness has never been a characteristic of the Church of England.

Nor can it be on the whole accused of intolerance. In the Middle Ages there was no persecution in England, even Wyclif was acting Rector of Lutterworth when he died, and his immediate followers were suffered to preach with but little molestation. When the burning of heretics was legalised, deaths for Lollardy were few and far between. After the Reformation in Elizabeth's reign, those who suffered for conscience sake were usually arraigned for political offences, and then, as has been shown, the paramount object was to induce the nation to agree in a religious settlement which would include everybody. In the seventeenth century, amid all the bitterness of political and religious controversy, if the Church did not display a toleration impossible in that age, at least it proved itself less bigoted than any other party when it came into power; and, since 1688, no Church in Christendom has allowed a greater diversity of opinion among its members. It is a remarkable circumstance that the State in England deserves most of the blame for one period of intolerance in the Church, and at a later date all the credit for a period of tolerance. The bishops under Elizabeth might have complained that they were compelled by the government to be severe on the Libellers with as much reason as Dr. Pusey blamed the remissness of the legal authorities in dealing sharply with the Essayists.

Like the English nation again, the Church has shown the power of learning in adversity not to repeat the mistakes which caused its troubles. It has shown amazing powers of recuperation: it has risen to renewed vigour after Danish invasions, Norman conquests, the Reformation with its disorder and spoliation, the ruin which followed the Great Rebellion, and the apathy which followed the Revolution. Over and over again men have asked "Can these bones live?" and in answer they have stood up an exceeding mighty army. However disquieting may be the signs at present, the historian cannot forget the lessons of the past in every age.

Nor can he neglect the warning of the past. The strength and weakness of the English character is a careless optimism, a belief that somehow or other things will come right if only they are let alone; and it is only in a serious crisis that the mental and moral energies of the Englishman are called into full activity. This partly accounts for periods of apathy such as the fifteenth and eighteenth centuries, and possibly for a lack now of interest in religion when people are so disappointed at its failure to avert the calamities of the world to-day or to work a change in men's hearts. But that a revival will come there is little doubt. And it is equally certain that it can neither be organised nor engineered, and the manner of its manifestation cannot be predicted. In the meantime, there are many pitfalls into which unwary Churchmen may fall.

When the Church in the past has endeavoured to enlist the support of the powers of this world, it has lost influence. It has too often ranged itself on the side of tyranny. It suffered from its subservience to the Stuarts in the reign of James I and Charles I and allowed its enemies to identify their cause with that of constitutional liberty. That its loyalty was not due solely to selfishness or baseness of spirit is plain, for it was continued by the clergy to their descendants when they had lost the favour of the people.

Less excusable was the resistance of the bishops to all measures of industrial and social improvement in the direction of greater humanity early in the nineteenth century; and Hurrell Froude was justified in his complaint that the Tory party was no true friend in the troublous days of reform. The lesson of history is that the forces of Christianity should never align themselves on the side of any secular party in the State, for the Church which does so is doomed to a rude awakening when it realises the bitterness of its open enemies and the coldness of its supposed friends. The salvation of the Church in England has been the diversity represented always in its members: before the Reformation it contained supporters of Rome and nationalists; during and after the Reformation Catholic-minded men and Puritans; at the Revolution High and Low Churchmen, and in modern times Liberals and Conservatives. It would presage future disaster if enthusiasm for the Church to-day was confined to the upholders of Capital or Labour. A Church which hopes to retain any influence must not consent to be the spaniel of any faction in the State, but must be ready, on the contrary, to denounce whatever party is disposed to advocate views in its supposed interest which are opposed in any way to the practice and teaching of Christ.

In such an event if Churchmen are to be heard they

should be able to speak with one voice, and for this reason unity is of the utmost importance. It has already been indicated how necessary this is, and how wonderfully it has been preserved in the past. The Church has been threatened with disruption throughout its history, and the danger is still present in two forms:

The first is that the Anglo-Catholic party may become so offended by some action of more liberal Churchmen that it will break from the parent body. Hitherto those who have done so have, as a rule, found peace and generally obscurity in the Roman communion. It is often asserted that if Disestablishment and Disendowment were to take place in England there would be a schism, resulting in two Churches opposed to one another.

For those who would break away a serious study is advisable of the fate of the Non-jurors, who numbered in their ranks some of the best Anglicans of that period. The way these earnest men divided and redivided into factions and the obscurity into which the sect fell should be a warning. The fact that their Church principles bore so much fruit as the years passed among those who declined to go out with them is an encouragement to remain loyal to the Church of England.

Dogma may prove a more serious matter than practice in producing division. Here the chief desideratum seems to be patience. But patience and passivity are not synonymous. The policy of ignoring theological differences is not a wise one. What is now needed is scholarly investigation. It is the business of the expert to place before the world what he believes to be scientifically true for examination, and of those who differ from him, after due consideration, to show where he is mistaken. Critical difficulties, like those formerly raised by science, can only be solved after rigid examination and fair-minded deliberation. On the other hand there are mysteries beyond human comprehension the truth of which can only be referred to the conscience. The most important of these is the meaning of the Divinity of Christ. The central necessity of His Presence in any formulation of Christian thought is admitted by the ubiquity of His appeal to the conscience of His professed followers.

But the supreme danger is that the Church of Christ may become an organisation equipped for service, but devoid of a message to the world. Nothing, Apostolical Succession, Sacraments, organisation, discipline, enthusiasm for humanity, social service, or even a profession of universal brotherhood and unbounded love can take the place of an active belief in God and Jesus Christ. On these as a foundation, the Church of England will have to build, if its future is to be secured.

INDEX

(References are to pages.)

Abbott, Archbishop of Canterbury, a typical Low Churchman, 134, et seq.
Acts of Parliament, Toleration, 103, 138, 141, 147
  Church Discipline, 194
  Public Worship Regulation, 194
  Clergy Discipline, 194
Adamnan, St., biographer of Columba, 22–24
Admonition to Parliament, Puritan demands, 107
Advertisements, Parker's, order to wear surplice, 106, 107
Allen, Cardinal, founded seminary at Douai, 92
American Church, the, its episcopate, 220
Anabaptists, extreme separatists, 97, 103, 105
Andrewes, Bishop, typical High Churchman, 127
Anglicanism, its distinctive features, 114–123
  dangers of, 225, 226
Anselm, Archibishop of Canterbury, an Italian, 45, 46
  his troubles with William II, 48
Apocrypha, more added to Lectionary, 1662, 130
Architectural Society, founded at Oxford, 192
Arminius, Laudian party embrace opinions of, 129, 130
Arnold, Dr., "noetics" at Oriel College, Oxford, 183

Augustine, Archbishop of Canterbury, his mission to England, 14–17, 31, 32
Augustine, St., of Hippo, his opinions and doctrine, 18, 19, 129

Baptism, baptismal ceremony in Rome, 40, 41
Barrow, Puritan, Marprelate libeller, 110
Becket, St. Thomas à, murder of, 48
Bede, Venerable, History of the English People, 31, 35, et seq.
Benedict, St., rule of, 29
Benson, Archbishop of Canterbury, judgment in Lincoln case, 195
Berkeley, Bishop, zeal for missions, 212
Bible, rarely read: but not unknown in Middle Ages, 62
  British and Foreign Bible Society, 179
Bishops, how nominated after Reformation, 115
  how consecrated, 116
  attitude to the Wesleys, 167
Blackburne, Archdeacon, subscription controversy, 148
Bloomfield, Bishop, wearing the surplice in the pulpit, 192
Brett, non-juror, 156
Brooke, Rajah of Sarawak, bishopric of Borneo, 215
Browne, Robert, Puritan, 98

Index

Burnet, Bishop, Latitudinarian and Low Churchman, 134, 137, 138

Calendar, church, little altered at Reformation, 84, 119
Calvinist clergy, oppose Methodism, 172
Cambride, the Platonists, 143, 144
evangelicals at, 174
Camden Society at Cambridge, 192
Campian, Jesuit, suffers death, 92, 111
Carthusian monks, 57
executed under Henry VIII, 72
Cartwright, Puritan, activity at Cambridge, 107
Celtic Church, the, importance and influence of, 19–25, 35
Chapters, Cathedral, allowed to choose bishops, 75, 115
Chaucer, the "Wife of Bath," well read, 62
the "Persone of the Towne's" sermon, 63
Churches, educational value in Middle Ages, 62
Church Missionary Society, foundation of, 179
Clapham, evangelical centre, 174, 181
Clapton, High Churchmen at, 181
Clarendon, constitutions of, 49
Clarkson, Thomas, essay prize in slavery, 178
Clergy, Anglican, an estate of the realm, 117
Colenso, Bishop, criticises the Pentateuch, 198, 202
Collier, non-juror, bishop and controversialist, 156, 157, 159
Columba, St., 22–25
Commons support the Tudors, 71
Comprehension Bill, 138

Convocation, heavily fined by Henry VIII, 72
Cooper, Bishop, 110
Cornwall, rebellion in, against English prayer book, 79
Councils, general, 10, 11
acts of first four accepted, 11, 12
Courts, of delegates, 194
high commission, 194
Cranmer, Archbishop, character under Henry VIII, 74
brings foreign Reformers to England, 80
burns heretics, 83
Creeds, the three, 12–15
Cromwell, Thomas, Earl of Essex, executed under Henry VIII, 73

Darwin, "Origin of Species," 198–201
Deists, how refuted, 145, 147, 150
Dissent, rise of, in England, 95–113
Doctrine, unaltered by Henry VIII, 73, 74, 76
Dodwell, non-juror, on the effect of baptism, 156, 157

Easter question, Celtic attitude on, 20, 21, 37, 38
Ecclesia Anglicana, the clergy, not the Church of England, 75
Education of poor, societies to promote, 178, 179
Edward VI, disastrous character of reign, 77, 78
Eighteenth Century, its callousness, 171, 172
coldness of church in, 171, 172
Elizabeth, Queen, her moderating church policy, 84, 85
selfish but far-sighted, 85, 88
Essays and Reviews, the publication of, 198–201

Index

Evangelical party, its defects and virtues, 173–179

Extreme Unction, development from New Testament times, 66

Family of Love, Sect, non-militant Puritans, 103

Field, Puritans, admonition to Parliament, 107

Fisher, Bishop and Cardinal, executed under Henry VIII, 72

Free Will, controversy on, 129, 130

Friars, popular preachers, 63

Froude, Hurrell, with Keble and Newman, 183, 184, 185

Fry, Mrs. Elizabeth, prison reform, 178

Geneva, influence in England, 105, 106

George III, King, unaffectedly religious, 139

Georgia, colony of, Wesleys go as chaplains to, 163, 164

Gibbon, historian, his Oxford career, 180

Gore, Bishop, a modern High Churchman, 133
  on the Old Testament, 204

Gregory I, the Great, Pope, his claim to jurisdiction, 27, 30

Gregory VII, Pope, demands homage, 3, 46

Hadrian IV, Pope, characteristically English, 3

Hampden Controversy arouses Oxford, 187

Hannington, Bishop, martyr in Uganda, 216

Head of the Church, title given by Parliament to Henry VIII, 71, 72

Henry VII, appoints council of regency, 78
  attitude to Rome, 69, 70, 74, 75
  did not set up new church, 74
  his power and unpopularity, 70–73
  liberal in religious gifts, 69, 70
  popular at his accession, 68, 69

Hickes, non-juror, learned controversialist, 155, 156

Hoadley, Bishop, typical Low Churchman, 140
  Bangorian controversy, 148

Holy Discipline, Puritans demand, 107

Hooker, Richard, representative of Anglicanism, 15, 127

House of Lords, strong clerical element in, 72
  bishops, reason for their membership, 116

Huxley, Professor, controversy with Wilberforce, 200, 201

Image worship, attitude of English church to, 16, 17

Independency, congregational system of church, 98, 99

India, the church in, bishops consecrated for, 214

Iona, Columba's monastery at, 19, 22, et seq.

Irish church, early importance of, 19, et seq.
  its eqiscopate, 209, 211, 212

James I, King, understood Anglicanism, 126, 158

James, II, King, fidelity of non-jurors to, 152–154

Jesuits, order of, appearance in England, 92

Johnson, Dr. Samuel, supporter of religion, 139, 140, 149, 169

Index

Jowett, master of Balliol College, Oxford, essays and reviews, 201

Keble, John, his Assize sermon, 183, 184
Ken, Bishop, refused to take the oaths, 154, 156
King, Bishop of Lincoln, tried for Ritualism, 195
Kingswood, the Wesleys preach to the miners, 164
Knox, Alexander, Irish High Churchman, 181

Latitudinarians, meaning of the movement, 142
Lay Folks Mass Book, rhymed explanation of the Mass, 63
Laud, Archbishop, his policy and churchmanship, 126–128, 135, 136
Law, William, the serious call, 156
visited by John Wesley, 163
Lichfield, Archbishopric of, established by Offa and suppressed, 35, 39
Locke, lays stress on Reason, 145
Lutheranism, cold to English refugees, 105
Lyndewood, Canonist, on the use of the surplice, 107

Macaulay, Lord, contrasts the churches of Rome and England, 166
McDougall, Bishop, mission work in Borneo, 215
Marprelate libels, attack on bishops, 100, 109, 110
Martyn, Henry, chaplain East India Company, goes to India, 176

Mary, Queen, recognises dissolution of monasteries, 73
reign made breach with Rome irreparable, 81, 82
personally superior in character in Elizabeth, 81
Mary, Queen of Scots, takes refuge in England, 89, 92
Mass for the Dead, disliked because of priestly pretension, 64
Methodists, name given at Oxford, 162, 163
their missionary labours, 165, et seq.
claims made by preachers, 167, 168
Milman, Dean, History of the Jews, 202
Milner, Isaac, Dean, noted Cambridge Evangelical, 176
Moorfields, London, Wesleys preach in, 164
More, Sir Thomas, executed under Henry VIII, 72
Mysticism, not a sufficient remedy for, 206

Newman, J. H., Cardinal, tract 90, 183, 184, 186, 200
Northern Earls, rebellion of, 89
Northumberland, Duke of, conforms under Mary, 78, 79
Nova Scotia, Bishopric of, earliest colonial, 213, 214

Ordo Romanus, baptismal service in, 40
Oriel College, Oxford, intellectual distinction of, 182, 183
"Origin of Species," Darwin, excites clerical opposition, 200, 201
Ornaments, Rubric, Ritualists call attention to, 192

Pallium or Pall, sent to archbishops, 33, 36
Parliament, Henry VIII's acts done through, 69, 70, 71
Parish clergy, high character of English, 63
  some teach severe doctrine before Reformation, 63
Patrick, St., work in Ireland, 19, 21
Paulinus, missionary to Northumbria, 33, 36
Pelagianism, of British origin, 18, 19, 36
Penance, sacrament of, 63, 65
Persecution under Mary cruel and disastrous, 81
  persecution of Catholics under Elizabeth, 92, 93
Philip II of Spain, Elizabeth's only ally, 88, 92
Pius V, Pope Saint, his bull *regnans in excelsis,* 90
Pole, Cardinal, Archbishop of Canterbury, orthodoxy questioned at Rome, 81, 120
Poor, condition of, evangelical interest in, 178, 179
Pope, not unpopular with the people, 67
  often defied by sovereigns, 70
  surrenders monastic lands in reign of Mary, 80, 81
Præmunire Statute, used by Henry VIII, 72, 75, 115
Prayer book, first, of Edward VI, 79, 155
Prayers for the dead, reason for their abolition, 121, 123
Prison reform, share of Evangelicals in, 177, 178
Protestant misrule, Edward VI's reign so designated, 78
Protestantism, Eighteenth Century churchmen gloried in, 165

Purgatory, medieval doctrine, 64
Puritanism, spirit of, before Reformation, 63, 64
Pusey, Dr., joins Tractarians, 185
Quignon, Cardinal, preface to Prayer Book due to his Breviary, 119

Raikes of Gloucester, Sunday schools, 179
Roman Catholics, ancient gentry loyal, 89, 90
  at first unmolested, 89
  feeling against, in England, 89–93
  reasons for their secession, 89, 90
Rome, reunion with, under Mary, 80, 81
Romilly, Sir Samuel, criminal law reform, 179
Rose, H. J., *Tracts for Times* projected, 184
Royal supremacy, importance of, 115

Sabbatarianism, severe sometimes in Middle Ages, 63
Sacheverill, Dr., high church reaction to his sermon, 131
Sacraments, centre of Medieval religion, 61
  the Seven, 62, 64
Sancroft, Archbishop, 152
  refuses to take oath to William and Mary, 153, 154
St. Bartholomew, massacre of, its effects in England, 91
Scotland, Church of, gives American orders, 212
Sectarianism, outcome of Reformation, 95, 96
Selwyn, Bishop, missionary work, 215

Sermons, rare but popular in Middle Ages, 63
Shaftesbury, Earl of (Anthony Ashley Cowper), interest in the poor, 178
Sharp, Granville, exposes slave trade, 177
Simeon, Charles, evangelical leader at Cambridge, 176
Six Articles, act of the, under Henry VIII, 73, 82
Slave trade, evangelical share in suppression, 177, 178
Societies, propagation of the Gospel, 209, 213
Church Missionary, 179
Somerset (Seymour), Duke of, idealistic but rapacious, 79
Surplice, clergy ordered to wear, 106, 107

Taylor, Jeremy, Bishop, "Liberty of Prophesying," 143
Thackeray, novelist, imaginary picture of Clapham Society, 174
Tillotson, Archbishop, Latitudinarian and Low Churchman, 137, 138, 146
Tracts for the times, 8
effect of, 184, et seq.

Transubstantiation repudiated in Church of England, 120, 121, 122
Trent, Council of, conclusion of, 91
Tudor, House of, defective title to throne, 71

Universities Mission to Central Africa, due to speech by Livingstone, 216

Vestments, controversy under Elizabeth, 106, 107
Via Media, success under Elizabeth, 83–85

Wesley, Charles, goes to Georgia, 164
Wesley, John, 139
spiritual experiences of, 163
Wesleys, the family, the elder Wesleys, 161, 162
Samuel, the younger, 162
Whiston, William, his curious opinions, 147
Whitefield, his origin, 163
William the Conqueror, character of his rule, 46, et seq.
Williams, Archbishop, a Low Churchman, 136

www.ingramcontent.com/pod-product-compliance
Lightning Source LLC
Chambersburg PA
CBHW060117170426
43198CB00010B/924